RETURNING FIRE

(I NEVER THOUGHT HE'D SHOOT ME)

A True Story

This Book
Belongs To

NANCY RITCHEY

LINDA RHOUTSONG

PAGE PUBLISHING, INC.
New York, NY

First originally published by Page Publishing, Inc. 2019

ISBN 978-1-64424-470-8 (Paperback)
ISBN 978-1-64424-471-5 (Digital)

Printed in the United States of America

To my precious kids,
both of blood and heart:

Without your forgiveness
and unconditional love,
I would not have had the
strength and hope to go on,
to forgive myself, and to begin
making the necessary changes to be
the person I am today.

There are no words to express
how very much I love you all!

—Mom

To Mark's family. There are no words to describe how sorry I am!

CONTENTS

FORETHOUGHT

The following is just one of thousands of stories,
many much more tragic than mine.
It is a story that may have never happened
had there been the kind of help and support
available for both men and women today.
It is a very sad and tragic story, one that will
turn me into an irresponsible,
selfish mom.
It is a story that will scar two large happy
and loving families and many
special friends
for the rest of their lives.
I thank God that my kids have forgiven me.
It took many years before I could forgive myself.

INTRODUCTION

I had always considered myself an intelligent person. Having been the mother of five and a wife of twenty years by the time I was thirty-six and as you can tell, I din't always make the best of choices. What can I say, I was very young. I had somehow managed to turn an unexpected pregnancy at six-teen, into a beautiful rewarding life for the next twenty years. I came from a very loving family, being the youngest of three. I had a wonderful childhood with beautiful memories that I will always treasure. I could not have asked for a better mom and dad. Although, there were occasional well deserved spankings, but always executed in a calm manner. There was zero abuse in my life and I had never been exposed to violence of any kind. When my fairy tale (I thought) marriage suddenly ended, I knew that none of it was my fault. Still, it was a very sad part of my life. There were no drugs, except for an occasional night of "social" pot smoking with our best friends Terry and Teri Lynn. That didn't even begin until after my fourth child was born. We only drank when we went out dancing and I had never even smoked a cigarette. I spent my first thirty-six years being a normal happy kid, a devoted wife and a very loving mom. I was feeling proud, feeling like I had done well. I loved God with every ounce of my being. All of a sudden, I was a single mother of five, beautiful and amazing kids. My life was full and I was in total control. The stress of my failed marriage was gone, my training stable and riding lessons were going great. I thought I had everything I would ever want. My kids, my dogs and horses, were all I needed and I was doing just fine. Then I met Mark and my whole world would change. My life consisted of the happiest times

I would ever know, but it all came with a price. Soon, his anger and abuse would throw us on a roller coaster ride, with amazing highs and horrible lows that will haunt us all forever. No one should ever have to experience this kind of horrible terror and it was all because of me. Also, because of me, (I almost named my book that,) I caused practically unbearable pain, to my friends and two amazing, loving and very close families. It broke us apart for all these years and they never even knew exactly what happened. I love you all so much!

This is my story

CHAPTER 1

THE LAST ACT

A small desert town

I can feel my warm blood oozing through my fingers, and it will not stop no matter how hard I press. Sitting on the corner of our king-size bed, which barely fits into the three walls surrounding it, I try desperately to hold the flesh on my arm together. The light-colored bedspread is turning scarlet. Against my back, I can feel the curtain that provides privacy when we are sleeping. I have pulled it back neatly this morning and looped it to the wall as I had done every day since Mark and I had rearranged the room to accommodate two cribs just fifteen months earlier.

Darkness blankets the inside of the barn where we live, the only light coming from the small window next to the bed. It is just light enough to see the terror on the face of my eleven-year-old son, Danny. He is standing bravely by my side, tears streaming down his cheeks, his hands glued to his best friend's .22-caliber rifle. His younger sister, Becky, is crying hysterically.

Danny's voice is trembling, his entire body shaking. He asks again in a desperate, pleading voice, "Are you all right, Mom? Are you all right? Oh my god, Mom, please say you're all right!" I wonder if my young son can smell the sickening stench of blood.

I can feel my bone, and I can tell that my arm is not all there anymore. How much blood can a person stand to lose without dying?

I ask myself. The whole front of me is covered with blood. I can still feel the heat from the hundreds of tiny pellets that penetrated my body only moments before. Inside my body, a firestorm is raging, causing me to wonder how much damage has been done.

Oh my god, I can't believe Mark shot me. I had to shoot back. My god, did I even hit him? He has disappeared. He's gone. The man that I had loved with all my heart had appeared as a deranged stranger only moments before. I don't want to admit what I know is the truth. He wants me to die, and it is possible that he may return and kill us all in his uncontrollable rage.

The image of the bright-orange flames from the shotgun, accompanied by two very loud bangs, is imprinted on my mind. The sound was piercing in comparison to the cap gun sound of my small .22-caliber handgun. My hands had shaken horribly as I used my left hand to support my wrist after Mark's first shot had severely mutilated my left forearm. Seven times I had pulled the trigger, using every ounce of courage and strength within me, tossing my gun to the floor when it did not fire that seventh time, never remembering the extra bullets I had placed in my back pocket, fearing Mark would come for me. Now the distinct smell of the gunpowder that fills the air in the darkness of this cold, eerie night is overpowering my senses.

My babies are screaming hysterically, and they are somewhere near, but I cannot tell where. They sound very frightened, and their screams frantic. It is so dark in the back of the barn that I can hardly see. All I can see is the flickering of the one kerosene lamp I had lit earlier as the daylight from this terrifying day had dwindled away.

The lamp is in the front section of the twelve-by-thirty-six-foot barn that we had converted into a very cozy home. It is sitting on the bar that separates the living room area and kitchen. Light is reflecting off the cups and pots and pans that hang on every beam in our country-style kitchen. I glimpse a view of the many beautiful plants in our very tiny home and remember the kids saying it resembled a jungle in here.

Can this really be happening to me? Where is Mark? All I had seen was the shadow of a man that I did not want to know when he acted so crazy. The faint light from outside had outlined his six-foot frame, beard, and dark shoulder-length hair; I never saw his face or the beautiful blue eyes that I'd loved so much. Just seconds before, Mark had broken the door down, pulling and pushing over and over until the deadbolt lock he had installed himself broke away from the doorframe. I had been only ten feet away from Mark when he fired without warning, the shotgun steadied at the side of his hip.

Once again, he had become the hateful, abusive, violent man that he had fought so hard to control in the short two years and three months we had been together.

Everything is moving slowly, and my head feels like it is going to float away, as if it may lift right off my shoulders at any moment. I cannot let myself fall over, and I know that somehow I have to stand up. We need to call for help. Oh my god, please, we need help so badly. I know that I am dying, and I can't let my kids see me die. Please, God, I pray with all my might.

I can only imagine what I must look like. I can tell that my clothes are covered with blood. I am very aware of my shirt sticking to me, almost as if it were covered with glue. I have to stay alive long enough so someone can get me away from my kids.

Please, God, please let me live until they can get me away from here.

Where is my babies' daddy? I know that I am in shock, since I am feeling no pain and I still can hardly accept that this is happening, always believing in my heart that he would never really hurt me. Again, he had crossed over that fine line, the one that separates sanity and insanity.

God, please don't let this be happening.

Our babies are only fifteen months old; my precious Danny and Darla and their lives have only just begun. I can't believe what their daddy has done.

For the first time in his entire life, Mark had said he was really happy. He adores his precious babies, yet he was destroying it all. Why does he do this? Why can't he control himself? He hates it when he loses control!

Danny is just a child, and he should not have to defend us. He loves Mark like a father, and he has just chased him out of the barn, shooting at him, over and over, and shouting, "I hate you! I hate you!" His screams were loud and clear, and the terror in his young voice was unmistakable.

I am standing up now. It takes most of my energy, but I am standing. Oh god, I am swaying back and forth and the room is spinning, making me light-headed, just the way a child on a merry-go-round would feel. Mark's worst fear has become a reality. He really hurt me badly this time, and I am remembering something that he had always told me. "It scares me, babe, because I love you way too much," he had told me, eyes narrowed with worry. I hear his words over and over in my mind. Is this what he meant, the very thing he had feared? Is all this really even happening? Please, God, let it just be a horrible nightmare and let me wake up covered with sweat. Don't let this be my blood. There is so much blood that this has to be a dream, a horrible nightmare. Or is it?

Stand still. Do not try to walk yet, or you will fall, I tell myself.

I cannot fall, because if I do, it will scare Danny and Becky.

I am beginning to walk, slowly and carefully, and I have made it to the outside kitchen section that serves as the walkway to the back third of the barn. I feel the wood slats of the floor on my cold, bare feet and fear that I am about to go down. The bar is L-shaped, continuing around from the living room area. I know that I can't let go of my arm, because it is still bleeding, and I have to hold my arm together to help stem the flow. Slowly, carefully I walk, but suddenly I have no more strength and I know I can go no farther. My normally strong, healthy body fails as I fall to my knees between the stove and the bar. I am able to balance myself slightly, sitting back on my calves and feet very carefully. Weakness holds me to the floor like a magnet as I realize I can't move. I am between two of our barstools right in the center of the home that I love so much. I can't believe that I am still conscious. My right hand seems glued to the left forearm, elbow, and flesh that I am so desperately trying to hold together.

I don't want to die in front of my kids. My eyes close, and they will not open up no matter how hard I try. My God, what is happening? I can't believe that I am too weak to open my eyes. I have no physical pain, none at all, yet I know that very soon I am going to die and my life will be over. The simple act of swallowing has become a chore.

Soon, everything that I live for will be gone. I won't have our babies, my children, my family, or my friends. Mark has totally lost control this time, and he has destroyed everything we had. Why couldn't he get better and learn to control himself? This time he has gone too far and it is too late for sorry, because nothing he can say could make this okay. My body is numb and feeling no pain, but the pain in my heart is practically unbearable.

Danny is using the phone; his young voice is still quivering with fright. The barn door is wide-open, and I can feel the cold coming into our usually warm, cozy barn. The open-faced, cone-shaped fireplace is just a few feet to my left, never having been lit tonight. My precious son's words are desperate, and I can hardly understand him. He is making all the necessary calls, never taking his eyes off the open door, afraid that Mark will come back in again for the third time. He never stops pointing his rifle toward the front door. After hanging up the phone, he cautiously, with rifle glued to his hands, steps out on the deck, watching for Mark and protecting his family. I can hear his bloodcurdling screams, and I am totally helpless.

"Somebody help us! Please help us! Help! Help!" Danny is terrified. His screams penetrate the night sky as he pleads for help from anyone who can hear his words of distress. He is just a young boy, and this is too much for him, and he does not want this to be happening. He loves Mark so much, but this is not the Mark he loved.

This is the guy he hates and the one he has feared many times. This is the one that Mark also hates so much, and we know that he wants someone to stop him when he loses control. My baby boy is trying so hard to stop him. I can't believe he did this. Oh god, what have I done to my children? I should have never allowed any of this to happen. I should have been more afraid, and I know now that I should have left when all this began three days earlier. If I had hidden from him, my kids would be safe right now. How will they ever forgive me?

My tiny babies have found me, and their screams are tearing me up. I can feel them climbing all over me, pulling my hair and grabbing my face as they try to pull themselves up. They need me to hold and comfort them like I always do, but I can't move because I am totally helpless, but they don't understand. There is a baby on each of my thighs, and I can feel their desperate, tiny bodies pushing against mine. The confusion has scared them badly, and they want their mommy to hold them and love them, but I still can't move or even talk.

Please, God, don't let me fall on my babies, I pray.

Their big sister, Becky, is only nine and is practically a baby herself. She is hysterical, and with each sob, her small body trembles. She tries to keep the babies off me, but it is no use, because they just keep coming right back to me and she is too devastated to handle them both. My Becky is terrified. "Where is he? Where did Mark go?" she pleads to her big brother, sobbing uncontrollably. "Is he coming back in?"

"I don't know," Danny says. "He disappeared into the bushes. It is so dark. I can't see him. He ran toward the corral." I know Mark could be anywhere on our two acres of trees and brush. The neighbors are distant; we are quite a ways from the main highway and also sit back from our street a fair distance.

We are still all alone. Why doesn't someone get here? Where is everyone?

God, please help us, I pray.

It seems that time is standing still.

Danny had dialed 911 first. Then he'd called his best friend, Monty, who lives across the street. Next, he'd called Leroy, my friend, whom I had been on the phone with when we first heard Mark's footsteps leaping up our fourteen steps. Leroy had called 911 the moment we'd hung up, knowing Mark was now on the property. We had no way of knowing that help was on the way even before the sound of gunshots had pierced the air. It would seem like hours before any help arrived, and for the very first time, I wished that we did not live so far from town, even though I'd always loved the seclusion.

"Monty, where are you?" Danny screams. "Help! Please, somebody help us! My mom is dying! Somebody please help!" His screams are becoming more and more desperate.

Monty's dad had heard the shots and would not let him out of the house. He sneaked out of his bedroom, knowing he had to help his best friend somehow. My friend Leroy, not knowing where Mark was, loaded his .44, afraid that he might come to his house. He watched out his window for a long time in the darkness of his own home, fearing for his life, never forgetting how crazy Mark could be at times. Our neighbors Jim and Iona, after hearing the gunshots, were making their way across the dark desert with no weapons. Iona was in her bathrobe, but they were coming to try to calm Mark down, having no idea what damage had been done and that he had shot me. They had been waiting for me to bring Danny and Becky over to stay with them so the kids would not have to be afraid anymore tonight. The past two days had been horrible for us all. We had been afraid long enough, and I wanted them away from here, to a place where I knew they would be safe.

I still cannot move or open my eyes. My eyelids seem to weigh a thousand pounds, but my ears are working perfectly. I can still hear my son's desperate cries for help, his little hands still clinging to Monty's .22 rifle. It is the one he used to fire at Mark as he fled the barn after shooting me. He is so scared, but he is determined to protect his family. "Monty, help us! Where are you? Please help us?" Danny is still out on the deck, screaming for help. "Are you all right, Mom? Are you all right?" There is no way that I could find the strength to answer. My dry, sticky lips seem glued together, my teeth clenched tightly. "Becky, is Mom all right? She is not dead, is she?

"Oh, God, please don't let her die!" my young son pleads. I know that this is not a bad dream or a movie. This is real, and it is happening to my precious children and me.

"Please, someone, anyone! Please get here! Please help my children!" I think to myself. I can still hear my son screaming through his tears, loudly and desperately. It is the same way he screamed as he chased Mark out of the barn, shooting at him over and over. My Becky's courage is beginning to fade, and her tears are hysterical. She is still trying to keep her baby brother and sister off my blood-soaked thighs. By now, their little sleepers are stained with blood, and for the first time, Becky can see just how badly I am injured.

"Don't die, Mommy, please don't die. Mommy, I love you so much. Please don't die," Becky pleads. I have never heard anyone cry so hard before. I can only imagine her beautiful face with her long blond hair and blue eyes swollen from the constant crying she has done tonight. I can picture the terror that I know is on her face, and I can feel the tears welling up under my eyelids, which will not come open. I pray that they will not escape down my face, for my children must not see me cry. I need to be strong for them.

It still seems like time has stopped and we are all alone and so afraid because we do not know where Mark is. Why isn't someone here? How long can I bleed like this without dying? Becky is calling 911 again, and they are trying to comfort her. "They will be there any second, honey. Try to calm down and be strong for your mommy. They are on their way."

Where is Rory? He should be here by now. It seems like hours have passed, but actually only about ten minutes have elapsed.

"Monty, where are you? Rory, where are you?" Danny screams once again. All the while he continues to watch for Mark, never taking his eyes off the darkness that had engulfed him just moments before. All the while, Danny clung to his rifle, still feeling the warmth of the barrel caused from firing it repeatedly at the man he had once thought of as his dad. He had no idea if one of the many shots he had fired had even connected with the moving target as he had chased him out of the barn.

Finally, he hears the sounds of Rory's truck. Then he sees it. "Mom, Rory is here! He's turning the corner. We'll be okay now that Rory is here."

As Rory turns the corner he sees Mark's truck parked on the side of the road about a quarter of a mile from our property, on the soft sand just off the pavement of our sparsely traveled road. He turns on all his off-road lights. He is lit up like a glistening Christmas tree, a sight my young son will never forget.

"We will be okay now. Rory is here!"

RETURNING FIRE

For the first time since this night of terror began, there is a sound of relief in Danny's voice. His hero has arrived, and my very brave, very young son will not have to be a man again for a very long time.

Thank you, God. I give thanks, knowing we will be safe now and my children won't have to be afraid anymore. Just don't let me die yet, not in front of my children, I pray. All my strength is gone now, and I fall sideways against the bar. I can't straighten back up.

"Danny!" Becky screams. "Mommy died! Our mommy is dead! Oh god, please no!" Her desperate screams are ear-piercing. My baby girl is hysterical, and I am helpless to comfort her.

Please, God, help me move. Help me talk or open my eyes, anything, so that my little girl knows that I am not dead. I need to tell her that I am not dead. How can I let her know? She cannot handle this. I have to let her know. God, please help me, I pray. Somehow I find the strength to move my index finger. Thank God she sees it.

"Danny, she's not dead. Mommy's not dead. She moved. I saw her finger move. She is still alive."

I can't believe the sound of relief in their voices. They know that they still have their mother—for now, anyway. My babies are hysterical, still trying to climb into my arms. They are longing for the familiar, comforting voice of their mommy. They still do not understand why I am not holding them and loving them the way that I always do.

Through my daughter's screams, I recognize the sound of Rory's truck as he guns the powerful engine to speed up the long, sandy driveway. Help is finally here, and I'm not afraid anymore. The sense of calm that surrounds me is comforting, knowing that Rory will take care of us now. Danny yells down to him as he screeches to a halt.

"Rory! Hurry! Mark shot my mom. She is up here! Hurry, please! She's bleeding so much." I can hear him leaping up our long stairway two or three steps at a time. When he reaches my side, his voice is soft and gentle. His voice is trembling as I feel his touch.

"Linda, where are you hit?" he asks.

I somehow manage to speak. "My arm…my chest." Those are the last words I remember speaking for a long time.

More help is on the way. Jim and Iona are coming up the stairs.

"She will be okay. Your mom is tough," Rory says reassuringly. "Where is Mark?"

"We don't know," Danny answers. "He ran away through the bushes. He went toward the corral, and then he just disappeared. I couldn't see him anymore because it's too dark." I am so thankful for the sound of relief I can hear in my son's voice.

Things are not very clear now. I know that Iona is here, taking care of me, and I can hear Jim crying. He is saying over and over, "I don't believe this is happening. I can't believe this is happening." In spite of his own shock, he is trying extremely hard to comfort me. I can feel his hands gently stroking my hair as if to comfort a scared puppy. He is very upset. I am glad to hear that he is leaving with Rory and Danny to look for Mark. They know that no one is safe until he is found. I pray for their safety, knowing that Mark is capable of anything now. They all know he has totally lost control. They all know he has gone crazy. Thank God Iona is still taking care of me. She is being very calm and reassuring. She knows exactly what I need, and her medical experience is a comfort to me. Her presence is like a shining light from heaven, and I feel for the first time that I may not die after all.

As my mind wanders, confusion once again sets in. Rory has just told the kids that I would be okay. Rory is very smart, which leads me to believe that I may not be as bad as I think. If this is true, then why is my friend Jimmy so upset? Why is he so sad? Thinking about his reaction has me afraid again. Afraid that I am dying. I still cannot talk or move, and I know this is not normal. There is something very wrong with me. I have always been extremely strong and healthy, but now I am just scared. I don't want to die, and I can't let my kids see me die.

No part of my body will function, but I am aware of everything that is going on around me. I'm glad Iona's said I am okay. I think she is wrapping my arm with something. I hear someone say Roy and Nicki are here to get the babies. Thank God!

The paramedics are finally here, along with the firemen and the police. The firemen from town, in the big truck, were the first to arrive. There was a train coming that would soon block the only way across for a long time. The driver knew I had been shot, so he quickly increased his speed, making it safely across the tracks, knowing a delay could cost me my life. He was so brave. He came onto the property before an officer had arrived, something not usually done if the suspect in a shooting cannot be located.

Although it doesn't hurt, I know that a part of my arm is gone and that my insides are filled with pellets. My lungs must be damaged, because it is becoming almost impossible to breathe. I try hard to concentrate on breathing smoothly and evenly. It is not working, and the feeling is one of pure panic. I am thankful for the mask on my face, realizing that it must be oxygen. Why don't I hurt anywhere? I can't believe that I do not hurt. They are moving me around now, and there are hands all over me. I can't believe that I am still aware of everything that is happening. The paramedics can't see.

"Where are the lights?" the paramedics ask.

"There are no lights in here!" I hear Iona answering.

"Get the damn generator. We need more light!"

Everything is moving slower than ever now, and I wonder why all this is taking so long. Please, God! Let them take me away from here before I die, I pray.

I can feel the presence of a lot of people, and it seems like everyone is talking loud and in slow motion. I have no feeling in my body, and I still feel no pain and I am very confused about this. I know that I'm dying. They cover me with a blanket, and I can feel them picking me up. They must be putting me on a stretcher. Someone is strapping me down, and I can feel them cinching the straps tightly across my limp, wounded body. God, why are they strapping me down? Am I already dead? I go over everything one more time. I can't move, I can't see, I can't talk, and I do not feel pain. I know that I should be hurting really bad. Am I unconscious? No, I can't be, because I can still hear everyone talking. I don't understand any of this. If only I could open my eyes. It is so frightening not to be able to see what is happening. Oh god, why did this happen? How did this happen?

Where are my kids? I know that they are not around anymore, because I can't hear their voices. I think that Iona is gone too, and I still don't know where Mark is. What happened to him? I haven't even heard his name. Wouldn't they be worried if he had gotten away? I'm the only one they seem to be worried about. No one is sad. Wouldn't someone be sad if Mark was dead? Maybe not. Maybe no one except for me. He didn't shoot someone I love. He hadn't shot my mom or my friend; he had only shot me. After tonight, they would all be happy if he was dead. He can't be dead, because someone would be talking about it if he were dead. God, if I only could talk, then I could ask someone about him. It is no use, because no matter how hard I try, I can't make myself talk. I am so weak.

I can feel the crisp, cold air on my face now. They are carrying me outside, and I know I am alive because they haven't covered up my face. I can feel the jarring of my wounded body as they descend the steps. Our stairs are very steep, and I feel like I am falling. I can tell that I am going down headfirst, and I know now why they strapped me down so tightly.

I'm trying so hard to open my eyes. I want to see what is happening, but it is no use—they will not open. I am very wet, and I feel as if I have been immersed in a tub of water, but I know that it's my blood. Thank God, they are finally taking me away. It has only been about twenty minutes since the shooting, but it seems like hours passed before any help arrived. Once again I wonder how much blood a person can lose without dying.

The cold air is gone, and I am much warmer now. I must be in the ambulance, yet the door must still be open, because I can hear voices very clearly. I sense a great deal of confusion.

"Where is she going?" someone asks earnestly.

"To trauma" is the quick reply.

"If she goes clear down the hill, she might not make it. She's going to trauma first, she probably needs blood, the strong voice orders.

My god, what did he say? They must think that I can't hear them. Bless me, Father, for I have sinned. Please, God, forgive me for my sins, I pray. This is it. I know I will die on the way to the hospital.

I hear the door slam and can feel the jarring motion of the ambulance as it moves slowly down our long horseshoe-shaped dirt driveway. The siren comes on, and it is very loud, and I can only wonder if the lights are flashing also. I hope my kids are not watching, because I know that I am one of those people now, one of those people being rushed to a hospital. But this is only supposed to happen to other people, or in the movies and on the news, and in bad dreams. Only to other people, not to us. Not to my family. This can't be happening. It is just a horrible nightmare. Or is it?

I pray all the way to the hospital. I pray that my kids will be okay, and I pray that I won't die. My kids would be so sad if I died. They all love me so much, and we are all so close. They're my best friends, and I am their mom. My own mom just died three weeks ago, their Mana. We loved her so much.

Please, God, do not let them lose me too.

I remembered my Becky only minutes before, how she had reacted when she thought I had died. What if I can't move my finger ever again? I think, remembering how I had been able to let her know I was alive earlier. I pray with all my heart that no one will have to tell her that I died tonight.

I hope my babies are okay and not still frightened. They don't understand any of this. I pray that everyone will forgive me for the horrible nightmare I've put them through. My mind flashes once again to Mark, wondering about his fate. Did he finally get control of himself? I know that he will never ever forgive himself for this. It was not the Mark that I love who shot me; it was that other guy, the one that he hates so much. It was the one he couldn't control, the one who could take over his mind with almost no warning. How could he become so weak? It was a question that had always haunted me.

What have I done to my kids? Will my Danny and Becky ever be the same again? Will they be scarred for life? Mark has put us through hell, and I know that we can never be together again. I can never forgive him for this. This is too horrible, and this time, he has gone too far.

Don't let me die, God. Please! They have been through enough, and I know they cannot handle any more. Please, God!

Suddenly, I remember the phone calls today. Mark had called nine times today, begging me to let him come home. He had said, "Without you, I have nothing to live for." I had to say no, because he had been acting so crazy. I wish I had left sooner. Mark needs help so badly, and I know he was not ready to come home yet. I wish he had understood we had all the time he needed. He needed to get better and to learn to control his temper before he could come home. He knew I still loved him, so why did he panic? Why did he have to do this? I am so confused, and I still can't believe he shot me.

I know that he really has gone crazy to do this.

Will I ever see my kids again? Will I ever come home again to the barn that I love so much? I can tell that we are moving very fast now, and my mind is also racing. If only I could talk. Where are my kids? They need me more than ever now, and I can't even be with them. I know my babies are okay now with their aunt and uncle. I am glad the kids aren't riding with me to the hospital, just in case I die before I get there. Are all these things they have hooked to me helping? I don't feel better, and I wish Iona were still with me. Why didn't they let her stay with me? If she were here, I wouldn't be so scared.

Oh god, I am so scared. I am dying, and I am all alone. I have never felt so abandoned.

"How are you doing, Linda?" someone is asking. "Stay with us. We're almost there."

I try to answer, but it's no use.

Again, the movie crosses my mind. The one Rory and I had talked about on that horrible night just two days ago, when this nightmare began. I told him I didn't want to be in a movie like this. I can't believe this is still going on. It is just too scary. I hate scary movies. I always have.

I tried so hard to stop it all. I should have left, and I should have been more afraid and thought more logically. I should have thought of my kids' safety a lot sooner. I knew from the past how crazy Mark could get, but I'd always made excuses for him. There is no excuse for this, and I know it. I'm so afraid of how this movie is going to end. If only I could have written the script. If I'd written the script, it would have a happy ending, because I love happy endings. They always make me cry, and Mark loves to tease me when happy endings make me cry.

Is this movie over? No, it can't be. There are still too many loose ends. Not everything has been explained yet. If the ending is sad, can I handle it? I have to be patient. I will just have to wait until it is really over so I won't jump to any conclusions. The main character, Mark, is still missing. It is not over yet. It can't be. I wonder if I had missed something important. Did I miss the final scene is this last act? Did something happen that I am not aware of? Maybe the ending is too sad for them to tell me and they all think that I can't hear them. Maybe they're afraid that I can't handle a sad ending right now. I have to stop worrying, because I have to get stronger first. I'm so weak, and I've lost so much blood.

This is not a good time to worry about the future and possible sad endings. It is a good time to think happy thoughts, thoughts about the past and how it all began. I will put possible sad endings aside for now and think about happy beginnings. I remember it all so well, and I am so glad I kept a journal. If this movie is over, I will know soon enough. Yes, for now, I will only think happy thoughts. I don't wait to think about dying. I don't want anyone to die today.

CHAPTER 2

FRIDAY THE THIRTEENTH

Thinking back, I realize how much my life with Mark has been like a movie, because it had all began just like a scary, silly horror movie would. It was Friday the thirteenth, and the moon was full. Some of you are probably thinking that it is no wonder this tragedy has occurred, while others might say that I should have been a little more hesitant about beginning any relationship on such a day. It never bothered us, though; in fact, we always used to joke about it, because our relationship was proof that Friday the thirteenth was a lucky day, it being the night that our life together had begun.

I remember the night that we met like it was yesterday. It was very hot on this particular July afternoon. My friend Gene owned an old stud that I had been working for him. I liked to ride in the late afternoon in order to beat the heat, but it did not seem to help on this especially hot day. The air was unusually still for this time of the day, and I was beginning to feel uncomfortable with every deep breath that I took, working myself along with the horse harder and harder, drawing the hot air down my throat and deep into my lungs. My headband, which was an absolute must for me to wear in the hot summer months, had quickly become drenched, but it served its purpose, as it kept my long bangs from sticking to my forehead as they would when covered with sweat. My bright-yellow tank top exposed my bare arms and shoulders, which, along with my fair-skinned face, were feeling the scorching rays of the sun more than usual today. It was not unusual for the temperature to reach upward of 110 in the hot California desert.

I was glad to have this opportunity to work for Gene, since I was very busy trying to establish a good reputation as a trainer and riding instructor in our small desert town. It had been my lifelong dream, and I was finally pulling it all together after many years of hard work and learning. I had begun my experience with horses and training like many others. With a shovel or a brush in hand, I would clean the stalls and groom the horses, always paying strict attention to the trainers as they worked their perfected magic on the strong, beautiful, athletic Arabian horses. Having the opportunity to work for my neighbors Jane and Don of Ja-Don Arabians was a wonderful opportunity for me since I was eager to learn all that I could.

Gene was very well-known and liked, and I knew that if he were pleased with my work, my reputation would spread quickly. In a small town like ours, word of mouth was the best advertising you could get. Someday I would be a highly respected trainer and riding instructor, realizing my lifelong dream. I was blessed with a strong, healthy body, good hands, and a deep understanding of horses.

On this afternoon, exhausted and drained by the heat, with all my work finished, all I had on my mind was relaxing. I loved the hot summer nights at our barn so much.

By late afternoon, it would finally cool down enough to enjoy being upstairs, where we lived. The soft, cool evening breeze made it possible to be fairly comfortable in our small but cozy upstairs living quarters, even in the dead of summer.

Our barn, as we affectionately called it, was a two-story structure with stables and a breezeway below the living area, and it only measured twelve feet by thirty-six feet. We had a living room, kitchen, bedroom area, and a makeshift bathroom. We had no electricity, so even the smallest of fans would be totally useless. For us it was kerosene lamps and a small twelve-volt television that ran off the car battery. When the battery would go dead, we would simply push the car and pop the clutch so we could recharge it as we drove to town, or rev it up in the breezeway below.

Later on, we would purchase a generator for washing clothes, vacuuming, and sawing firewood, and it was only to be used an hour or so a day, and never just for lighting. That was unheard of and totally unnecessary, as far as I was concerned. When the generator would run out of gas, we would siphon gas from the car. What a joy it was to accidentally get a mouthful of gas! Needless to say, I became an expert at siphoning.

We had it all figured out, and most of the time, things would run very smoothly. An ice chest served as our refrigerator, and many mornings we woke up to floating leftovers. It was a beautiful, simple life, and I loved every minute of it, although the kids would disagree with my feelings. They wanted to be a little more modern, and they were a little embarrassed to say that they lived in a barn. I know that if I had never started calling it a barn, they would have never thought of it as one. After all, it was our house, and it just happened to be above the breezeway and six stalls below.

We had running water like everyone else, along with a propane water heater and stove. To have the last two luxuries, all we had to do was fill our five-gallon propane tank every five days. If it ran out in the night or we were broke for a day or two, we would always make do. Our toilet was our biggest problem. My son Jimmy, who was fifteen, would vouch for that. It was a porta-potty, made for camping, and it was his job to dig a hole and bury the contents about every third day. The hardest part was carrying it down the stairs without spilling a drop. He would probably tell you that the worst part for him was trying to make sure it did not splash him as he dumped it into the hole or threw in the first few shovels of sand.

With all these little inconveniences, I have to admit that I never loved any house I ever lived in anywhere nearly as much as I loved that old barn. Because it was so small, our family could not have been closer, and I firmly believe that love grows stronger in small places. Someone wrote a song about it years later, so I know I am not alone in my thinking. When you are forced to live so closely, you know one another very well, and you almost have to get along because you cannot get away from one another. You learn very fast that "sorrys" are so important and forgiving is a must.

My beautiful eighteen-year-old daughter, Shelley, and her boy-friend, Rudy, lived with us that hot July. Unlike her mom, she was built like a model, tall and slim, with legs up to her neck, and she was truly my best friend. When I came home that day, wanting to relax, I soon realized that Shelley and Rudy were arguing. I am sure it was over something silly, since it usually was, and Rudy was upset and just wanted to get away for a while.

"Come on, Ma," he said, as he affectionately called me. "Let's go to town. We can go to Mac's," he murmured softly toward my ear with his hand cupped, as if to tease my daughter that we were telling secrets. Rudy was trying his best to try to convince me to go to the town hangout that Mac and Jean, whom I considered my friends, owned. At that time, I was boarding their yearling Arab colt, and I was working with him. I had been meaning to go for a long time, hearing Jean brag about the one-man band they had hired on week-ends, and because I played guitar, I had been a little curious. There was not much to do in our very small town, which was fine with me, since I had absolutely no interest in going out.

In fact, I had not been out once during the six months since my husband of twenty years and I had separated. I had been with him since I was fifteen, had five kids with him, and he had me totally convinced that no man would ever want a woman my age with five kids. My life had been very sheltered, and at this point in my life, the last thing in the world that I wanted anything to do with was another man. He had hurt me very badly, and I was scared to death to even think about another relationship, knowing full well that I wouldn't know how to act if a man did ever ask me out. My life was com-plete, and I had everything I wanted at this time. I had my precious kids and my two horses. My business was going well, I was proud of myself, and I was doing just fine and had all that I would ever need. Or so I thought.

I don't know how he finally did it, but I let Rudy talk me into going to Mac's that night, even with it being Friday the thirteenth and all. I decided it might be fun to get out, knowing I had nothing to worry about being with Rudy, the young man whose dark hair and cute, boyish, all-American good looks had won my daughter's heart.

He was always a lot of fun, and I knew that he would take good care of me. After all, he was soon to be my son-in-law. I knew that I was a mess after working with horses all day, but because my ex had truly convinced me that no one would ever be interested in me, this gave me a "why bother to fix myself up" attitude. So I didn't.

I have always been a very simple, natural kind of girl, so getting ready for my big night out on the town was quick and easy as I washed my hands and face and changed the sweaty headband that I had worn all day. A little deodorant and a splash of Chanel No. 5 would do me just fine. My medium-length blond hair was tucked up under my headband, and I hadn't even bothered to change my clothes except for my dirty, sweaty tank top. Since it had been a difficult decision for me to go out, I was determined that it all seem very casual. My wardrobe consisted solely of jeans, a white tank top, and cowboy boots. I had bought my boots at a yard sale a few years back, already broken in, for a buck. They were the most comfortable things I ever put my feet in, and I loved them. Standing only five feet two inches, I also felt very tall in them, as the heel was about an inch and a half. The white top would show off my beautiful, dark tan. In spite of my fair skin, I always tanned really well, and my blond hair looked very light against it. Looking as perfect and as beautiful as I cared to look, I was feeling very comfortable, so off we went, much to my daughter's delight, as she was looking forward to a little time to herself. She gritted her teeth, gave us a smirky little smile, and sent us on our way.

When Rudy and I got to Mac's, we saw our friend Bud sitting in a booth. Bud was an old Indian who had definitely experienced life to the fullest. His tough, suntanned skin showed his years. I had spent hours listening to his many interesting stories, realizing that he was very wise when it came to people, not trusting many—and rightly so. I considered him a very good judge of character. Rudy and I sat at his table. Good, I thought to myself. This night seemed very casual so far.

Just when I was beginning to feel totally comfortable, two men walked in, and I could not believe my eyes. I had lived here for a year now, and I had never noticed even one guy who was anything like my type. I have always liked the hippy look, long hair and beards, and when these two men walked past our table, I did a very noticeable double take. The younger of the two had definitely noticed me, as he nodded, raised his brows, and flashed a beautiful smile my way. His dark-brown hair was perfectly layered and fell to his shoulders. His beard was trimmed short, and his beautiful blue eyes stood out against his tanned-looking complexion. He was very handsome and exactly my type. He gave a hearty, quick laugh, having noticed the obvious double take I had done. He appeared flattered and didn't seem at all embarrassed by any of it. I felt the warm flush of my face, picturing the bright red that I knew it had become. He was with an older man, whom I later learned was his dad. They both appeared to be a little drunk, but it was a funny, very controlled kind of drunk.

Moments later, with no warning, they were sitting at our table, and to my surprise, I was glad. It was a small booth, and Mark sat across from me, next to Bud. The music was loud, and Bud and these two men were leaning over to talk to each other. It was very awkward at first, which made me feel uncomfortable immediately. I am never one to be shy, but for some strange reason, I was feeling extremely shy at that moment.

Suddenly, this nutty guy was introducing us to his pet bug. It was perched on his hand like a parakeet, and it was by far the ugliest bug I had seen. It was an ugly, dark green with a very fat body and huge wings, and it was so big that I pictured in my head the awful mess it would make if it were squished. While Bud was trying to make the proper introductions, this weird but cute guy was trying his best to convince us that this ugly bug was his pet. He and his bug had my full attention. This guy was so funny, and there was no doubt that he was flirting with me with his beautiful smile and an occasional wink.

Unexpectedly, this so-called pet bug took off across the room and was flying around like crazy, scaring everyone. Rudy and I were laughing so hard as Mark kept yelling and cussing at the bug, telling him how sorry he was going to be for not minding, all the while gritting his teeth and frowning in the direction of the bug. Here was this guy explaining to us that the bug's behavior this evening was not at all unusual. He always acted up whenever he took him out, he explained, with brows raised and a look of disgust. It was so funny, and I was laughing very hard.

"Don't worry. When I call him, he will come back," he said with a serious face.

"Sure, sure," we kept repeating between our laughter, all the while shaking our heads in disbelief. "Some pet bug," I murmured with a big, flirtatious smile.

I still cannot believe what happened next. We had a lot of laughs about it the next couple of years, because Mark could not believe it himself.

"You don't believe me? Watch. Come on, bug." He raised his voice, gritting his teeth at the same time. "Get your little ass over here right now, or I am never taking you out again," he demanded with a stern, serious look on his face.

He held his hand up real high, and at that very instant, the stupid, ugly bug flew clear across the room, circling frantically a few times, and then headed directly toward us and landed right on the very hand that Mark had raised as a perch. It was something you had to see to believe as Mark was beaming like a bright light and grinning from ear to ear, all the while trying to act like he had expected it to happen. Later, he said he could not believe his own eyes. He told me, from that moment on, he knew I would be his, because his luck had never been better than on that Friday the thirteenth night, with the full moon shining so brightly outside.

If you have not guessed already by the little bug act, Mark was never one to be shy. He was very outspoken and had more personality than anyone I had ever known. We talked for quite a while that night before he finally realized I was single. I felt very flattered when he told me that for a while he had thought that Rudy was my date. It took him a couple of hours before he finally convinced me to give him my phone number.

The thought of dating scared me to death. I did not have much of a chance with Bud and Rudy both helping him talk me into it. I was definitely outnumbered. When Rudy went to the bathroom, I was at Mark's mercy. Since I had been on the inside of the booth,

I had felt protected by Rudy, but Mark saw his chance and acted immediately. He stood up, grabbed my hand, and with a little hesitation, a squinted-up face, and a slight tug-of-war, gently pulled me to my feet. As we danced, we talked a little more seriously. His light cologne was mesmerizing, and he was not shy about holding me close. I couldn't believe how natural it felt, not having been held like that for a long time. I could feel my heart pounding and hoped that he could not feel it too. He told me that I smelled like flowers and that it was making it very hard to control himself. "It isn't me, silly, it's my perfume," I responded shyly. His cute little chuckle let me know that he was just teasing, and he promised to be good.

I had wondered how old he was, so with a squinched-up smile, I boldly asked him. I told him that he shouldn't get any ideas, because I knew that at thirty-six, I was too old for him. He assured me that I wasn't, because he was thirty-two. Four years' difference was perfect, he said, with a beautiful, satisfied smile. "Oh, is that so?" I said smugly. "And just how did you become such an expert on age differences?" I teased, smiling and looking right into his beautiful blue eyes. He was lying, of course. I guess that was as high as he felt he should exaggerate since he was really only twenty-nine. Later, when I found out the real difference in our ages, it did not matter. By then I was head over heels, 100 percent, genuinely, hopelessly in love.

Mark said he had been separated from his wife for many years, which turned out to be true. He also told me he had five kids, just like me. This, however, was not true, but he figured since I had so many kids that I would like him more if he had a lot of kids too. Actually, he had two boys, Mason and Randy, about ten and six. There was also a little girl in Oklahoma named Tanya, who was four years old. He said that he did not know for sure if she was his or not, so she did not have his last name, but he quickly added that everyone who had seen her thought that she must be his daughter because of the resemblance. I will always believe that in his heart, he knew she was his daughter, and I know for sure that he loved her very much.

Our evening was full of laughter, dancing, and talking, along with a lot of teasing and flirting. I hadn't had that much fun in a long time. I was remembering that I was more than a mom. All too soon,

I knew, much to my regret, that it was time to say goodbye. Mark promised he would call the next day and asked me if I would like to go fishing for our date tomorrow night. "Hmmn! Sounds a little fishy to me," I teased, flirting, playing hard to get.

Actually, it sounded like a very exciting first date, I thought.

I had never caught a fish, and it was something I had always very much wanted to do, so I thought it would be a lot of fun. The feelings that I was having about this guy were a little scary and something I had never expected. What is happening to me? I wondered in a surprised way.

"I will call you in the morning after Leave It to Beaver," Mark said. "I have to do some chores for my dad, but I will call you by two o'clock. If I don't, then you will know I lost your phone number."

He insisted I take down his number and made me promise I would call him if I had not heard from him by two. For the first time tonight, he was being really serious, wanting to make sure I got all the details right. "You won't stand me up now, will you? I would be so sad if you did," he said, smiling that beautiful smile and giving me a very sexy wink.

"I will," I said, knowing all along I would not. Then he surprised me. He stood up, leaned forward as to whisper in my ear, and quickly kissed me on the cheek. With a shocked look on my face and my mouth wide-open, I let out a surprised laugh, and he was gone as quickly as he had appeared. I couldn't believe that I was smiling from ear to ear, feeling once again the heat from my beet red face. I wondered if I would ever see him again. I remember thinking he had more personality and charm than anyone I had ever met. He was so funny, and I hadn't had so much fun in a long time. It was nice feeling so womanly again. It was nice having someone care about me in that way, causing me to feel very special and, much to my surprise, very happy.

"What have I done?" I kept asking Rudy in disbelief. What have I gotten myself into? was all I could think about the entire six-mile drive to the barn. Inside I was feeling so happy and more special than I had in a long while. I could not keep from smiling, and I knew that I was glowing as bright as the beautiful full moon that followed us home that night. Who says Friday the thirteenth is bad luck? I thought to myself.

When I got home, I told the kids about my fishing date. I was a little embarrassed about the whole thing, having been so adamant about never wanting to date, and I was also a little worried that they might not approve. They could not believe their ears. They would never have believed me if I had not had Rudy for a witness. They were all very happy about this incredible news their mom had since they had been trying to get me to go out for a long time. After teasing me relentlessly, they all went to bed.

They had almost given up on me. They used to say, "Mom's just happy vegging." At that time, none of them was thinking of what a hard adjustment it might be for them if, all of a sudden, they had to share me.

"Are you two really okay with this?" I lovingly asked Danny and Becky as I sat on the bottom bunk, stroking her forehead after tucking them in to bed.

"Yes, Mommy," my beautiful, precious seven-year-old daughter answered with a yawn, rubbing her tired little eyes.

"Sure, Mom, it's just one date!" Danny boldly answered from the top bunk, sounding like his very mature, for nine years old, self.

One date, I thought to myself as his words echoed in my mind. I wondered curiously if that was all it would be.

All my kids were my very best friends. We were so, so close, my kids and I. They were such a blessing to me, and I thanked God for them every day, always feeling like the luckiest mom in the world. I wondered what my future held for the first time in a long time, knowing I only wanted the best for my children.

My kids were my whole world. How lucky I was to have my five terrific kids! My eldest son, Richie, was twenty. His hair was long and blond, and he had the looks of a rock-and-roll star. That was his dream, and he was an excellent guitar player. He had a good job down the hill, our term for the cities on the other side of the mountain. Shelley came next, followed by Jimmy. He was my shiest child, even though he also had the looks of a rock star and was an excellent drummer. Then there was Danny, nine, and Becky, seven.

Danny was like a little surfer dude, hair to his neck and parted in the middle, layered just a bit. I had been the only one who had ever cut his hair, and he had finally outgrown the bowl cut that he had worn for years. Becky was as cute as could be with her beautiful, laughing, smiling round face and her outgoing personality. They were very happy, well-adjusted kids in spite of my recent divorce and having a dad that didn't seem to have time for them anymore. I was truly blessed when God gave me my kids, and each is very special and very individual. Since they had wanted me to date, and I definitely had a date, I decided to focus on that very subject.

I asked myself if I would look as good to him tonight, when he was totally sober, as I did last night. Other silly questions filled my mind. What should I wear and how would I act? How do you act on a date? I knew that I could only be myself. I wished I could at least blow-dry my hair. I thought that if I could impress this guy when I was scroungy, he was bound to think I looked beautiful tonight.

After we had fallen in love, we would look back and laugh so hard about this first date. That night, he came home with me and never left. I told him how scared I had been that he would not like me as much when he was sober, and he just smiled that sexy smile of his and said, "Are you kidding? I couldn't believe my eyes when you came driving up that night. You were such a fox. My brothers had me worried that you would be some old hag and only looked good the night before because I was so drunk—you know, coyote ugly—and that I might have to chew my arm off to get away." It was so funny comparing what had been our secret fears. We had both been nervous for nothing. It had all happened so easily.

My next big fear was wondering if he was one of those guys who would expect you to sleep with him on the first date. Because of the sheltered life I had led, this really had me worried. I was able to relax a little once we had spoken and everything had been arranged. He said to be at his house at six o'clock and told me exactly how to get there. His house was real close to Mac's, so I knew that I could find it easily. Aside from a terrible case of nerves, which had my tummy filled with butterflies, I was feeling happier than I had felt in a very long time.

All afternoon, Shelley and I had been cleaning the barn. We had danced around, playing my favorite tape, Juice Newton, really loud, a behavior not unusual for the two of us when we were in very good moods. There was one particular song, called "Shot Full of Love," that I was playing over and over. It was one of my favorites, and a part of the chorus says, "Then I met you, and the next thing I knew, there I was, all shot full of love." We played it again and again, just being silly together. We always had such fun doing silly things like that. We were so close. Gosh, I love her so much.

Rudy was able to solve one problem for me, the blow-dryer. When we had first built the barn, we bought everything we could find that would run off twelve volts. I had found the cutest little blow-dryer at an RV store. There was just one small problem: it took an enormous amount of juice, so it would cause the battery to run down very quickly unless the engine was running. If the battery was fully charged, it would work our little twelve-volt TV for at least five days, but because of the huge drain it caused, the blow-dryer was totally useless as far as I was concerned. But this night, I was desperate. So wonderful Rudy started up his little car, plugged that useless blow-dryer into his cigarette lighter, leaned over and opened the passenger door, and said, "You may now enter Rudy's traveling beauty salon, at my expense, please."

"Thank you, sweetie." I smiled and gently kissed him on the cheek, feeling very appreciative of his kind gesture. There I sat for about twenty minutes inside the car with the engine running, radio blaring, blow-drying my hair and never thinking about how silly I must have looked. After that night, it was never worth the hassle again. The best blow-dryer that I ever used was the one where I stood out on our barn deck with that ever-dependable late-afternoon breeze hitting me. It worked the very best of all, and it did not cost a cent for gasoline and never ran down a battery.

After receiving all the well-meaning rules that my kids had laid down for me to follow, "Don't stay out too late," "Don't believe everything he tells you," "Don't be nervous," "Be yourself," and "By all means, don't let him kiss you good night," I felt pretty sure I was as prepared as I could be. I was only me, take it or leave it. The kids said that if he did not like me, he was a total idiot and we would not want anything to do with him anyway. They were definitely my biggest fans.

The kids had their evening planned. They were looking forward to watching the movie The Exorcist, and they were very excited. I did not think it was a good idea for Becky and Danny to watch such a movie, but as usual, they were able to convince me that it would be okay. I warned them that I would be really upset with them if they ended up having bad dreams about it as I reluctantly gave in to them.

I warned the kids that if this guy came by the barn with me tonight, they were to be on their very best behavior. We were definitely not your typical family. I had raised my kids to always tell me what was on their minds, and they were all very much outspoken. I am very proud of the relationship I have with my kids.

I could not prolong it another minute. As I felt very nervous and perfectly beautiful, it was time for me to leave. So much for their lesson on showing their best behavior if I brought Mark by tonight. Earlier on the phone, Mark told me that before we could go fishing, we had to go get some white rock for the landscaping he was doing for his dad's yard. He assured me it would not take but an hour or so and added that he really wanted me to come with them. I had no idea, thank God, that I would be meeting almost his entire family on our first date. Here I was, driving up in my old, ugly, dilapidated '65 Malibu with quite a few dents and a chipped, rusty brown paint job. I drove up the long narrow driveway, only to be halted immediately as I neared the garage.

"Can you pull over into the dirt? My dad worries about oil in the driveway!" I heard someone yell from a distance but could not see him.

Oh my gosh! How embarrassing! I thought, feeling the color drain from my face, all the while aware that if I had driven up in a Rolls-Royce, they would not have been so worried. Knowing all too well that my car had the looks of an oil leaker, and rightly so, I hurriedly backed up and pulled over to the side in the dirt. Since I had been seen and it was too late to leave, I slowly got out of the car, feeling quite embarrassed and even more nervous than before. Suddenly,

38

I noticed a really gorgeous-looking guy kneeling down inside the garage, chuckling to himself, with a mischievous little smile. He appeared to be working on something.

"Is this where Mark lives?" I asked shyly, eyebrows raised.

He nodded, accompanied by a very serious look that made me feel as if he were looking right through me. "Yeah, this is where I live." He laughed heartily, and I could not believe this was happening, my second embarrassing moment. I had only seen him for a couple of hours last night, so I guess it was an honest mistake. You would never know it, though, by the way he was laughing. I was glad that I was quick with a witty reply and a surprised laugh.

"Sorry, it's just that you were nowhere near as good-looking last night. It was kind of dark in Mac's."

Thank God, the ice had been broken. Our laughter got away from us, and the tension in the soft, cool evening air was eased. Relaxing a little, we knew that we were in for a fun-filled, battle-of-the-wits type of an evening. This man had the most beautiful blue eyes I had ever seen, and his very wavy dark-brown hair was styled to his shoulders. As he gently took my hand and led me into the garage, my heart felt as if it would jump right out of me.

After I had been introduced to everyone, and knowing I would never remember their names, it was time to go get the rock. Before everyone had arrived, Mark had quickly showed me all the beautiful rockwork he had done for his dad, and I saw a totally different side of him. This guy was an artist, and his rockwork was beautiful. He was beaming with pride, and rightly so, as he gently led me by the hand from area to area, showing me all that he had done. I was very impressed and totally aware of the butterflies that fluttered frantically in my tummy.

The white rock we were about to go get was to be used along the driveway. You could see where they had left off and where we would put the rock we were getting tonight. The next thing I knew, Mark held the door open for me and I was jumping into a big Chevy truck, his dad at the wheel. Mark shut the garage and jumped in beside me as I slid to the middle, and off we went.

I had just met three of his four brothers. There was Ray and his brand-new girlfriend, Nori; Roy, his wife, Nicki, and their three-year-old son, Jason; and Kyle, the baby of the family. His wife was not there. Kyle followed close behind in his Chevy truck so that we could haul twice as much rock.

"At least your family has excellent taste in trucks," I said, making a cute face as I smiled up at this handsome guy beside me. I had always been a Chevy fan myself.

"I like the way she thinks," Mark said, smiling that beautiful, sexy smile of his as he reached for my hand and held it tightly. I had never expected to feel so comfortable with him, and much to my relief, my butterflies were finally beginning to calm down.

Mark told me he was hoping to do enough rockwork for his dad to buy this truck from him, and it quickly flashed through my mind that this guy might not even have a vehicle. If he had absolutely nothing, would it matter to me? Not if I continued to feel the way I did about him. He was definitely growing on me.

The place we were going was only a few miles away. It was an old, closed-down rock mine, and it was kind of hard to get up the hill where the white rock was. Once we got there, it was obvious that it was worth the trip. It was incredible, and there really was a "mountain" of white rock. After backing the two trucks right up to the mountain, the guys climbed up on the hill directly above the trucks. As they shoveled, the rock just kind of fell right into the truck beds, and in no time at all, they were as full as we could safely fill them if we wanted to be able to drive out of there. Mark was definitely the hardest worker in the group, and I quickly realized that he was trying to impress me. How sweet, I thought. Soon I would learn that it was not an act and that Mark was never afraid of hard work, always giving it his all. He was very good at everything he did.

At last, the work was finished and it was time for a break. For Mark's family, a break always meant a beer. How they all loved their beer! Above the rock, there was a huge building that had just a roof, no walls. We all went up under the roof since a light, cool rain had started to fall. The view was magnificent, and as I tried to absorb it all, it was fun to imagine this place operating in full swing, mining all kinds of rock. I am sure that it was at one time a prosperous business. As far as Mark and his dad were concerned, they had found a gold mine in all that rock. I don't remember much of the conversation, but I remember thinking they all seemed real nice. They were all a little bit different, but very nice and a lot of fun.

Besides Mark, Nori was the friendliest. I liked her a lot from the very beginning, as she was very talkative and extremely bold, trying immediately to make me feel comfortable. Nicki was more mellow, but also very pleasant. We were to become very close later on. I learned she was never one to form a quick opinion about anyone, time would tell all, and she did not miss a thing. If she liked you, she would be your friend forever, and if she did not, screw you. Believe me, she would never hesitate to tell anyone "Screw you" either, and I loved her honesty.

By the time they finished a few beers, the rain had stopped and the wind blew wildly, as it was not uncommon for the weather to change with the blink of an eye in our mysterious desert. They decided it was time to go, and because of the foul weather, our fishing plans had been canceled. We went back to the house, and I watched proudly as they unloaded the rock, Mark working very hard and never seeming to tire.

They each drank another beer or two, and the next thing I knew, we were on our way to the Big Rock Inn. It was a bar just a few miles down the road, and a live band was appearing that night. It was not very much fun for me, since I never really enjoyed places like that. There were a few couples dancing, and everyone else was just sitting around, watching. Having never been a great dancer, I was too self-conscious to dance in front of this family I had just met. Mark could tell I was feeling uneasy, so after one beer and one fast dance with Nori, he told his dad that we were leaving, and I was really glad we had driven my car. As it turned out, they were all ready to leave also.

After I told them all a little about my barn, Ray and Nori decided they wanted to see it, so off we went as they followed close behind. I had not spent very much time with this family, but I knew one thing for sure: I did not have to worry about them thinking my family was a little crazy. Between the two of us, it was definitely a photo finish where craziness was concerned, and I liked them all a lot. I was still a little nervous, though, because at the bar Nori and I had a chance to talk alone for a minute, and I had boldly managed to find the nerve to ask her a question that had lain heavy on my mind the entire evening.

"Is Mark the type that would expect me to sleep with him on the first date?" I nervously asked Nori.

Nori could not help but laugh. "Probably, but I can tell he likes you a lot, so I don't think he will get pushy about it."

It had been an honest answer, and I felt a little more at ease after that. I knew he liked me, but it was nice to hear it from Nori too. Besides, you just never know how a person can fool you. That had been one of my biggest reasons for not wanting to get involved with anyone ever again. People could always fool me so easily, and I always believed everyone.

It was probably because of the crowd in my barn, standing in one room only, or maybe it was the late hour, but Nori and Ray left right away. It was decided I would give Mark a ride home in a little while, and I was really looking forward to having some time alone with him so I could have a chance to get to know him better. I could not believe I was so wide-awake, knowing all too well I would be sound asleep by now on any other night. I was excited, was happy, and was experiencing an incredible boost of energy all of a sudden. I knew in a matter of seconds that I would have this barn cleared out, and I did, in record time.

I was happy that The Exorcist had not scared the kids too badly. They knew they would never get to watch a scary movie again if they appeared frightened, so I was sure they were putting on a good act when they asked me to please leave a kerosene lamp lit for them. Tucking them in to bed, I was nervous and excited about what was ahead for me on this night.

All the older kids, Richie, Shelley, Rudy, and Jimmy, slept in an old trailer we parked about one hundred yards from the barn. Since the only conveniences it had were beds, they never spent much time there. Danny and Becky had bunk beds back in the last third of the

barn, our bedroom and bathroom section. There were no walls sep-
arating their area from mine, just a blanket that hung from the walls
to provide a little bit of privacy. In no time at all, I had managed,
much to my satisfaction, to have the front two-thirds of the barn and
Mark all to myself. It was about time. Enjoying the peace and quiet
for the first time all night was really nice.

"Boy, you sure cleared this place out fast," Mark joked.

"That is one thing I am really good at when it is necessary," I
replied, knowing it was hardly ever necessary. Most of the time, I
wanted to be surrounded by my kids, so when I requested an imme-
diate evacuation, they all knew I was serious and they always showed
me respect by clearing out.

As I looked around, I could not help but notice how romantic
the barn atmosphere seemed. It was the first time I had seen it in this
way. I guess it was because I never had a gorgeous, charming, sexy,
not to forget funny guy right here with me and all to myself. Finally!

The kids had left three lamps burning in the cozy living room
area. I very nonchalantly walked around the room, blowing one out
completely and turning the other two down very low so as to give a
candle effect. I felt Mark's eyes fixed on me, all the while continuing
with my mission to make the room seem as romantic as possible. I
turned the TV off and turned the radio on, a little mood music, if
you please. It was a twelve-volt car radio, of course, with a built-in
cassette player, I explained as I changed the kids rock-and-roll chan-
nel to my "soft love song" station. "It is amazing how much you can
learn to live without and still be very happy," I said with my sexiest
smile.

Leaning over, I gently took his hand, and he rose to his feet,
following me as I led him out on the deck. I was longing to show
him the beautiful view that I loved so much. Our porch at the top of
the stairs served as our deck and was about twelve feet by eight feet.
It had a nice wood rail around it that was a perfect leaning height.
I spent so many hours out on the deck, leaning and looking, crying
and laughing, playing my guitar, watching my precious kids, and
drawing many hours of peace and tranquility from the beauty that
surrounded us. That deck had so many priceless memories for me.

Who would have thought that night, exactly two years and three months later, my kids and I would live through the most horrible experience I could ever imagine? It all started on this very deck, the one we fell in love on.

Standing against the railing, looking out at the view, Mark quietly stepped behind me, placing his arms around me. I had never felt so surrounded, so engulfed, and it was a beautiful feeling. Sitting lightly on the overstuffed couch to our left, we melted together. If I had been anymore relaxed, unconsciousness would have claimed me.

With no neighbors nearby, Mark and I both agreed on this beautiful July night as the wind had died, that it seemed we had the world to ourselves. The view was breathtaking, and the privacy outrageous. The moon was almost full, and I was so very happy. It was not until that exact moment that I realized how much was missing from my life the past months. I always knew that I was an incurable romantic—I loved being in love. I loved the idea of being in love, and now I was once again really, truly, head over heels in love. I could not believe it all happened so fast and that it felt so good.

Mark was the gentleman of all gentlemen that night, and I could not have been more comfortable. It was amazing how well we got along, having led such totally different lifestyles. We shared one thing after another about our past lives. This time, he was totally honest.

"What would you think if I told you I used to be a heroin addict?" he asked bluntly.

"You're kidding," I said, not being able to hide my shock, eyebrows raised in disbelief. "That's awful. I can't believe it, you're kidding me!" I pleaded for the answer I was hoping to hear, that it was just a joke.

"It is true," he answered sadly. "I guess I should not have told you, but I wanted to be honest with you," he said with much regret in his voice.

Fearing what the answer might be, I was still able to ask my very important question. "Do you do it now?" I boldly blurted.

"No. Never. I beat that years ago. I would never do it again no matter what," he replied.

"Thank God" was the only reply I could come up with, feeling relief over my entire body. "I could never handle that, not for anyone" was all I could say.

"Quitting being a junkie is my proudest accomplishment. Hardly anyone can quit for good," he said proudly. "I figure, if I can do that, then I can do anything." He would repeat this phrase during our future together, always trying to convince me he was strong enough to learn to control his violence. The proud look on his face as he made his statement was all I would need tonight and every time that followed. I knew without a doubt he was sincere.

"Tell me more," I urged, giving him my total attention as I moved as close to him as possible.

"Most of my life has been pretty rowdy. I have been in trouble quite a bit. I can't believe I survived it all."

I was surprised that none of this information seemed to bother me. In my whole life, I never even knew one rowdy person.

Even though our pasts were as different as night and day, we seemed to have so much in common. All the basic things like hopes and dreams and the fact that we only needed the very simplest things in life to make us happy. It was very obvious he loved his kids very much and he was looking forward to settling down so he would have the chance to be with them more often. He wanted to give them quality time, something he had not ever been able to do regularly. He said the same thing about his mom, dad, and brothers. It was clear that he loved them all very much.

"I am kinda the bum of the family, the one who has always gotten into trouble. Someday I am gonna make them all proud of me," he said, because he knew that he had not given his family much to boast about in the past.

We were out on the deck for a couple of hours when, suddenly, the time had come. It was the moment that I had been anxiously, nervously awaiting. I knew he was about to kiss me—a girl just knows these things. It was a moment I will never forget. As we sat there together with his arm around me, we had suddenly quit talking. As we looked right into each other's eyes for what seemed to be an eternity, he gently held my face with his free hand and gave me the most gentle, loving kiss I ever had. We had melted together like magic, and I felt my heart pounding in my throat like never before.

I was a little surprised that I let him kiss me, even though I had wanted him to want to. Some people might think I am cheap, but I sure don't feel cheap, I thought to myself. Oh well, it is my life, and I am going to live it the way I want to, I reminded myself as he stood up and pulled me to him, holding me close. After we had stayed like that a few minutes, he gently led me inside, the beautiful light of the moon shining brightly through the open door as we sat on the couch in the living room.

"I wonder what time it is," I told Mark.

Straining to see the hands of his watch, he answered, "I can't believe it is after three o'clock," in a surprised voice.

"Well, time sure does fly when you are having fun." We both agreed. There was never any mention of the fact I was supposed to take him home, and I had no intention of bringing it up. I didn't ever want this night to end, and I did not think I was ever going to want this guy to leave. It never entered my mind that he was really here to stay from this night on.

(There is a line in a song called "Leather and Lace," and later, he had made it one of our special songs because of one line about knowing the moment he came into my house he would never leave. He gave me his leather, and I gave him my lace. It was a perfect song for us.)

The rest of the early morning hours were spent sharing, laughing, and matching wits. We always had so much fun doing that. We found ourselves slowly cuddling more and more. It was the most natural thing in the world. I could not remember feeling so happy or so excited. I knew I was very much in love, crazy as it sounds. After all, I knew what love was. I was not some inexperienced teenager on a first date. I knew myself very well. I knew the last thing I wanted was to fall in love again, but here I was, and it had already happened, much to my surprise. There was not a damn thing I could do about it.

Even though I was feeling like a teenager at this exact moment, I knew I was not, and I knew exactly what I was doing. That beautiful morning, as the dawn broke, I knew I was about to make love with this man I had only known for about thirty-six hours. I could not believe I did not feel one tiny bit guilty or bad. Our lovemaking was as beautiful and natural as our first kiss had been only hours before, and I was feeling happier than I had in many years. So much for strong morals was all I could think.

As we lay on the couch in each other's arms, we watched the sun come up together through the open door. Mark said in a gentle but determined voice, "Someday I am gonna marry you, you know. I have never had me an old lady with class before. Now I do." He smiled.

"Yeah, you do" was all I needed to say. That was all that he wanted to hear, and by now there was no doubt how either one of us felt about the other. It was definitely love at first sight. I was now a firm believer in it, and I knew that there was nothing better.

As all good things must come to an end, now good old reality hit me. I remembered once again I was a mom, and a damn good one at that, so I had to get ahold of myself if I was to continue. "I think it would look a lot better if I am in my own bed when the kids wake up," I said, half-heartedly trying to pull myself away from Mark's tight hold. Reluctantly he released after giving me one more very tender kiss. I got him a pillow and a blanket and gave him a quick but exaggerated "I'm really sad about getting up" kind of look.

He made a cute frown face but laughed and agreed with me. Pulling me to him for another very romantic kiss, he then responsibly let me go. We knew that if I stayed any longer, we would both fall contentedly asleep, and that would not look good. As I climbed into my own bed, I remember thinking that nothing could probably ever go wrong for me again. It is true what they say: love can be so blind.

I knew I had to get a little bit of sleep, as hard as it was to stop thinking about all that was happening to me. In just a few hours, I had to be at a horse show, which was all part of my job. I had promised my friend Barbara, who was also one of my students, I would be there to watch her. I knew I wouldn't require much sleep, because I was on a natural high. I felt like I could conquer the world now and that I could do anything I ever wanted. I was totally, irreversibly, happily in love. Wow! What a wonderful way to feel! I thought to myself.

I like this. As I smiled contentedly and hugged my extra pillow, I drifted into a deep sleep.

When the kids woke up, they did not seem too surprised that my date was asleep on the couch. Thank God I was in my own bed was the first thing to cross my mind. They liked Mark from the very beginning, as he won them over immediately with his charming, outgoing personality. Right from the start, he had them cracking up. I loved so much the way he filled our barn with laughter. I was glad one bridge was crossed successfully, with the three of them hitting it off so well. Mark would soon realize it was not too confusing at the barn with just the younger kids and myself there, nothing like when all the "big kids" were here also.

"I need to use the john," Mark said as I realized he hadn't used it all night.

"Oh, I'm sorry, I should have told you, it's all the way to the back," I said apologetically.

Being so used to it myself, it never entered my mind how shocked he would be when he saw our porta-potty. He came out immediately. "Not to worry, I am housebroken," he said as he headed outside to pee.

"Oops," I said, with a squinched-up face. Nothing I could do about that one, I thought.

After a quick bowl of cereal, I gave the kids their orders, and it was time to leave. I asked Mark if he would like to go with me or if he wanted me to take him home first.

"I would like to go with you, but could you run me by my mom's first?" he answered.

He said he needed to do something real fast, so we stopped briefly before heading to the horse show. We did not stay long, just long enough to watch Barbara's class and introduce her to Mark. I was very proud of my student because she was a fast learner and was doing great with her strong little mustang pony. This was the day that we had our first of many pictures taken of us together. Barbara used her Polaroid camera, and we both looked very happy and content. I was touched when she gave it to me, as it would be a souvenir of our first day together.

CHAPTER 3

ADJUSTMENTS

Mark continued to stay at the barn with us, but once a day, without fail, he would have me drive him over to his folk's house. I would always wait in the car, so I had no idea what he was doing. It never took but a few minutes, and he would come out smiling, never offering any explanation. I was puzzled and beginning to realize that this was very weird. This "weirdness" was eventually explained, very logically, on our fifth day together.

Exploring the desert, we had covered many miles on the dirt roads, loving the peace it held for us and enjoying the scenery with the endless, sharply colored wildflowers as far as you could see. The afternoon was perfect, with a medium-cool breeze beginning to blow as we came upon an old deserted cabin. There were no doors or windows, and of course, it had been ransacked, as most deserted places in our desert had.

Mark could barely control his excitement upon seeing what remained in this old cabin, as it contained only a few but very important things. There was an old counter with a very deep stainless steel sink inside, something that the barn was lacking, which made it a major chore to wash the dishes every day. But even more important, blessing of all blessings, there was a real, genuine, honest-to-gosh toilet, and the way Mark was acting, one would think it was made of pure gold.

"Tonight I am gonna get Rory and his truck and come back to get this toilet, bathroom sink, kitchen sink, and counter," he said, trying to be cool and hold back his excitement, all the while grinning from ear to ear.

"Our barn is not set up for a real toilet. Where would it drain to?" I questioned, puzzled.

"Don't worry, babe, I'll figure it out. You having to drive me to my mom's every day just so I can take a dump is really getting old," he said in a very serious tone.

"Oh my!" I laughed so hard, knowing the big mystery was solved. All these days, the only reason he needed to go to his mom's was so he could go to the bathroom. We would laugh about this forever. "Why didn't you just tell me that's what you were doing, silly? I was beginning to think you were really weird," I teased, laughing all the while.

Needless to say, that night, our good friend Rory, Mark, and my son Jimmy got us a new toilet, basin, and kitchen sink, and by the following day, the toilet was fully installed. We dug a big hole on the back of our two and a half acres, just behind the barn, and ran a pipe from the toilet into two fifty-five-gallon drums, which we covered in rock. Since the bathroom was upstairs, getting it to run down was no problem. A short hose running from our water line would fill the back of the toilet so it could be flushed. It was the same hose we used to fill the bathtub, and it would escape from our grip many times over the next couple of years, hosing down the entire bathroom. Sometimes it was funny, but if you had just put on nice clothes and let the hose get away from you as you flushed the toilet, you were bound to be wet and it did not seem at all funny.

Thanks to Mark, we finally had a real, genuine toilet. Mark joked about the amount of money we would save on gas now that I did not have to drive him to his mom's house every time he had to go to the bathroom.

The next few days were hysterical as it seemed that about every half hour or so, we would hear the toilet flush. "What the heck are you two doing?" I asked Danny and Becky as they sat back on the couch, giggling under their breath. "Does one of you have a problem today?" I asked, having heard the toilet flush every few minutes.

"No, Mommy. It's fun flushing our new toilet, and getting to fill up the back of it with the hose is fun too," Becky answered excitedly.

"Yeah, it's fun, Mom," Danny added, giggling a little.

It had been so long since the kids had a toilet that flushed that they could not resist flushing it over and over. Besides Mark, Jimmy was the happiest of all, because he never had to dump that old porta-potty again.

In the weeks that followed, I discovered there was a lot of need for adjustments. I soon learned this guy, as much as I loved him, was very different from anyone I had ever known. He had no manners whatsoever, something I had always been very big on, and I could not believe the horrible belches that he could unleash. "How can I teach my kids to have manners if you keep doing that without excusing yourself?" I pleaded, as it had been a sore spot from day one.

"Gosh, babe, that really makes sense. I've never been around anyone that had manners." He laughed. "I will try, and if I forget, you remind me."

That was so easy, and I was very thankful that he agreed to my very "bold" request. I had been afraid to bring it up at first, but it got to be more than I could handle in a very short time. Much to my happiness and the shock of his family, he learned quickly that if he was going to be with me, he would have to excuse himself, and that was all there was to it. It took a while to break this rude habit of a lifetime, but I am very proud to say he did it.

I remember a time that we were with Mark's little brother Kyle and his wife, Brenda. She could not believe her ears when she heard Mark say, "Excuse me," for the first time.

"Mark said 'excuse me.' I do not believe it!" she said in total shock.

I was so proud of him even though he was a little embarrassed, but he was happy to see how much it pleased me. We talked about it later when we were alone, and I told him how much it meant to me for his family to see he was changing for the good. "Babe, this is only the beginning of the new me, you just watch," he gloated proudly. Gosh, how I loved him.

During the weeks to follow, I had the opportunity to meet the few friends Mark had with "class," as he put it. He told me how proud he was going to be to introduce me to them and he knew they would be very surprised to find out he had a really nice girl for once. He was certain I would like them all and positive that they would feel the same about me.

Every time he would introduce me, he would proudly say, "This is my old lady, Linda. I finally got me an old lady with class." I wasn't sure if I would ever get used to the term old lady, but I did, after realizing that it was meant with the greatest affection. All guys like Mark proudly referred to their women as their old ladies. It didn't bother me for very long, but it was definitely an adjustment for me.

Gene and Linda were the first of Mark's friends I met, and I liked them from the very beginning. We hit it off right away, and they were very happy that Mark had found a girl like me. They saw a whole different guy now, and they could hardly believe the change in him. Gene and Linda soon became, without a doubt, our very best friends they had two kids, Tim and Tara.

Moms and Pops were next. It was easy to tell by their names that they were an older couple. They were so special, just a couple of old "hippies" who would do anything for you. Mark loved them a lot, as well as their teenage daughter, Gretchen, and I was blessed that they took me under their wing from the very start and always made me feel like family. My only complaint was, sometimes when Pops and Mark got together, they could get so crude. When they were drunk, there was no one who could be ruder and cruder than those two, all in fun, as far as they were concerned. Moms agreed with me on the subject, and we did not think there was anything funny about it. When they were sober, they were the nicest guys in the whole world. When we would talk about how much it bothered and embarrassed me, he would always say, "Babe, we were just having a good time, I'm sorry," and promise he would try harder next time.

Mark had one biker buddy whom he still kept in touch with, named TJ. He and his wife, Connie, were the friends Mark had known the longest, and we spent a lot of time with them. They were one of our favorite couples to party with, and Connie was a very good cook. Mark and TJ had many funny stories to tell from their rowdy past together, so there was never a dull moment when we were with them. TJ was the perfect example of what Mark was becoming. The years, Connie's two daughters, and a son of their own had mellowed him out, and he was a family man now. Underneath his hardcore biker look, he was just a big old teddy bear at heart. He was very proud of his family, and Mark and I loved them a lot.

Next was Big John. He had two kids he loved with all his heart. He was the perfect example of what babies could do to a tough guy's heart. Big John is the kind of guy that will look you right in the eye and tell you nothing bothers him.

"It's no big deal. I don't let things bother me. I really don't care." That was Big John's attitude, and I learned very quickly that it was all bull. The two of us grew very close, even more so later on, and I know him very well. He is a very big man with a heart to match, and probably more feelings than most people I have known in my life. He is such a special man who meant the world to both of us.

Leroy was the last friend I met. He was the mystery man I had heard so much about for weeks, and I knew that everyone loved him a lot. He was definitely the most successful of our group, having a great job with the phone company, his own house, and excellent credit. He was very mature, always responsible, and definitely the one we all looked up to the most.

From the beginning, it was very apparent how much Mark loved our barn. In no time at all, I learned he had very weird thumbs. They were bright green—I never saw anyone make things grow the way he could. "In a few years, this place will look like a lush green forest," he would say. Believe me, it was well on its way. He could turn a twenty-inch twig into a twenty-foot tree in to time at all. I laughed at him at first, but then I learned the laugh was on me. Who would ever think someone could grow a big, fat tree out of a tiny naked twig? Every time he planted something new, he would always have to show me.

It was a beautiful, cool evening, and as he did every evening and morning, he was busy watering the many twigs he had planted a few weeks earlier. He had spent a great deal of care choosing the twigs off a friend's tree and soaking them in water until they sprouted tiny hair-like roots before carefully placing three-foot sticks in rows all over our property.

I was about a hundred feet away, schooling my athletic Arabian mare, Lindina, over some jumps. She was dapple gray, with her beautiful long mane and tail flying freely in the wind. As I put her through her paces, her performance was flawless on this particular afternoon. Sitting her cantor was easy, feeling as though I were on a rocking horse, up and down, up and down, slow and easy. Finishing the course, I slowed her to a trot and began posting to her perfect rhythm, using only the slightest fingertip pressure on her reins as she responded perfectly to all that I asked of her. She loved to work for me, and we played friskily like well-schooled dancers in the soft cool air, rising and falling, feeling my hair flowing in the breeze.

I had worked many hours for Ja-Don Arabians in order to earn her. Her bloodlines were excellent, and when I got her as a ten-year-old, she had never been broken. She was totally trained by me, and I was very proud of all that we had accomplished. Together we became one as we worked and played, feeling the perfect motion of her canter and lead changes as she turned with the slightest pressure of my leg. Mark had described it as "magical," never missing a chance to watch us work as we melted together as one, but today, something else would have his undivided attention.

"Babe, can you come here a second? I have got something to show you," I heard him calling in the distance, boasting with pride. Cantering over to his side, I slipped off my mare, giving her a loving pat on her neck. "Look, babe!" he exclaimed proudly, pointing to the tiny green bumps on its three-foot twig. "They are growing already. I can't believe it! In no time at all, we are going to have big green trees everywhere!" He was so excited, like a child with a brand-new toy.

"Oh, honey, that is so neat! I am so proud of you," I said, hugging him. "This place would be nothing without you. I am so excited!" I said with my cutest excited look.

I knew that it would be beautiful someday, and I loved his child-like gentleness as much as I loved his strength. At first, he would have to call me to show me the brand-new little green whatever-it-was that showed the first signs of life every single time. Even later, he always kept me informed of his daily plantings, and he was as proud of the rest as he was with the very first one.

It seemed Mark always had the garden hose in his hand as he rooted, transplanted, separated, fertilized, and watered for what seemed like hours a day. The garden hose soon became his trademark. In between doing his dad's rockwork, he started our own. Our place was really starting to look neat, and it was so nice to have him take such an interest in the place. After all, it was my dream come true, and I felt like a fairy princess. All I had to do was make a wish, and Mark would make it come true.

"Honey," I said in my pleading, I-want-something voice, "I would give anything to have real wood on the inside walls of the living room." I pointed to the unfinished inner wall. The plywood on the outside showed, along with the two-by-fours that framed the walls. His face looked as if an idea had come to him, and it surprised me to hear his simple, short, and to-the-point reply.

"Maybe someday, babe," he answered, shrugging his shoulders.

Oh well, I thought to myself, so much for walls.

The very next day, he told me he had a surprise. We went to his dad's house and spent the next hour or so very carefully tearing down some wood fencing he had. "This will be great, babe. Your walls you wanted!" he boasted proudly, knowing how pleased I would be. Much to my surprise, these old, weathered one-by-six boards were about to become our very rustic, very beautiful living room walls, and I loved it.

When we were all done except for trimming it out, I made a suggestion that made him laugh his distinct, hearty laugh.

"Let's just break up these boards that are left and use them for trim. It'll be so rustic." He was still laughing. "Please, honey. Trust me, please, it'll look really neat no matter how they break up," I pleaded. "It will go with the rustic style, honey."

"You are a nut," he teased, but trust me, he did as a masterpiece was born.

Our living room was one of a kind and had my most favorite walls ever. He wasn't about to admit my idea was a good one until he got other opinions. As it turned out, everyone thought our "dog fence" walls were great, so he had no choice but to agree. "Well, I have to admit, babe, you are sure easy to please," he chided.

"I know," I teased back, making a face. "Stick with me and you will be the happiest man alive."

He said, "I am already," as he put his arms around me.

"Good," I replied with a brilliant smile. "Thank you for the walls, honey. They are perfectly beautiful."

He could only laugh.

Mark always seemed to have an endless amount of energy, and in no time at all, he had our place cleaner than it had ever been. In order to do this, he went to the dump a lot. The only vehicle we had was the Malibu, so he could only take a little bit at a time, using both the trunk and the back seat. There was only one problem: our storage area was filling up very quickly. He was always bringing things home we either needed or we might need someday. It made perfect sense to me, being the biggest pack rat that ever lived, and soon we were both obsessed with going to the dump.

Our dump had no gate, so it made much more sense to go at night with flashlights. After a few months, our excitement dwindled when we realized half the town seemed to be there, fighting over all that wonderful junk. After all, there wasn't much to do at night for excitement in our small town. We had one gas station and one store, and they both closed at nine. There were no signals and a few roads that were paved. The partiers were at the two bars, and the rest of us went to bed early. What a great life I had, and I was on top of the world—for now, anyway.

Mark was happy to see the success of my small stable. It was the one thing I was good at, besides being a mom, and he was very proud. He had always been uncomfortable around horses, but now he wanted to learn to ride. He wanted us to be able to ride together, knowing it was one of my favorite things to do. When I had suggested riding a few times in the past, he always came up with an excuse. One day, Mark brought it up again, and the timing was perfect.

"Babe, I really want to learn to ride, but I am kind of nervous about it," he said, walking over to me as I was brushing my Appaloosa mare, Christy. She was an old posse horse and was in foal with her second baby for me. She was a horse that anyone could ride, being very lazy and calm. The worst that could happen would be that she wouldn't go too far from her stall at feeding time or would try to run home for the same reason.

Mark had already had a few beers on this particular day, and it was just starting to cool off, so I thought that now was as good a time as ever. I figured, if he had enough beers to get the nerve to tell me he was scared, he probably had enough that it would not matter if he were a little frightened. I had just finished with a student who was learning to jump. It was a perfect afternoon, being a little cooler than normal for this time of day.

"Okay, honey, it's time," I said. "Saddle up, Christy. You are going to learn to ride."

Mark spent a lot of time helping me with the horses and had mastered the task of saddling them. I was glad that I had an old Western saddle, knowing he would never have been able to ride with my English one. He chose his tack, and I got my Arabian mare, Lindina, out and saddled her up. She was my jumper, and like most Arabs, she could be spooky on a bad day. She was definitely my horse. Other riders confused her, and she would act terrible, as she was trained to respond mostly to my legs. She would not be good for a beginner.

Christy became Mark's horse, knowing she was not afraid of anything and that all she needed was a firm hand and someone who wouldn't let her get away with doing what she wanted. I knew Mark would be perfect for her. I watched proudly as he cinched up her saddle, slid the bridal on, and adjusted the bit. He carefully checked each of her hooves, making sure they were clean. Smiling nervously, patting Christy's neck, I knew he was ready as he led her toward me.

"Are you ready, my handsome cowboy?" I flirted, Texas accent working perfectly as we led our horses out of the breezeway.

"I reckon I am ready as I'll ever be, you gorgeous little filly, you," he flirted back in his own sexy cowboy accent.

"Just a few words of advice, honey," I said more seriously. "You will do just fine if you trust me, yourself, and most importantly, your horse. There is a lot more to riding than just staying in the saddle," I warned.

"Let's do it, baby!" he sounded as ready as he'd ever be. He cupped his hands together, giving me a leg up, and as I threw my leg over, I looked up at the heavens, saying a short little secret prayer.

There was only one question in my mind: I wondered if he could be taught to stay on her without falling off. After filling the saddlebag with ice and a few beers, I had been a little worried. Much to my surprise, drinking or not, with a few little tips, Mark turned out to be a natural on a horse. I was very proud and very excited, knowing we had one more thing in common. He loved to ride almost as much as I did. "I can't believe how easy this is," he said over and over, his nerves having all but disappeared, and he was feeling like a real cowboy now. Because of it being his first time, and with me knowing how sore he would be tomorrow, we only took a short ride of an hour or so. The last quarter of a mile, I let him go ahead, laughing at the cloud of dust he was leaving as horse and rider stormed wildly into the breezeway.

Christy had brought him right to her stall, and even though he had so much fun, I could tell that he was glad to be home as he swung his leg over and stood on solid ground. "Boy, my butt hurts!" he said with a strong Texas accent as I rode slowly and controlled right up to him. He was walking bow-legged, as if he was still on a horse, and I was busting up, laughing. He always made me laugh so hard. "Did you see how good I was at keeping her in a gallop on the way home, though, babe? I did good, huh?"

"I don't want to burst your bubble, honey, but that is called barn sour. She knew she was heading home and it is time to eat. I don't usually let them get away with that, but you were having so much fun I didn't have the heart to stop you. Next time, you need to control her. It will be a good lesson for your second time out," I informed him in a stern yet teasing tone. "You can't allow her to do what she wants," I explained, eyebrows raised.

Mark responded, still in his best cowboy accent, "Well, if my butt is hurting this bad next time, I'm gonna want her to run home even faster. I feel like someone tried to split me in two." I was still cracking up, and I couldn't believe that I could be this happy.

In our short time together, we spent many hours on those horses. It was nothing for us to take off at the spur of the moment, with the dogs running ahead, flushing out rabbits. Sometimes we'd bring the guns, trying our best to pick them off, pretending we were real cowboys. My mare would always freak out when the gun fired, so Mark would always have to warn me to get a good hold on her before he fired.

Our favorite ride was to town, six miles there and six miles back. It was quite a trip, so sometimes we'd stop at his dad's house. Soon Mark became an excellent rider. When we were broke, we knew we could always have a good time, since shooting and riding were two of our very favorite things to do, and they were both free fun. Needless to say, we never rode out of there without that old saddlebag full of ice and beer. We didn't need much to have a really great time.

The time had come for me to meet Mark's kids, and I was very nervous. "What if they don't like me?" I asked Mark with a worried look.

"They will love you, babe, don't worry."

His kids lived down the hill in which was about a half hour's drive from where we were. We knew that my old Malibu would heat up coming through the pass, so Shelley let us borrow her little Chevette. "It'll run fine," she promised. "Just watch the water, because it might heat up just a little coming up the hill. It won't happen if you remember to check the water."

I was nervous when I met Mark's beautiful ex-wife. However, she made me feel comfortable and was very nice to me. His sons, Mason and Randy, were both dolls. Mason wanted to come home with us, but Randy wanted no part in leaving his mom.

Later, I learned that Randy had never gone with his dad before. In fact, Randy hadn't spent much time with his dad at all. Mark seemed to understand when Randy said he didn't want to come. We said our goodbyes, and off we went, Mark, Mason, and me in Shelley's wonderful Chevette, water checked and all. It was at least a hundred degrees that hot August afternoon.

About a quarter of the way up the pass, we noticed the car was starting to get hot, and about halfway up, it got even worse. By the time we were three quarters of the way up, it was definitely time to pull over, because the radiator was boiling, steam coming out everywhere. "Now what are we going to do?" I asked, tears threatening. We thought there had been no need to carry water. After all, we had just checked it. As we sat there half-laughing at our predicament, inside I was trying to keep from crying. I had wanted to make Mason's first experience with us unforgettable, but not in this way.

Then Mark surprised me. "There's no time like the present for a beer." As usual, we had an ice chest with beer, but this time we hadn't brought ice, only one of those blue freezer things filled with gel, and there were three beers inside.

"The beers," Mark said excitedly. "I'll just relax and drink one. By then, the car will have cooled down enough and we can take the radiator cap off without losing any more water. Then I'll add these two cold beers after I start the car. That'll get us to the top of the hill to the gas station."

I couldn't believe what I just heard. "You're going to put beer in Shelley's radiator?" I asked, bewildered.

"It'll work, babe, trust me," he replied reassuringly. I could see that Mason was definitely his son by the way he was laughing.

The heat was practically unbearable along the side of the freeway that afternoon, so I reluctantly agreed. I was willing to try almost anything to get out of there and get home.

"Start it up, babe!" Mark hollered over the noise of the traffic speeding carelessly by. The sound of the engine starting was music to my ears that day. Besides the horrible heat, I had been scared that someone was going to swerve over and kill us all at any moment. "My hero!" I proclaimed as Mark gave me a high five, and Mason was laughing very hard as he joined in on the action. We had bonded, his young son and I, and I learned a very important lesson that day, one

I will never forget. If you ever need water in your radiator and all you have is beer, use it, because it really works.

Mason and I loved each other from the very beginning, just as his dad and I had. He was definitely his father's son. He was very outgoing and funny, just like Mark, and he fit into our family like he had been there all his life. He and Danny, being only a year apart, became best friends, just as Mark had known they would. When it was time for him to go home a couple of weeks later, he didn't want to go. His mom agreed that he could live with us for a while and go to school with Danny. We'd see how it went. Immediately, a triple-decker bunk bed was built, and Mark's eldest boy became part of our family. I loved him so much, and from the very beginning, he called me Mom.

Once Mason was living with us, Randy started to come up quite a bit on weekends. He was such a doll. It was nice to watch Mark enjoy both his boys so much finally, really getting close to them. "This is the first time that I've ever had a normal life to give them," he had told me one day, feeling very proud of himself. He thanked me so many times, saying if it hadn't been for me, he would never have gotten so close to his kids. He loved them very, very much, and he was a good dad to all our kids.

I was so glad to see how much Randy was enjoying his dad. One day, he told me, "You know what, Linda? Before my dad met you, he was like a bum. Now he's something. I love him."

I will never forget that conversation with Randy as I'd never forget the way his dad beamed with pride later that night when I told him what his son had told me. He was very proud of his "new" self, and I know that his boys were also. He was also very happy to be so close to his parents now, and he spoke of how badly he wanted them to be proud of him.

"They are!" I would tell him. "I can tell that they love you very much."

"Babe, I know that they love me, but I haven't always given them much to be proud of in the past," he would say sadly. "Now I will!" he beamed.

September was Mark's birthday. Since our family always made a big deal on birthdays, we planned a party. We'd have it at his dad's house, and it would be just his family and mine. Except for when he was young, Mark could not remember having a birthday party. Our parties were always the works, including the "Happy Birthday" song, blowing out candles, and of course, opening presents. He was a little embarrassed by it all in front of his family, but he knew he had to get used to it now that he was a part of our family.

It was very funny watching him, and he really didn't know how to act receiving presents. In spite of his embarrassment, he was very appreciative. One present, which was very special to him, came from my son Richie. It was a spray nozzle for the garden hose. We all laughed, seeing Richie so happy, knowing he had given Mark the perfect gift that day. "It's perfect," Richie bragged. "He's always got that garden hose in his hand." We knew that was right, because the garden hose had become Mark's trademark.

For weeks, Mark had been showing me a piece of property about halfway to town that he had been keeping his eye on because someone had planted a bunch of trees a few months back. You could tell someone must be planning to build a house there and started the landscaping early. For the past month, Mark had been saying, "No one is taking care of those trees, and they're starting to die." It was driving him crazy to see those beautiful young trees die off for no reason.

One night, out of the clear blue sky, he said, "Come on, babe, we're gonna go save some lives. We've got to get that little pine tree on the way to town before it dies. You can drive the getaway car. We'll be like Bonnie and Clyde."

"We can't do that. What if someone sees us?" I said, surprised at what he wanted to do.

"It'll be okay. It'll only take me a minute to get it out, and I'll throw it in the back seat. All you have to do is sit there with the engine running," he replied.

I was very nervous about this plan, but I knew he was right. Those young trees would die if they didn't get care soon. We waited until about ten o'clock, and off we went, partners in crime on a very still, dark night. As I approached the lot, I killed the engine and the lights at the same time. Realizing how noisy my old car was, we decided to change our plan a little. We couldn't leave the engine running. Not far from the lot, there were two houses with their lights on, and I was so afraid they would catch us. You could have cut the tension with a knife. I watched nervously as Mark got not one but two trees, and as he came toward the car, I started the engine and put it in gear.

"Let's go," Mark said after tossing the two trees and his shovel in the back seat, dirt and all. For a brief moment, we felt like Bonnie and Clyde, especially me, never having done anything like that before. My adrenaline was pumping as I drove nervously back to our hide-out, the barn, watching for headlights the entire three or four miles. Holding the flashlight in the darkness of the night I watched as Mark carefully planted, fertilized, and watered his priceless treasures.

It took about two months before all the traces of our night of crime disappeared because of all the dirt in the back seat of the car. The kids griped for a long time about the dirt since every time they rode in the back, it would get on them and in their eyes. We felt awful every time they asked why we didn't use the trunk. It was a good question, and we wondered about it ourselves. We figured Bonnie and Clyde made mistakes—big ones, in fact. Look how they ended up. Besides, it was faster, not taking the time to open the trunk, so we laughingly consoled ourselves with that thought.

So much for our life of crime—at least we saved the trees. It was hard for Mark to watch the slow death of every other tree on that lot. You'd have thought they were people, the way he talked about it. "People just don't care!" he would say every time we drove to town. He was definitely my hero for saving those baby trees. What a heart he had at times.

The month of November held a lot for us. Mark met my dad, and they liked each other immediately. He was excited to learn that Dad had been a professional baseball player, having played center field for the Angels back in the late forties and early fifties. His name was Cece Garriott, and he played when the actor Chuck Connors played baseball, before his acting career began. He and his wife were close friends of the family back then, before he became a movie star. Mark liked to brag about how I used to know the Rifleman. It was true even though I was only about five years old when my dad retired.

My and Mason's birthdays were both in November. On my birthday, we had a little marriage ceremony. It wasn't legal, of course, since we were both still married to our ex-spouses. As we pretended we were being married, Mark placed a very special ring on my finger. It was an ET ring, and he said it stood for extraterrific. It was very romantic, definitely a Kodak moment, and many pictures were taken. I was now thirty-seven years old, with a thirty-year-old boyfriend that wanted to marry me more than anything in the world, and I truly felt adored. In two days, I would find out just how much my life was about to change.

From the beginning, Mark made it very, very clear to me that he did not want any more kids. I got on the pill the first month we were together. But remembering to take the pill had been a problem since I had had an IUD for five years previous and hadn't needed to remember about pills. Using birth control was for the best, since I definitely noticed Mark's lack of patience with the kids a lot lately.

One night, when Mason, Danny, and Becky were sitting at the bar, doing their homework, I was on the other side, making dinner. The four of us were happily discussing our day, not being unusually loud, having learned that being too loud would sometimes upset Mark. He was reading the paper about ten feet away, in the living room area of our twelve-by-thirty-six-foot barn. All of a sudden, with no warning, Mark blew up. "Shut your damn mouths now! I can't even read the newspaper with you laughing and talking so loud!"

Without thinking, always trying to keep him happy, I went along with him for a moment, nicely hushing them up. "Better knock it off, or the ogre's going to be a grouch." Soon after, thinking about how this was one of my favorite times of the day—fixing dinner and sharing with the kids—I spoke up loud and clear. "Wait a minute, Mark. I have made a lot of adjustments for you, and I'll probably keep doing so, but there's no way I'm going to make those kids stop talking because you can't read the newspaper." My boldness surprised me.

"Shut your mouth! Just stay out of it!" he screamed, teeth gritted. His stare was cold and deliberate.

"You need to try concentrating a little harder and stop trying to listen to us at the same time you are trying to read," I said with voice raised and tears threatening.

"That's it, bitch, I've heard enough!" And he stormed out of the barn, taking two or three steps at a time, madder than hell, and went for a walk until he calmed down.

I was very shocked at the way Mark had behaved, having never seen that side of him before, and I was feeling very angry. I was glad he didn't mention it again when he came back in for dinner. "Sorry, babe" was all he said as he brushed his lips to my cheek.

"I hope so," I replied, still feeling very disgusted about the whole incident and fearing that this kind of behavior might become a habit for him.

As time went by, he became an excellent reader during confusion in our small barn, and it was something that we would laugh about a lot in the future. It had not been one bit funny at the time.

The next afternoon, Shelley and I both had doctor's appointments. She was almost certain she was pregnant, something she and Rudy had been hoping for. "Mom, I am so excited! I just know that I am pregnant!" my glowing daughter exclaimed. I was to be fitted for a diaphragm since I couldn't seem to remember to take my pills. I kept forgetting for four or five days and then taking three or four at a time to make up for it. It was so confusing.

Shelley was in one room and I was right next door after we had both given our cup of urine. Before they could fit me with a diaphragm, it was mandatory to make sure I was not pregnant. Both doors were open, and the doctor saw my daughter first. "I'm sorry, the test is negative," I heard him say. "Maybe next month you will get your wish." My heart broke, as I knew the disappointment my daughter was feeling.

He entered my room with a serious look, and I was puzzled, thinking they could not fit my diaphragm today. "Well, it seems your daughter's wish came true for you today. You are approximately five weeks pregnant." I felt the color drain from my face as my daughter, upon hearing, entered the room.

"You've got to be kidding!" I pleaded. "I can't be pregnant!" I replied, on the verge of tears.

"The test is positive, there is no doubt," the doctor repeated, much to my surprise.

I could hardly believe what I was hearing, all the while knowing how much Shelley wanted a baby and instead finding out her mom was pregnant. As we left the doctor's office, the three of us (Rudy had come along) were a mess. They were heartbroken, and I was shocked, not to mention scared to death, wondering how I would ever tell Mark. "Please promise that you won't say a word to Mark until I have more time to figure this out," I pleaded, this being more than I wanted to deal with at this time.

You could have cut the tension with a knife that night in the barn. No one was saying much, and the kids were unusually quiet, which I was grateful for under the circumstances. Not long after dinner, they got a little more rambunctious and started giggling. "You guys knock it off, now!" Mark scolded them with a clenched fist.

"Leave them alone! You are so mean! What is wrong with you? They are just being normal kids!" I shrieked. With all the tension I had built up, it was just the excuse I had needed to get me going.

"This sucks! I've had it with you and your normal kids!" he screamed sarcastically as he went out the door and headed down the stairs.

I wasn't through. "You are such a jerk!" I screamed, storming out on the deck. "Since you're leaving anyway, you might as well know. I'm going to have a baby." I turned, went inside, and slammed the barn door very hard, listening as he slowly walked down the stairs, never trying to respond to my shocking statement. Bastard, I thought to myself.

Early the next morning, I was awoken by a knock on the door. It was Mark, and it would be the first of many times he would show up with his heart in his hand, begging for my forgiveness.

"Don't you want to know how I feel about the baby?" he asked sadly, hanging his head.

"No!" I said, shaking my head, eyes filled with tears. "You've always made it very clear you don't want any more kids. I'm really sorry, but you know it was an accident, and you also know that I could never get rid of it. I already love it so much, and it is a part of you and me," I said in a soft voice as he put his arms around me.

As our eyes me, I recognized a familiar look of his, a look that I loved so much. It was for only me to see, and it was part of Mark that I truly cherished and the Mark that I adored. It was a look that had no ego behind it, no masks, no pretense, no hard guy, just pure, honest, loving, caring, getting-it-all-out-in-the-open feelings.

His words had never been so sincere as he said, "I love our baby too, please give me a chance to show you," patting the tummy that he knew held his child.

He could always turn me to putty at times like this; he knew exactly what to say and do. As he held me close for what seemed like a very long time, quivering, he said, "I can't believe how bad I want this baby, babe."

"I'm glad, honey" was all I could say, wondering if a baby would help him learn to control his anger. His behavior lately had been as different as night and day, like Jekyll and Hyde, and it was not a good thing.

It was an unusually warm, sunny day, and we had ridden the horses to the aqueduct near the barn, to sit and watch the water and smoke a joint, enjoying the peace and quiet. All of a sudden, he surprised me with a statement that really confused me. "You know, babe, sometimes it really scares me that I love you way too much."

With a puzzled look and creased brows, I responded, "That is so silly for you to think that, honey," in a serious, shocked tone. "You can't ever love someone too much, because the more you love some-one, that's the best there is. You can't ever love someone too much. Our love is the most love there is. It's the best there is," I said in a serious tone. Most of the time, what I said made perfect sense to him, but this time, I could see he wasn't totally buying it.

"It still scares me, 'cause I know I love you way too much. It scares me what could happen. It just scares me," he replied. As we walked up to where we had tied the horses, I was still confused and a little frightened by his statement, knowing that Mark thought something bad could come from our love.

After we were over the initial shock of my pregnancy, we settled into a time of anxiously awaiting the birth of our baby. Sometime in late November, Mark and I had another fight, as they were starting to come more often. It was one of our one-nighters—meaning, Mark had been made to leave and had returned the next day and convinced me to forgive him, as always. It seemed that he would never do quite the same thing twice, so I was always hopeful that he could change for the better. Most of the time, when he would slip, he was very good at catching himself and apologizing right away, and I could live with that.

He'd say to me, "Babe, give me a chance. I can change. If I can get over being a junkie, then there's nothing I can't do. Hardly anyone ever gets over being a junkie, and I did. I can do anything I set my mind to, so please let me show you. Give me a chance." He always knew all the right things to say, and he was always so sorry. I can't believe how naive I was.

That cold night in November, when we had our one-nighter fight, Mark had left Mason and gone to his dad's. Somehow, it was decided between Mark's mom and Mason's mom that it would be best for Mason to stay with his grandparents from now on. The way things were going with his dad, I tended to agree. Mason was okay about it; he loved them a lot, and they loved him. They bought him some real nice clothes, much nicer than we could have afforded, and were always very good to him. Mark's parents were wonderful people, and all their grandchildren were very special to them, so I knew they were very happy to have him.

Our first Christmas together was a disaster. Mark didn't know what it was to have a real family Christmas. He hadn't had one since he was a kid, and in our family, this day was as big of a deal, if not bigger, than birthdays. There were presents galore, and it was very exciting. When morning came, the kids were filled with excitement. "Santa Claus has come!" the kids had squealed as they woke up and ran to see their presents. Danny and Becky were still pretty young, and their excitement got me going. I was there, of course, building a fire in the chilly barn and sharing their excitement, but Mark would not get out of bed no matter how hard I pleaded.

"It's too damn early," he said, in a mean, stern voice.

With tears in my eyes, I begged him to get up. "Please, honey, don't do this. Christmas is so special to us. All the kids are waiting for you, please!" I begged. "Please get up for me!" The kids decided they would try, but nothing worked.

"Come on, Mark, get up, please," they begged.

"Get out of here! Go open your presents. I will see them later. Now go!" His answer was final.

I knew it was useless, but I did not give up. "Please, honey, I am begging you," I pleaded one last time.

"Not now, I'm too tired," he replied angrily. "Now leave me the hell alone. Now!"

"You are such an ass! I hate you when you act like this," I mumbled angrily as I walked away.

I couldn't let him ruin Christmas for the kids, so I did the best I could to get through it. I didn't do too well, though. I'll have to admit, I shed a lot of tears that Christmas morning. Once Mark finally woke up and listened to all the big kids tell him what a creep he had been, he felt really bad. That didn't help me any, though. It was too late, and we'd never get that Christmas morning back. The damage had been done. He had been very mean and thoughtless.

I'll never forget his face when he came in the barn later. In one hand was his heart, in the other a very special gift. It was a gift he had been bragging about for a week to me. "It is the best present you could ever imagine," he had been telling me. "I thought of the perfect gift for you. You're gonna love it." It was, too. It was a beautiful wood rocking chair for me to rock our baby in when it was born. It was probably the most thoughtful, perfect gift I had ever received. Why he had to ruin our Christmas morning the way he did, I will never understand. I hated it so much when he acted like that. If not for that, it would have been one of the most beautiful Christmases I ever had. Mark learned a big lesson, though, and our next Christmas would be different.

CHAPTER 4

THE VIOLENCE BEGINS

It was sometime after New Year's, and we were heading home from Leroy's house. Becky was in the back seat, singing in her sweet, little eight-year-old voice. She was always such a happy child, and hearing her sing made me smile. Mark was exhausted and not in a good mood; he was out of pot, and the fact that we didn't have extra money for it did not make him happy.

"Quit that gosh-dang singing! You're irritating the hell out of me!" he yelled at my baby girl, teeth clenched.

"Leave her alone! She's just singing! You make me so mad when you act like this! What a mean man you can be!" I immediately responded angrily, volume raised slightly.

"Shut your friggin' mouth now!" he yelled back.

Looking back at my sad little girl, giving her a supportive look, I said, "Honey, please stop for just a few minutes. We will be home soon." I winked. "I'm sorry he has to be such a grouch, sweetie." Reaching back, I gave her a reassuring pat on the leg and a comforting smile.

He was not going to go without a fight on this night, however. "Get your knees out of the back of my seat," he demanded angrily. "How many times have I told you about that, Becky?" He turned his head toward her, revealing a mean, hostile look. That was all that I could handle, pulse shooting up like a geyser, my maternal instincts kicking in.

70

"You are such a monster! I can't believe this!" I said harshly, voice raised sharply. I was very irritated at his behavior. "Just because you are out of pot, you don't have to be so mean! Leave her alone!" I turned to my precious daughter. "Becky, please, honey, don't sing and keep your knees out of the seat." I reached my hand over the seat, slipping her tiny hand into mine. "We are almost home, and we won't have to be around him." I blew her a kiss with my right hand and another big smile, hoping that he hadn't wounded her spirit.

As we drove up our driveway, it really began to get serious. "You are such a bitch!" he screamed at me, grabbing my forearm.

"Just leave us alone!" I screamed, pulling my arm away, shaking my head in disbelief. "You are not going to treat my daughter like that! You are the meanest man I have ever known! Just get out!" It was only a moment before my tears began to flow.

"I'll leave, bitch, don't you worry about that." Pounding up the stairs, me hot on his trail, he went straight to the bar and grabbed my keys.

"What are you doing? Give me my keys!" I screamed, following him down the stairs.

Just as we reached the bottom of the stairs, I grabbed his hand, trying to pry my keys loose from his grip. He grabbed me by the arm, swung me around, and threw me to the ground. I felt my stomach hit first, and then my head. I went down with such force that I saw dark for a minute. I wasn't sure if I'd been knocked out, having never been unconscious before. Immediately Mark realized how hard he had thrown me and was trying to get me to my feet to make sure that I was okay. I stayed on the ground, fighting his attempts to help.

"Leave me alone! Just leave me alone. My baby, my baby!" I shouted hysterically. "You hurt our baby!" Tears flooded my eyes and poured down my cheeks as I held my stomach.

Over and over I repeated these words as Mark sat in the dirt next to me, both arms around me, rocking me like a baby. I was certain that something was going to be wrong with our baby. In no time at all, I had calmed down a little.

"I'm sorry, babe. I'm so sorry, babe. What have I done? What have I done?" he pleaded over and over. "Please forgive me. What have I done?" He was very sorry, and his words were sincere—there was no doubt about that. They always were.

After I got my breath, he helped me to my feet. "Come on, babe, we need to go inside. I will help you," he urged. We started up the steps, and slowly we went up one step at a time, holding my tummy, his arm gently around me, and I went to the bathroom. Ten shocked seconds went by. "Oh my god! I am bleeding a little!" I cried. I knew there was something wrong. In all my previous five pregnancies, I had never spotted even once. What had this blow to my body done to our baby?

"Babe, I am so sorry. What have I done? My god! What have I done?" We were both very frightened.

"We've got to get you to the hospital right away, babe."

"Wait, wait, just let me think," I said, shaking my head in confusion. "I have to think, just let me think!" I knew how important it was to do the right thing; our baby's life might be at stake. "Let's go to Gene and Linda's and tell them what happened. We'll get another opinion. It's only a little bit of blood, so maybe it's okay," I said with a soft, strained voice and tear-streaked face. "I don't know what to do. Maybe Linda will know."

I knew that by the time we drove the half hour to their house, I might be better. If I were worse, there would be no doubt about what I would do. "There is an urgent-care center right near their house. If I need to, I can go there," I murmured softly. I was worried that Tim and Tara would find out what Mark did to me.

We left immediately. By the time we arrived at Gene and Linda's and explained briefly what happened, I had spotted a little more. We all agreed that I should go and be examined right away. "Linda, please drive me?" The last thing I wanted was to be around Mark at this moment, feeling nothing but anger and disbelief, again, at what he had done.

"Of course I will," she said in a very comforting voice. "But first, take some aspirin," she ordered.

My headache pounded both temples, and I was starting to feel a little sick to my stomach. I was still really upset with Mark. I couldn't believe that he had done this to me. All the "sorrys" in the world wouldn't bring back my baby if something were to happen to it, I thought to myself as I glanced back at him and shook my head in disbelief as Linda and I left the house.

After the doctor examined me, he told me the baby seemed to be okay and only time would tell. "Go home and stay off your feet for a few days, and if any more bleeding occurs, go immediately to the hospital. That is an order, young lady!" I smiled up at him with much gratitude. "By the way, are you sure you are not further along in your pregnancy? The fetus seems quite larger than it should be."

"No, I can't be further along. It must be a big baby is all," I explained the best I could. "Thank you so much, Doctor," I said, shaking his hand as we said goodbye, all the while dreading facing Mark again.

When Linda and I arrived back at her house, I was still so angry with Mark that I could hardly stand to look at him. We told the guys what the doctor had said. Mark was walking around, looking like a lost puppy. As usual, his heart was in his hand, but for the first time, he was getting no response from me, and he was hurting. I was thoroughly disgusted with him. "If you know how wrong it is for you to lose control like that, then why do you let it happen?" I asked sternly, eyes narrowed intensely. He hung his head, shaking it from side to side, and gently grabbed my hand. "Leave me alone! Just leave me alone," I said sternly. "I hate you for what you did!"

I decided to take a shower before we left. Feeling the presence of someone else, I look up to see Mark. He was standing on the toilet, peeking over the top, trying to say "hi" and make me smile. "Babe, it's me. I love you so much," he said. He managed to get a little smile out of me. I was still in a daze about the whole thing.

What am I going to do? was all I could think. This was very serious, and the big question in my mind was, Could I take the chance of something like this ever happening again? Had he learned a lesson from this? He could not have been sorrier, I was sure of that, and I was so confused.

When I got out of the shower, we had a long talk. Mark said that he would understand if I didn't want to be with him anymore, because he knew that what he had done this time was really bad.

"I know that sorry doesn't seem like anything this time, but I am, you know," he said, head hanging low. "I'm sorrier than I've ever been in my whole life, babe, please believe me," he begged.

"It doesn't matter how sorry you are. You did it and now I have to be afraid it will happen again." I backed away as he walked toward me. "How can I ever trust you again?"

He gave up. "I don't blame you. I am so ashamed," he said, voice quivering.

"Honey, I need some time to think about all that has happened. Please understand," I said in a soft but stern voice. "You know that I love you, but I cannot take the chance of this ever happening again. This is very serious."

"I understand, babe" was all he could say as he opened the door and got in the car, head bent in sorrow.

We drove to his brother Kyle's house in silence as I fought back tears of confusion. It was very hard for me to do, but I knew it had to be done. I was so scared and still very worried about our baby. The doctor had told me time will tell and to go home and stay off my feet. That was exactly what I did, not taking any chances with my baby.

For two days, I lay on the couch in the barn and I was very sad. I was starting to feel that the baby was going to be okay, and I missed Mark so much. I was lost without him. We were always together, and there was a definite void in my life that couldn't be filled by anyone else.

The kids were all very attentive to my every need, and naturally, they were angry at Mark for what he had done to their mom. "I hope he never comes back, Mom. You wouldn't let him, would you?" Danny asked.

"Honey, you know that I love him very much and I am going to have his baby, and besides that, he is really sorry," I argued my case softly.

"I think you would be crazy to forgive him, Mom," he sternly argued back.

"Don't you want Mom to be happy?" I continued on, pleading more intently.

Loving me the way that he did, my young son finally agreed. "Yes, I want you to be happy, so I guess it's okay," Danny very reluctantly gave in. I know that my young son loved Mark very much; he just didn't want him to hurt me.

I didn't know what to do since he hadn't even called. The last thing he had said was, "Call me if you change your mind." How long could I be so stubborn, knowing how badly I wanted him to come home? All I needed was for him to hold me and tell me how much he loved me and everything would be okay.

Why hadn't Mark called? He'd always called me before when we'd had a fight. As soon as he'd get to town, he'd call and tell me how sorry he was and ask if he could please come home.

"I'll show you I can change, babe," he'd always say, and indeed he would. I was beginning to realize what a Jekyll and Hyde he had become. There were no gray areas, only black or white, heaven or hell.

There was still no phone call, no message, no Mark. Later, he would tell me that he just felt too ashamed to call. "There was no excuse this time, babe. I could've killed our baby."

Sadly, I knew that he was right.

There was only one thing for me to do this time. I called him at Kyle and Brenda's. When Brenda answered, we talked briefly and she told me how sad Mark had been, then she put him on the phone.

"Honey, I want you to come home. I miss you, and I'm lost without you. The baby's fine, I can tell. Will you please come home? I need you so much, and I love you," I pleaded with him. "I know how sorry you are and that you would never do anything like that again," I continued, begging with all my might.

"Are you sure that's what you want, babe?" he asked with much surprise in his voice.

"I've never wanted anything more. I want you home."

He was so happy. I told him that I'd be there in ten minutes, and I was. It was a very touching reunion. We both knew we didn't want to live without each other and that something that bad would never happen to us again. The violence problem had been solved, and it had almost cost us our baby's life, so we were sure that it would never happen again, absolutely sure.

Everything started going really well for us in the months to come. Mark was doing a lot of work for people in our small town. He was stuccoing houses, doing rockwork, and doing any kind of odd job that someone needed done. The extra money came in very handy. He never really made a lot at once, but he made sure that it came in pretty regularly. He was a real hard worker and was always the happiest when he was working. He took so much pride in whatever he did, and rightly so—everyone was always pleased with his work.

In January, Shelley's biggest wish in life came true. She found out that she was pregnant. Finally! We were very excited, knowing that most of our pregnancy would be spent "pregnant together." Her baby was due almost exactly two months after mine, and we had a lot of fun with it.

"Look at this, Mom," she'd say when we were out shopping. Then the salesgirl would comment, "That's your mom?"

"Yes!" Shelley always replied truthfully.

"Shelley, I told you to stop trying to tell people that I'm your mom. She's always doing that to me, to try to make me look old," I would respond in a surprised chuckle.

The usual reply was, "I didn't think there was any way you could be her mom!"

We had such fun with that routine, and I was happy that I still seemed so young to others. "I am proud that you're my mom," my beautiful daughter would say with her beautiful, brilliant smile, never embarrassed to walk hand in hand with me.

Both Shelley and I had an unbelievable craving for ice, nothing but ice. I had very strong teeth and could eat any kind of ice, but Shelley didn't, so hers always had to be crushed. Her favorite was from Mac's, where Mark and I had met. It was the perfect ice for her, she'd say, and Rudy made plenty of trips those six miles to town to get Shelley ice.

Toward the end of my pregnancy, I could hardly do anything that took two hands, because I couldn't put my cup of ice down. I know that this weird craving I had for ice was the biggest reason I kept my weight down so well. I got into my old jeans within a week of giving birth. All I had was that old, familiar loose flab to deal with. Any woman that has had a child can relate to what I'm talking about.

As it became hotter and hotter, my feet began to swell. It was a problem I always had when I was pregnant in the summer months. Shelley had some swelling also. I worked the horses until I was five months pregnant, still jumping my Arab till then. Later, I would wonder if I should have kept jumping that long. When I couldn't button my jeans anymore, I figured I'd better quit with the trick riding stuff and wild horses. Mark and I would continue our nice pleasure rides until two months before the end of my pregnancy, since at that time I was too large to get on my horse safely.

I always loved being pregnant, feeling really special, as if I were the only one in the world that could do this. The two men I had babies with had always made me feel really special when I was pregnant, and I'm sure that helped a lot.

Mark's big thing was making sure I walked a lot. "Come on, babe, let's go to H&E lumber and look around," he asked one afternoon, as it was beginning to cool down.

"Honey, I'm tired, and my feet hurt," I whined, giving him a cute frown as I pushed aside the hand he had offered to pull my enormous body up off the couch. It was our favorite store, and we went there often, just browsing around, looking on every aisle. "Okay, I guess, if it will make you happy." Still in a pouting tone, I reluctantly gave in. It always amazed me what big steps Mark could take, and for me to keep up with him, I would almost have to jog.

"Come on, babe, keep up! It's good for you to walk," he said with a serious grin. "I'm not gonna slow down for you," he teased. I'd try my best to keep up, but being only five two, it wasn't easy.

I'd usually be close behind, teasing right back, "Yes, Master, I'm coming. Me good geisha girl. Me keep up best I can." I always used the best Japanese accent that I could muster up. "Honey, slow down, please. You know that I can't keep up with you," I pleaded.

"Don't let go of my hand, and you won't fall behind, silly," he said, shaking his head with a big smile. Soon I would always have to let go and lag behind again.

I remember when I first found out that I was pregnant. Mark and I talked of how I was going to get a big belly. Little did we know just how big it would get. From the back you couldn't tell that I was pregnant. From the front, I looked like I had a great big beach ball in my belly.

I had to chuckle to myself as I remembered something he had told me months before. "Don't expect me to walk around with you in stores and stuff when you start getting a big belly, babe, because I won't," he had said in a very serious tone. It sounds funny now, but at that time, it was a big problem that he had said that to me. I cried a few tears, thinking that he would be embarrassed of me. It never happened, of course, but I didn't know that at that time, and his words had really hurt. As it turned out, Mark was always very proud of that big belly, because that was his baby in there.

Every time I went to the doctor, I always asked, "Are you sure there aren't two babies in there?" Especially the last two months. I was really getting huge, because it was all up front, right in the middle. When we'd be sleeping at night, I was forever waking Mark up with the baby kicking him in the back as I cuddled up to him, with my belly against his back. It seemed like this baby never stopped kicking.

Having had five normal pregnancies, I was sure that something was very different this time. Every time I would ask about the possibility of twins, she would assure me, "No, Linda, only one baby." Dr. Su would say that very matter-of-factly. "Only can hear one heartbeat," she would say in her strong accent. I had to trust her, and I figured that she knew what she was talking about. I just kept getting bigger and bigger, and I felt like I was going to pop, wondering how my skin was going to stretch one more inch. I couldn't get off the couch the last month without someone helping me. "Still only one baby," my doctor assured me every time I had an appointment, and I was beginning to feel like a freak.

Before we knew it, it was Mother's Day. Rudy and Shelley had this great idea for a present for me. "Let's go. We're taking you guys to Vegas for your Mother's Day present," Shelley said.

Vegas, I thought. I was still two months from my due date, but I was beginning to be uncomfortable quite a bit of the time. With the temperature being very hot for May, I already had quite a bit of swelling in my feet and ankles. Still, we took almost no time at all in giving them our answer.

"Okay, we'll go," I told them, "but only for the night and one day."

Mark was ecstatic. "Shoes for the baby!" he yelled as he pretended to be rolling dice, grinning from ear to ear.

"You are so funny, honey," I said, half-laughing, shaking my head.

All we had to go in was Rudy's old Ford truck, and it would be very crowded with all four of us riding in the front of the truck. Actually, there were six of us, counting the unborn babies, and it was almost a three-hour drive.

In no time at all, we were off, and even with our pregnant bellies, swollen feet, ice, and all, we had a really good time. As it turned out, we won enough money to be able to keep putting it back into these damn machines. They're good at letting you win just enough to keep going for a while, anyway. Looking around at all the different types of people and the bright, twinkling lights, the sound of coins spitting out of machines and people yelling with joy was very exciting to me, sheltered life that I had led.

My favorite game was craps, even though it was kind of hard for me trying to lean over that crap table to place my bets and grab the dice. True to form, just as he had practiced earlier, Mark would yell excitedly, "Shoes for the baby!" I was laughing so hard and having so much fun around the crowded, elbow-to-elbow crap table, lifting one foot at a time, taking the pressure off my very tired, swollen feet.

Guys kept placing bets for us every time they won, saying, "Roll one for the little lady with the baby in the oven." We won so many times that way because I learned that when players want to keep someone rolling the dice that is doing well for them, they keep adding some of their winnings to your pile.

It was a lot of fun, except for my darned, old swollen feet, and I wished we'd had a room. "Babe, let me go get us a room so you and Shelley can lie down for a while," Mark urged a few times.

"No, honey, I'll be okay. That's a waste of money," I would say, always being the practical one, having raised so many kids. Besides, we weren't going to be there long enough to need a room.

Before too long, we were on our way home. About halfway there, Shelley and I got in the back of the truck because we were just too uncomfortable up in the front. My feet were so swollen that I felt like I'd better get them propped up or they were going to pop. Mark and Rudy just kept looking back at us and laughing. They thought that we were nuts wanting to ride back there. It was a lot more comfortable for us, I must say. We could stretch out, and I think we both went to sleep for a while. I now that I did.

Sometime during the month of June, Mark made us our love seat around the big tree in the front. "Come on, babe, get the kids. We are going rock-hunting!" he hollered from below as I sat out on the deck, playing my guitar and enjoying the soft, cool breeze that always blew in the late afternoon.

As we drove to the "special" place he had found, he gave instructions to Danny and Becky. "I don't want your mom to bend over and pick up any rocks, so as she finds them, you two will get them for her, okay?" he said in a protective way, not wanting me to hurt myself or the baby.

"Sure, Mark," they agreed happily, knowing it was always fun to go rock-hunting with the man that was like a father to them.

The four of us spent quite a while finding just the right rocks for it. The ones on top where we would sit were a pretty pink and very flat. We spent many hours sitting there, enjoying the shade from the huge tree that was now surrounded by the four-foot love seat and the connecting two-foot rock wall.

We loved the outside so much, enjoying the lush green trees that Mark had planted from tiny twigs, watching as they seemed to grow taller every day. If I was outside, just being lazy, that was where you'd find me, cuddling Mark or playing my guitar or just watching him as he carefully inspected and watered his precious trees one by one. He was very proud of all he had done to our place, and rightly so.

Since I closed my stable down and only had our three horses (we had acquired a nice quarter horse for payment on some work I'd done), we had decided to turn one side of our barn down below into rooms. One was to be our living room. For that, we would use the far two stalls. It would be big, twelve by twenty-four.

One day, when Mark was pouring cement to put our heatilator on, something very funny happened. While he was working over by the heatilator, I was busy being romantic. In the wet cement that he had just finished pouring for the foundation, I wrote "Linda Loves Mark." When I was all done, I turned over to show him how romantic it was. He smiled real big.

I said, "See how romantic I am? You would never even think of doing anything like that for me. It would make me so happy if you ever did anything like that for me."

"Come here, smarty-pants! Boy, are you ever gonna feel stupid. Now just look and see what I wrote. Mine's even drier, you can tell. I did mine first!"

I couldn't believe my eyes. He had written in the concrete where it was always going to show, "Mark loves Linda." He was right; I really did feel stupid, but it was the best stupid I'd ever felt. "Oh my gosh, honey! That is so romantic!" I hugged him tightly with my arms around his neck, flashing a brilliant smile.

"I'm so great," he teased, grinning as he kissed my forehead gently.

It was only about a month before my due date, and we were really getting anxious about what sex the baby was. Although Mark didn't really care what it was, I was hoping for a little girl. I suppose I didn't really care either—I was just curious, and as most parents would say, we just wanted a nice, strong, healthy baby. One day, Shelley said she knew a trick with a gold ring and a chain that would tell us what sex our babies would be. "How exciting!" I replied anxiously. "Let's do it!"

"Now, hold out the palm of your hand, Mom," she instructed as she hung the ring so it was right above it. In a matter of seconds, the ring started moving all by itself. I couldn't believe my eyes. I don't remember now which is which, but it either went back and forth or in a circle, depending on the sex.

"Oh my gosh," I said in disbelief as I watched it go through all five of my kids' sex perfectly, and in the right order, with eyes as big as saucers. For the sixth baby, the one that was to be my last, it said girl. But much to our surprise, it went one more time, indicating the seventh child was supposed to be a boy. "That's it, I know it's a bunch of bull, since this is my last baby," I said, shaking my head, making a face. That one really had us confused, so I laughingly wrote Shelley's theory off as a bunch of bull, knowing I was going to have my tubes tied after the baby was born.

"Gee, Mom," my daughter answered very seriously. "Maybe something is going to happen to this baby and it's a girl." Her pretty face went scared.

"That's crazy!" was all I could say, shaking my head and waving my hand at her as if to push her theory away.

She continued on, eyebrows raised, "Then you and Mark will decide to have another baby, and it will be a very healthy boy."

"What a sad thing to think," I responded abruptly. "No, it's all just silly superstition," I told her, forcing a slight laugh. "What an awful thought! This game is over, sweetie."

We had a really bad hot streak with cars in April and May. I'd blown up the old Malibu because someone forgot to check the water. Mark laughed so hard when he came to town to help me get it running.

"It moved at least six feet after it died," I said, not exaggerating. That sucker had gotten so hot I didn't think the engine would ever stop jumping. My son Jimmy had an old Toyota that he'd loaned us, and it blew up too. Of course, we were driving it at that time.

It was definitely time for us to get a car. We bought a '75 Dodge Dart from Mark's friend Sam, who owned the Pit Stop auto parts in town. Mark had done some work for him, and Rudy worked there also, so Sam let us buy it on time payments. It was really nice—nice body, paint, and interior—so we were both very proud of it. What a nice change from that old, dirt-filled Malibu. "Wow! How cool" the kids had said when we brought it home, excitedly climbing inside to look at every detail, giving their approval all the while.

We'd only had it for two days when Mark announced that he wanted us to go to Vegas in our new car. With the baby due in three weeks, I was very reluctant, with my swollen feet and all. I was so huge that people in the stores would do double takes at me, and I thought I looked freakish. I felt like I had a baby whale in me, but as usual, he was able to convince me how much fun it would be.

"We'll get a room this time. It'll be romantic," he argued. "We can stay two days, and don't worry, even as big as you are, I'll still hold your hand in public," he joked, tenderly patting my tummy.

How could I refuse an argument like that one? Besides, it would be our last chance to get away for a long time since I'd be nursing the baby, so off we went. We were having so much fun laughing, singing, and just being silly in our new-to-us car. I had to pee really badly, so we stopped just inside the Nevada state line, at Whiskey Pete's.

It was like a blizzard outside as the strong wind blew wildly, swirling the dust in the parking lot like a whirlpool. When I opened the door, the wind whipped it right out of my hand and banged it into a big cement light post, shattering the window. The noise was deafening as I felt the tiny particles of glass on my arm, tears threatening. It not only shattered it, but it also blew it out! I couldn't believe my eyes. Our brand-new car. Suddenly I saw Mark coming at me from the driver's side, yelling and screaming, shaking his fist wildly in the air.

"What the hell is wrong with you? Look at what you've done! I can't believe that you could be that freaking stupid!" he yelled through bared, gritted teeth.

He was so mad at me, and by now I was crying very hard—first, because of the car and, second, because of the way he was yelling and cussing at me. I couldn't believe it; it had been a total accident. Having worked with horses for so many years, I was pretty strong. I didn't just let things fly out of my hands.

"It was an accident!" I screamed at him, tears streaking down my face. "Do you think I did it on purpose?" Trying to defend myself, I knew it was no use; he was just too mad to listen to any of my explanations. Feeling like my bladder was about to burst, I stomped off, hurt and angry, to go to the restroom. When I returned, he was still very upset, and I knew to keep my mouth shut. As he drove off, with the freezing, cold air blowing wildly into the passenger's side, I slid all the way to the door.

"Let's just go home," I said in a very angry tone, not being able to keep silent any longer. "There is no way we're going to be able to have fun now. I don't need you yelling and screaming at me because of some freak accident," I said, with eyes starting to blur from the wind and tears combined.

"No!" he screamed at me. "I'm going to gamble, whether you like it or not! Now, just shut your mouth!" He was like a crazy man.

Oh my god, I prayed. Please don't let this be happening again. I couldn't believe that it was happening again. Shocked and fearing for my baby, I shut up, just as he had ordered.

There were still quite a few miles to Vegas after you crossed the state line. Needless to say, it was a very silent, tearful drive. Every once in a while, I would mention softly how badly I just wanted to go home. Mark was just too angry, and my pleading only made him madder, so I soon gave up. It took a while, but he finally calmed down enough to apologize.

"I'm sorry I got so mad, babe. It's just that I was so proud of our new car. I know it wasn't your fault," he said very apologetically. "I love you, you know that. Now, come over here and sit by me, where you belong," he said, reaching for my hand. "We're going to have us a good time, broken window and all."

Boy was, I relieved that he wasn't angry with me anymore; I had wanted so much to have fun.

"You forgive me, don't you, babe?" he said, eyebrows raised, as I slid over next to him, where I always sat.

"Yes, I do, honey. Thank you for saying sorry," I said, leaning my head on his shoulder for a second. I couldn't believe how easily I forgave him. What is wrong with me? I thought to myself.

As soon as we got into town, we found a room. It was downtown, where all the casinos were near one another. Going up in the elevator, we realized that our room was really on the thirteenth floor, not the fourteenth, as it stated. I guess in Vegas no one would want to stay on the "thirteenth" floor—bad luck, you know. They had no way of knowing that 13 was our lucky number. After we got settled and mentioned how romantic our room was, we were off to gamble and get a bite to eat.

I was always hungry, but I couldn't hold much at a time, with the baby taking up so much room. Vegas is, by far, one of the cheapest places in the world to eat. I love it, and I think the food is real tasty. When we got down to the casino, we started having so much fun gambling that we forgot to eat.

"Honey, look at my feet," I said, astounded that they were so swollen.

"Babe, I have to take you up to lay down and prop up those feet right away," he answered in a worried tone and a look of shock. It wasn't until we were back in our room again that we thought about eating.

"Mark, we forgot to eat, and I am starving," I said, making a face. "We need to go eat something."

"You are not going out until your feet look better." He looked shocked that I would even suggest it.

As I lay there with my feet propped up, playfully flirting with Mark and complaining about how hungry I was, he got an idea.

"I know. We'll call room service. Won't that be classy? Imagine us calling room service."

"Well, who has more class than us, anyway?" I replied in my best English accent.

Much to our disappointment, we soon found out that room service was not open. It was the middle of the night, we were told, as if we didn't know that. We laughed.

"I guess you've got to stay at a more expensive hotel to have all-night room service," Mark said. Then he told me to quit pouting and just relax. "I'll be back in a jiffy with something really good to eat. You just rest." He kissed me goodbye. "I love you so much, babe!" He was still trying to make up for his bad behavior earlier.

He was so good at it, I thought to myself as he headed for the door, smiling and waving.

"Honey, come here! I have a secret," I said, reaching up to him. He leaned over so I could whisper in his ear. "Thank you for not being mad at me anymore. I love you," I said with absolutely no pride. "I shouldn't have let the door get away like that, and I am really sorry." What is wrong with me? I thought to myself as he kissed me again and headed out the door with a big grin on his face.

I was feeling so content, lying there like a queen; all thoughts about our fight earlier had totally left my mind. Mark had been pampering me so often over the past few months, and I enjoyed every second of it.

Soon I was fast asleep. It was a good thing that I had fallen asleep, since Mark was not to return for a couple of hours. The next thing I knew, he was waking me up, covering my belly with quarters. There were more quarters than I had ever seen, and he proudly, gently dropped them all over me. He had hit about five fifty-dollar jackpots on a quarter machine, and he was very happy and being silly.

"I just couldn't leave, babe. I knew you'd be happy when you saw how much I'd won. Just look at all these quarters!" As Mark counted all his quarters, I pigged out on all the food he'd brought with him. His winnings helped make our last vacation before the baby was born a lot more fun, and we were able to pay for another night and stay an extra day.

About two and a half weeks before I gave birth, the mystery of Shelley's ring trick was finally solved. When I went in for my checkup, my doctor said she wanted me to go in and have an ultrasound. She was worried that the baby was going to be too big to have naturally and that I might need a caesarean operation.

I was really nervous. After all, I had had five babies normally, the last two totally naturally. "A piece of cake," I'd always described the births. I couldn't imagine anything worse at this time than having to have this baby cut out of me. What about Mark? He was looking forward so much to watching our baby's birth.

Please, God, don't let me need a caesarean! I was scared to death. The ultrasound was scheduled for the following day.

When we arrived the next day, we didn't think they would let Mark come in, so he waited nervously in the waiting room. The doctor immediately noted how large I was for carrying only one baby, but she assured me not to worry, saying that this would tell the actual size of the baby and the exact fetal age. Maybe it was due right around now instead of two and a half weeks from now.

"Wouldn't that be nice?" she said.

I laughed. "Not if I have to have an operation to get it out."

By this time, she had already put some kind of lubricant on my belly and was moving this little thing over it while she looked at a small TV screen. Suddenly, she turned it off, and I was scared.

"Is the daddy of your baby here, by any chance?" she asked.

"Yes, he's out in the waiting room. I was afraid to ask if he could come in, but he really wanted to. Why? Is something wrong?"

"No, nothing's wrong, but I'm going to get him. I'll be right back. This will be very interesting to both of you," she walked out the door excitedly.

What was wrong? I was really confused. Did she have bad news that she didn't want to tell me without Mark being here? No, I thought, she hadn't acted sad or worried. As a matter of fact, she was smiling, so it couldn't be bad news. Maybe she had found out what sex our baby was. That must be it—I bet she was going to tell us if it was a boy or a girl and she thought we should be together. That's all it could be, I said to myself, as she seemed too happy for this to be a problem.

Soon she reappeared, still smiling, with Mark only a few paces behind her. My fears had totally disappeared by now as I looked up at him smiling excitedly.

"Hi, honey. She said you could watch," I said, reaching for the comfort of his hand.

"Now I want you two just to hold hands and watch this little TV screen over here. I know you can't tell much by all this blur, but you are about to have not one fine healthy baby, but two!"

I couldn't believe my ears! Two babies? All this time, the doctor had assured me that there was only one. All five of my other pregnancies, I had prayed for twins, always hoping, since my ex-husband's grandma had been a twin. I'd never been that lucky, and now I was being told that there was no doubt about it. I had two very nice-size babies in my tummy. "I can't believe it! Are you positive?" I asked, tears of joy streaming down my face. I looked at Mark and realized he hadn't said a word, nor had he changed his facial expression. He was holding my hand very tightly, looking at me, eyebrows raised, still speechless.

"How do you feel about two babies instead of one?" the doctor asked.

"I'm so happy I can't believe it. I've always wanted twins," I said with a smile so big I thought my face might crack wide-open.

"I'm not sure" was all Mark could say, in a slow, soft murmur.

I was much too happy to stop and worry about how he felt. He remained pretty silent the rest of the time it took to finish, and it took quite a while to examine every part of both babies. "I am sure that one of the babies is a girl, but the other one is not in the right position to be able to tell its sex," she went on to say.

At this time, Mark politely excused himself to go have a smoke. He kissed me and said, "I'll see you when she's done, babe," adding a wink and a half-smile as he left.

"The reason Dr. Su could only hear one heartbeat is that one is in the front and the other in the back," she explained. Now I understood my freakish size and the way I was all out front. Thank God there was a logical explanation for all this. No one could tease me again about having to be pulled up off the couch, because I had two babies inside of me. What a miracle! God, I wished I had known this all along. I had proof to show everyone, because the doctor gave me a picture.

The first ten minutes of our twenty-minute ride home was a silent one. I was so ecstatic about our two babies. Nothing, not even Mark's silence, was going to take away from this moment. All of a sudden, he spoke; there was excitement in his voice.

"I think I'm okay now. I know I'm okay now! Wow, two babies. I must really be some kind of a stud, huh, babe? I can't believe that I'm really happy about this. I must be nuts!" By now he was smiling so big, and of course, I had tears of happiness running down my cheeks.

"You're really happy, honey?" I asked as he held my hand tightly.

"Yes, babe, I am really and truly happy. I can't believe we made twins!" he said, bursting with pride.

"Wow!" was all I could say, with a brilliant smile. The kids would be so excited. What a beautiful life we were going to have with two babies, not one.

When we drove up our driveway, Shelley was hanging over the rail of the deck. The deck that Mark and I had made love in almost exactly one year ago. It was hard to believe how much had happened to me in only one short year. What a good year it had been! As usual, I never thought of the fights or the violence, because the good was so good, and right now it was all very good.

"You're going to have twins, huh? One's a boy and the other's a girl?" Shelley was yelling at us before we could even get out of the car. She knew immediately by our faces that she was right. No surprises here, I thought.

"Yes!" I shrieked back, hands lifted in excitement.

"Aren't I a stud?" Mark added through all the chaos as Danny and Becky ran down the stairs to hug their mom. From this day on, Shelley insisted that we would have a boy and a girl and the girl would be born first, remembering her silly ring trick.

The next two weeks were spent doing lots of walking, lots of sitting with my feet propped up, and lots of bragging about the fact that there were two babies instead of one. I also was frantically gathering up more baby clothes and diapers. I always used real cloth diapers, only wanting the softest of cloth next to my babies' skin. "Why do you have to be so old-fashioned?" my baby girl asked one day, with a puzzled look on her face, as I was showing her how to fold the diapers.

"Because I have you to help me, that's why, and you are going to be my big-girl helper," I told her as I gathered her in my arms and gave her a big hug.

"Well, okay, then, I guess it will be okay to use these," she answered with her proudest look and a beautiful smile.

Mark and I felt like we were dreaming at times, thinking we were the luckiest two people in the whole world. We knew for sure that we had to be the happiest.

I only had a few worries. Would I have the babies on time? They were due on the seventh of July. That was weird, since my eldest son, Richie, had been born on July 6. He'd be twenty-one in two weeks. My second child, Shelley, was born on July 9. Now, these babies were due almost right in between their brother's and sister's birthdays.

We laughed about how I must be exceptionally fertile during the month of October. My last three kids, Jimmy, Danny, and Becky, I had carried much longer than my due date, and I knew that I'd explode for sure if my twins were late. The doctor told me not to worry about it, though, since twins were usually born early, if anything.

My other fears, aside from whether or not they would be healthy, were, Would I be able to have them normally? Would Mark be able to watch the delivery? And would it be possible for me to nurse two babies? I'd never had any problem nursing before. In fact, Danny nursed until his sister Becky was born. He was twenty-six months old when he quit. I was a little nervous about nursing two babies at once. Would I have enough milk? Would one have to cry while the other waited? I could never handle letting my babies cry.

Soon it was the Fourth of July. I wasn't feeling a bit like I was ready to deliver. I never had in the past, though, so I don't know why it bothered me. When I went into labor, then I'd know it was time. We went to Hesperia Lakes with Leroy, Rudy, and Shelley, who was feeling miserable in the heat, having only two months to go before her baby was due. Jimmy was there too, and so were Danny and Becky.

We had a lot of fun. The guys all got drunk, and they oohed and aahed very loudly every time the fireworks exploded in the sky. Everyone was hoping all the noise and excitement would make me go into labor. I was very glad that I didn't. Who would have wanted to go to the hospital with this group? Thank God, when it was over, we went home to sleep instead of to the hospital with a bunch of idiots who thought they were the funniest guys in the world.

Nothing exciting happened on July 5. It was miserably hot, as usual, so I sat around with my feet up most of the day. Much to everyone's disappointment, I was still feeling quite normal. When we went to bed, Mark and I made love, which was nothing unusual for us. So much for the saying that you're not supposed to make love the last six weeks of your pregnancy. Anyway, afterward, we both contentedly fell asleep.

At about two in the morning, I woke up feeling really weird. "Honey, I think my water broke," I said, waking him gently and speaking very softly so as not to shock him.

"You're kidding, babe!" he said excitedly, not minding that I had woken him up.

"I am not kidding, unless you wet the bed, because this bed is soaking wet," I teased, making a face at him.

In the future, Mark would always take credit for inducing my labor with our lovemaking. My pains had no pattern, but I was definitely in labor. When we finally called the doctor at about 5:00 a.m., she was a little upset that we hadn't gone to the hospital immediately, as she politely scolded us.

"You don't take chances with twins, Linda," she said. These were to be her first in a few years, and she was very excited about them.

Children are the anchors that hold a mother to life. I truly
believe that children are the anchors that hold a mother to life.

CHAPTER 5

BABIES AND A WEDDING

"Come on, babe. We have to go now. You know what the doc said," Mark urged excitedly as he grabbed the bag I had packed a week ago from the back. It was dawn by now, and I knew that he was right.

"Oh, honey, our babies are going to be born today. I can hardly wait!" I said, wide-eyed, feeling the butterflies inside, with anticipation of what was ahead. "There's no hurry, sweetie. My pains are still very erratic, and they are not very hard," I reassured him as he hurried down the stairs. As I fell in step behind him, he winked and gave me a brilliant smile, reaching for my hand. "Big day today, babe." His enthusiasm could not be hidden.

"This is it. Today we get our babies," Mark said with a beaming smile. "What better way to start off the day than watching the sun come up together?" His happy expression showed the excitement in his heart. Our desert is so beautiful in the morning, and the summer air at dawn was crisp and refreshing. I took a deep breath as he opened the door for me, and I climbed in the car to begin the journey of the huge task that lay ahead of me today.

We stopped at the doughnut shop for some juice, knowing we were in for a long, hard, but very blessed day. We talked about how, from this day forward, our lives would never be the same again. The next time I walked through our big barn door, we would be carrying not one but two brand-new babies, two brand-new little lives to love and enjoy forever. Mark was grinning from ear to ear. This day held much excitement for us, and even though we were a little bit frightened, we knew that we were finally about to be rewarded for the little inconveniences of the past months.

July 6 had already been a day for celebration in our family for twenty years. Today was the twenty-first birthday of my eldest child, Richie. How weird, I thought. I bet that not many moms could say they have three kids sharing the same birthday. So what if two of them happened to be twins? What a fun day July 6 was always going to be for our family from now on.

As I had feared, I was in for a long, hard day. The entire morning of what was to become my hardest labor of all was spent with Mark dragging me around the hallways of the hospital, making me keep up, pain or no pain, as he wheeled the IV pole in front of me.

"Slow down, that's not fair," I kept insisting. "If I don't keep up, this is going to rip right out of my hand."

He'd just smile. "I got you this time, huh?" he insisted over and over. "We've got to get these babies born, babe, so we need to establish a pattern to your pains. The doctor said so," he said very seriously.

"All of a sudden, you have become an expert in childbirth," I teased. "You know so much. Why don't you just take over for me, smarty-pants?" My teasing turned serious as I began having another contraction. "Stop a second, please!" I said in a strained and serious tone. Seeing that I was having a contraction, he put his arm around me showing his support.

The x-ray they had taken when I first arrived at the hospital showed the babies to be in perfect position for a natural birth. The baby that was to present itself first was in the head-down position. The second baby, the one in the back, was head-up. The doctor said it would be easy. The first baby would be born by itself, and then she would reach in and help the second baby out by its feet.

"Easy for who?" I replied with eyes wide-open.

She assured me that the babies were small enough that there would be no problem. They were both very healthy, with very strong heartbeats. Mark was very excited about watching their birth, and I was excited that it would be over soon so I could feel normal again. Soon I would be able to do all the simple things in life again. Things like wearing normal jeans, riding my horses, and getting off the couch without help. The mere thought of being able to sleep on my tummy again brought a soft, contented smile to my face.

My earlier fear had become a reality. My laboring had been long and hard, and I was totally exhausted from the weary task of maintaining control through the excruciating pain of childbirth. By all appearances, I was doing very well, but on the inside, I thought I might die at any given moment. How much longer can I do this? I thought to myself. My eyes filled with tears with every contraction as I somehow managed to be silent through it all. The day had been much harder than I had ever imagined, and I knew I could not maintain my brave, strong face and attitude much longer.

It was 9:00 p.m., and I knew that something was wrong. "This isn't normal, honey," I said, fighting back tears as Mark stroked my hand. "I don't want to scare you, but there is something wrong." He saw me take the deep, cleansing breath that showed him that another pain was coming.

"Come on, babe, you can do this. Just a little longer," he said gently as he coaxed me through this contraction, just as he had done so all day.

"I don't know how much longer I can do this. Besides hurting, I am so afraid there is something wrong," I said, voice quivering as I blinked back the tears I had so desperately tried to control. The past few hours, my pains were almost constant. They would reach that almost-unbearable peak and start to fade away, and before they would go away altogether, which was what made them bearable, they would start to build up again. I was totally exhausted, trying as hard as I could to stay calm and in control, something I had always managed to do with my five other labors. Falling apart was never an option for me, the pro of all pros at having babies. I knew that something was seriously wrong, and soon the doctor came in to examine me and verified my conclusion.

"Get her into x-ray right away," she said in a worried tone to the nurse.

"Oh my god, honey." I looked at Mark, not being able to hold back the tears for the first time today. "Don't worry, babe, it'll be okay." I was still trying to act calm. "The doc will take care of it. She knows what to do."

Never failing me, he stayed calm and in control and convinced me that everything would be okay.

"I love you so much, honey" was all I could say, and I knew that was enough for him as he smiled bravely and continued to stroke the arm on the hand that he held most of the day.

We had all been paying special attention for the last hour or two to the two fetal monitors. The babies' heartbeats had started to go very low during my contractions and taking quite a while to be normal again. It hadn't been a drastic change in the beginning, but now they were definitely going very low, as Shelley had been the first to point it out, hardly ever taking her eyes off that monitor. The nurses were so nice about letting my family come in and out all day. The babies were working so hard, but nothing was happening, and we were all very frightened by now.

"Please, God, take care of our babies. Don't let anything happen to them," I prayed as they wheeled me back from x-ray. Looking at the ceiling as they wheeled me quickly down the long hallways, I was more afraid than I had ever been in my life. The hustle and bustle of the busy hospital and all the sounds that went with it only added to the drama. Minutes after I arrived back at my room, the doctor arrived. She stood there until my contraction ended, then began to speak.

"Linda and Mark, I have just seen the x-ray, and there is a problem," she said softly, but her voice was intent. "Now listen carefully," she continued, leaning closer to Mark and me, never changing the serious expression on her face. "The first baby has moved since the x-ray this morning, and it is trying to come out buttocks first." I felt my pulse go sky-high as my eyes widened, never taking them off Dr. Su as she continued on. "This is not a good position. It affects the entire birthing process. So we must remove the babies immediately to make sure that they survive."

Looking up at Mark, I saw a look of fear for the first time as he appeared to swallow hard. "Do what you have to do, Doc," he said without hesitation, voice straining.

Of course, there was no decision to be made. Here I was, more afraid than I'd ever been in my fife, and I knew that they were going to take me away from Mark for a caesarean delivery.

"Please, Dr. Su, please. Can't Mark stay with me, please?" I begged, tears streaming down my face, my entire body trembling with fear.

As the doctor spoke, much to the shock of poor Shelley, who was seven months pregnant, she was in the process of catheterizing me in order to empty my bladder before and during surgery. I kept on pleading with her, stopping only when the almost-constant pains were at their worst. "I know that he can handle it. It would not bother him at all. Please, I need him to be with me," I sobbed uncontrollably, pleading with all my might.

I knew that I couldn't do this alone, and just the thought of it made me lose all control.

Finally, after a long silence, she answered, "I will agree under one condition only. If you give me your word that you will leave immediately without arguing if asked to do so. Okay? This is a serious situation right now."

Mark answered quickly, "You have my word. Thank you very much, Doctor!" With a quick sigh of relief, he said, "Just tell me what to do and where to go."

Things moved very fast after that. They rushed me to surgery to be prepared for a spinal and Mark to the scrub area, where he was dressed in sterile clothing. As they wheeled me swiftly past the kids, I wondered what could possibly lie ahead for me. "It'll be okay, Mom, don't worry. We love you, Mom!" My precious kids were trying with all their might to calmly reassure me, but the quivering in their soft voices could not be hidden from a mom that knew them all so well. Once again, I prayed that everything would be okay.

In no time at all, Mark and I were reunited in surgery. For the first time in about sixteen hours, I was finally feeling no pain. The spinal had taken effect, and I was very numb. "Honey, I have no legs or feet," I teased. His smile was relaxed, seeing that I was not in any pain.

"Good, babe, you can't kick me out anymore." He bent over and whispered in my ear with a slight chuckle. I was glad that the pain was over, but we were still very nervous, and I knew that we were both trying to be brave for each other as we made light of all that was going on.

The room reminded me of every operating room I had ever seen on television, and the hospital smell was overpowering. The light was very bright, which showed off the spotless, clean, and sterile sur-roundings. Someone was painting my huge tummy with brown stuff that I was assuming was a cleanser of some type. Soon they were draping my stomach with a tent of cloth, and I couldn't see a thing from just above my chest. Mark was sitting near my head, but in a tall stool, so he could see everything that was going on easily. There was a clear tube running between us like one would use in an aquarium, and Mark was holding my hand.

"Don't worry, babe, this will be a piece of cake. Pretty soon we will be holding our babies. Pretty soon we're going to see our babies, and it won't even hurt you," he said excitedly. In his other hand, he was holding our camera so he could take pictures as soon as our precious babies were born.

"Don't you dare take any pictures of my tummy cut open," I playfully warned him, pointing my finger at him clumsily, as I was only able to raise my hand a tiny bit, feeling they were lightly restrained. With a serious look, eyebrows raised, I said, "I mean it now, no yucky pictures."

All of a sudden, we knew what the clear tube was for. Mark's eyes got very big, and he had a shocked look on his face. There was a terrible sucking noise, and the tube began to fill with blood, my blood. It was so gross, but somehow we managed to find humor in the situation and laughed about it. We had relaxed quite a bit by now. After all, it seemed like there must have been at least ten doctors, and they were all very relaxed. They were talking about something one of them had heard on the news. That was how light the mood seemed as they were cutting open my stomach. It seemed like an everyday thing to them, and it took me a few seconds to laugh at myself for being so silly. Of course, it was an everyday thing for them. They were doctors. None of them showed any signs of worry. Thank God! Their actions gave me all the strength and encouragement I needed, and I had begun to relax a little as I anticipated the birth of my two little miracle babies. It felt good to smile as I looked up at what had to be the most excited man that ever lived, Mark.

"Relax now, you two. There is no need for worry now. We will get these babies out in plenty of time." How I loved Dr. Cora Su, and I knew without a doubt that everything would be fine. I was about to become the mom of seven, with two more priceless treasures to love forever.

Dr. Su had said just the words we needed to hear, and all our earlier fears were gone. Excitement was all we were feeling now. "What a weird way to have a baby," I told Mark, making a face. All those times I felt sorry for friends that had a caesarian, and this was not bad at all.

"Piece of cake, babe. You're my hero," he said, still holding my hand very tight, flinching a little as he would alternate sitting and standing, eagerly watching the procedure.

"I'm glad I can't see, by the faces you're making," I murmured softly. Even though I was happy, it would all be over soon. I was feeling a little cheated having had to go through all that terrible labor also.

"You're right, honey," I said in a surprised voice, crinkling my nose. "This is a piece of cake."

"If you could see what I could see, you wouldn't be thinking of cake," he joked as he made a yucky face.

"Here is baby A," the doctor said as she lifted her from me. "It's a girl."

"We got our baby girl," Mark said, face beaming with pride as his eyes filled with tears of joy. She was already crying and making awful faces.

"She's so, so tiny. I can't believe how tiny she is," I said. "Is she okay?"

"Not tiny, very nice-size for a twin. She looks very healthy," the doctor said in her very cute accent.

Immediately she handed our tiny, perfect, beautiful girl over to the pediatrician and went after the second little baby. I could not relax until I knew that the second baby was okay. She seemed to be having trouble getting this one out. It scared me since I could also see a look of concern and urgency in Dr. Su's face. Before I had a chance to ask what was wrong, she finally raised baby B, as she called it, high enough for me to see.

"Baby B is a boy," she said.

"A boy! I can't believe it's a boy, babe! We got us a boy and a girl. A little boy and a little girl all at once." It was the happiest moment of my life. "Thank you, God," I prayed in a tiny, soft voice. "Thank you so much!"

We named them Darla Renee and Donny Ray. The Ray came from Mark's middle name. I knew I had wanted a Donny. Just in case the other was a girl, I, of course, wanted them to rhyme.

It took a long time to find the perfect name of Darla. She was from The Little Rascals, a show I always loved when I was young.

We both had tears streaming down our faces. We had indeed created a miracle, two miracles. As soon as they put both of these tiny, brand-new little babies over on the cart and had sucked out their airways, Mark, standing beside our babies, boldly asked, "Can I take their picture now?"

"Sure, you can," my pediatrician answered reassuringly. "They're all yours." He stepped back out of the camera's view.

Mark was so elated that he wasn't even worried that he looked like a "poop butt," his term for me when I cried happy tears, as the tears covered his own face. Later, he'd tell me that it had taken a while for him to notice that his beard was all wet. It was his macho way of trying to downplay his tender side. According to Mark, he hadn't been crying; he'd just had water all over his face. It was funny, the way he told me that, and it was a part of him that I loved very much.

With a quick kiss goodbye and an "I love you so much, babe," I had a special request for him. "Don't tell Shelley she was right, honey," I reminded him. "Keep her in suspense for a while."

"I'll try not to." He smirked as he left the room, grinning from ear to ear, following his son and daughter to the nursery.

As they were beginning the procedure to tie my tubes, something we had already decided to do if the babies were healthy, my secret was revealed as the nurse took our babies out to the family one at a time. Shelley had been very anxiously waiting outside the surgery door, and as the nurse wheeled the first baby past her, she asked, "Is that the first baby? The girl?"

"Yes," the nurse replied, looking very puzzled that she had known its sex before she had said a word, knowing that Mark had stopped to wash his hands behind her and had not told anyone the sexes yet.

"Is that the little boy?" she asked as the second nurse wheeled Donny out.

"Well, yes, it is," the nurse replied, looking just as puzzled as the other nurse. "I thought no one knew for sure what sex these babies were," she replied with a puzzled look on her face.

"I knew," my beautiful daughter said, grinning with pride. "I knew for sure!"

Indeed, my daughter had been right all along, her with that silly ring trick. The funny part was how cocky she had been about it. I knew I would take a lot of teasing from her about it. Gosh, how I love my Shelley. She is so full of love and compassion and doing for others.

After the babies were taken to the nursery and they had taken me to the recovery room, Mark came back in to see me, and we had a chance to talk for just a few moments. He very naively said a couple of really cute things.

"Babe, you wouldn't believe how scared I was when they were trying to get Donny out. Your intestines were wrapped around his neck a couple of times. That was why it took so long to get him out," he said with all seriousness. The umbilical cord had been wrapped around the baby's neck, and Mark had thought it was my intestines. He'd also mistaken my uterus for my stomach.

"I just don't understand why they had to take your stomach out for a minute after the babies were born. It was lying right on your stomach, and they were working on it," he said with brows lowered.

I had to laugh as I explained that it was probably my uterus, much to his embarrassment. In spite of all I had just been through, I just had to laugh at my very handsome, very silly, and very excited man.

"I love you so much, honey. You know that, don't you?"

"Of course," he said, teasingly acting offended that I needed to ask such a question.

With a quick kiss and an "I love you, babe," Mark was off to see his babies, feeling prouder than he had ever felt in his entire life. "I bet I can make you laugh too," the male nurse said as he carefully lifted my numb legs, bending my knees toward my chest. "Oh my gosh! That is so weird!" He was right. I laughed!

This was the happiest moment of my life, and I could not have loved Mark more than I did on this day that our precious babies had been born.

Babies are bits of stardust
Blown from the hand of God.
Lucky the woman who knows
The pangs of birth,
For she has held a star.
—Larry Barretto

Mark was so proud of the present he brought me the day after the babies were born. He'd bragged that it had been such a thoughtful, true present. "Right from the heart," he said, raising his brows with certainty. "Just the kind of presents you like, babe." He brought me flowers, a card for twins, and a giant poster that he hung immediately over my hospital bed, and I was truly touched because it was definitely a gift from his heart. "Look, it has a dog and a cat, and it says"—he paused for a second to build up my curiosity—"'It's because we're so different that we have so much to share.'"

The tears that had filled my eyes could no longer be contained. "Oh, honey, I loved it so much. Thank you!" Reaching up to him for a hug and smiling brilliantly, I knew that no truer words had ever been spoken.

"I did well, huh, babe?" Mark asked.

"You did good, honey." I was feeling nothing but happiness. He could be so wonderful.

I had to stay in the hospital for the next three days, but they were definitely days of celebration. My son Richie, not being able to locate anyone on the telephone about his birthday plans, had finally come up and found us all. The babies had been born a little before ten o'clock at night, still making the July 6 deadline. His birthday present, he would proudly tell everyone. We were all ecstatic. The guys all celebrated for three days by staying drunk. Every time the nurses saw my family arriving, they'd crack up. They were a fun kind of drunk, though, and never a problem. The nurses had fun with them all.

"Here comes your family again. You have such a big family."

Of course, I really did, but on those three days, I acquired a lot more "family," who were really our friends. In the hospital, only "family members" were allowed to come into my room and hold the babies. It was really neat. I loved this hospital. They even let my little ones, Danny and Becky, come in and hold the babies. Those babies were in and out of the nursery all day long.

"They might as well get used to it now," I told the nurses. "This is the way it'll be when we take them home. They'll get lots of love. They have a very big, loving family." And they could all see that, it being very obvious.

Mark had been so excited about telling his family about our babies. It was the proudest time of his whole life, he had told me. "I called them, babe." Mark returned with a beaming, proud smile. "They were all happy!" I knew that Grandma was glad that there was at least one boy, having had five herself. We thought she would be a little partial to Donny. "I'm so glad they will have one of their grandmas nearby, honey," I said softly, feeling a little sad that my own mom was so far away, living in Georgia. Roy and Nicki sent me a beautiful plant in a music box planter; it was very special to me. They were family, but they were also our very good friends. After they were born, Grandma made them beautiful knitted blankets. It had been a very special gift that touched me deeply.

The next day, I felt like a new person, except for the fact that the first time I stood up, I felt as if my tummy was going to fall on the floor. "Hold a pillow against your tummy, sweetie," the nurse said. "It will make it a lot easier." She smiled. That worked perfectly, and after her expert advice, I was fine and feeling very thin in comparison to how large I had been the last few months.

Our little girl weighed five pounds, five ounces, and our boy was five pounds, fifteen ounces. They'd had separate placentas, so I had just gotten rid of a lot of extra weight. For three days, I was in the bathroom every hour or so, and soon all the excess water was gone.

By the fourth day, when I went home, I weighed four pounds less than when I had gotten pregnant. Much to my surprise, I put my old jeans on that same day. It wasn't easy, but I was determined. "Honey, I need you to help me," I whined teasingly, jumping up and down as I tried to zip my jeans with one hand as I pushed my flabby tummy in with the other.

"What do you want me to do? I can't help you with this problem, babe." He laughed, throwing his hands in the air, backing away from my request, wanting no part in this task.

"Oh, yes, you can," I replied, eyebrows raised. "Come over here and just do what I tell you." I waved my hand toward the bed. "This is a three-handed job, and I nominate you," I teased as I instructed him on what to do. I lay on my back and pushed my flabby tummy in with both hands while Mark very carefully zipped them up, and he got very excited when his job was completed.

Spinning slowly, hands on hips, turning this way and that, I gave my best modeling poses as I tilted my head from side to side, shoulders rising, flashing a very sexy smile. Knowing how much he loved it when I acted silly like this, I was really hamming it up as he whistled flirtatiously, grinning from ear to ear.

"You look good, babe. Boy, do you look good!" he said excitedly. "What a fox!"

I was so proud, having never done this well with my weight with any of my other pregnancies. My tight jeans had the effect of a girdle, and it felt good to have my tummy so well supported. I knew that nursing two babies would have me back to normal very soon. Soon I would be able to zip my own jeans, and I was thankful for my "ice craving," which had helped me control my appetite during the hot summer months toward the end of my pregnancy.

The next months were spent adjusting to these two tiny, new little babies. They were so small we could pass them around in one hand for a while. Mark soon nicknamed Darla Peanut, very appropriately, since she really reminded us of one. When we'd be at Gene and Linda's, we'd change their diapers right on their dining room table. We all laughed because it seemed like the most normal thing in the world to do. That was where we were usually sitting, so why not just change them there too? They were so tiny that it didn't seem like we were laying a real baby there, since they were more like the size of dolls. The sometimes-stuffy Gene didn't even mind, and it showed just how much he loved those babies.

After nursing the twins for six months, I was ready to quit. I was beginning to feel like a cow since it seemed that I was always nursing one baby or another. When one of them would cry, Mark would bring them to me immediately. "Want to eat? Here's Mommy," he'd always joke as he handed me the baby. If they were both crying, he would say, "Double-barrel time." Another favorite saying of Marks was, "Chocolate or regular? Who wants which?" It amazed him how I could nurse them both at once no matter where I was. I nursed them in bed, in the rocker, in the car, even in the bathroom, sitting on the pot. We never let our babies cry. I felt a little guilty that I quit nursing so early, but I knew that I had given them a good start and they were both very healthy.

At the end of September, Mark surprised me one day by driving home in a really nice truck.

"Whose is it?" I asked, wondering what he was doing with it.

"It's ours, babe. I just signed the papers," he said very excitedly. "I got it from Sam, and you have to sign these papers so it will be in both of our names," he said, smiling proudly as he handed me the papers.

If he hadn't had the papers to prove it, I would never have believed him. Sam was so nice. We'd bought our car from him and had just paid it off. Mark needed a truck so badly in his type of work. Sam had said we could buy it for a hundred dollars a month and that Mark could work some of if off by helping him out. It was perfect. We both loved Chevys, and it was a '77, I think.

That truck helped make us a lot of money, and Mark had even taught Danny how to drive it. I'll never forget when Danny was only nine years old and we had an old Corvair. We only used it for cruising around in the desert because it wasn't street legal. One day, I was in the breezeway, grooming my mare as I heard Mark and Danny yelling for me. "Mom, come here quick!" "Babe, hurry, you have to see this!" Their voices filled with excitement and urgency, I walked to the front of the barn, only to see a huge cloud of dust going down our long horseshoe driveway.

I couldn't believe my eyes as I stood there in disbelief, hands on head, thinking, Oh my god! There was Mark in the passenger seat of that old Corvair, holding his hand out the window with a beer in it, laughing really loud. The car kept whizzing backward, making a tight circle with my little boy behind the wheel as Mark gave him his very first driving lesson.

"What are you doing?" I screamed seriously at the top of my lungs, fearing for my son's safety.

"But, babe, he's nine years old. He's gotta learn how to drive," he argued. "He's doing great, he's a natural!" he argued, half-serious, half-joking.

"But backward! You don't drive that fast in reverse at any time, let alone when you are first learning how to drive!" I said, still very upset.

"Babe, the car got stuck in reverse and we can't get it out. I promised him he could drive for ten minutes, so we have to go backward," he explained very seriously, feeling his argument made total sense.

"Oh, I see, that explains it all," I said sarcastically, trying to hold back the laugh that was ready to explode out of me. Turning around, heading back to finish my chore, I couldn't help but smile. After all, there had been a good reason for it all, and I knew that I was as crazy as they were for accepting this silly explanation. Besides, it had been a very funny sight, and I knew that my son was always safe with Mark.

In September, it was once again time for Mark's birthday. It was his thirty-first. We had his party at his mom and dad's again. It was always nice to take the babies to his parents' house. You could tell his mom loved them very much, especially Donny. I realized that Mark's whole family was just like he had been when we first met. They didn't show much emotion or affection openly like my family had always done, but it was very much there as they showed it in other ways. Mark's mom loved yard sales and would always surprise us with a treasure. She knew what her son liked and always bought him special presents. One of his favorites was an old army jacket, winch he loved a lot.

As usual, at the birthday, all the guys got pretty drunk. Brenda's sister Joni was there. I had written a song for her for a contest she was in at school. It was a beautiful song called "Mama." Naturally, it was for her mom, who was a very nice lady. It had turned out to be a combination of how we felt about our moms, since we had talked about it together. I'm proud to say it won first place in her division. I'd even performed it in front of a lot of people at the high school just two months before the twins were born. It hadn't been easy holding a guitar in front of my big belly, but I did it, knowing it meant a lot to her.

I was in the house, taking care of the babies and visiting with the other girls, when suddenly Joni came running into the house beet red.

"I can't believe it! I just can't believe what Mark just did!" she repeated in a state of shock. She went on to explain somewhat unclearly that Mark had just unzipped his pants and grabbed a handful for her to see.

"What?" I couldn't believe it. That might be something the old Mark would do, not my Mark. He had been drunk and in a silly mood, but that was no excuse. He knew I would need a good explanation for this one. He thought he had one, or so he hoped as he entered almost immediately behind Joni, knowing that she had run in to tell on him.

"Babe, don't be mad. She told me I didn't have no balls, I was gonna show her." They had been arguing about something, and Joni had ended up telling Mark that he "didn't have no balls." That was all he'd needed with the silly mood he was in, drunk as he was. What could I say? I knew one thing for sure—that was the last time she'd ever tell Mark that. But I hated the way he acted when he was drinking so much, and I was very embarrassed and shocked that he had acted like that. "Do you think that impresses anyone?" I asked in a disgusted tone. "I'm sorry, babe. Really, I am" was his only defense, hanging his head. I could not believe how immature he could be sometimes.

On this same day, we thought that Shelley was going to have her baby. It turned out to be a false alarm, and her daughter, Rachael, wasn't born until the next day. It was a very special day for me. I was lucky enough to be able to coach her in her labor and go into delivery with her and Rudy. We both held her up as my first grandchild came into our lives; it was exciting and very emotional as the three of us shed lots of tears of joy. Shelley and I shared the same doctor, and her childbirth experience was beautiful and calm for us all, having taught her that childbirth is one of the most beautiful experiences they will ever have.

When Rachael was born, Mark and I decided at the very first that we would not be called Grandma and Grandpa. From the very beginning, I was Inna, a childhood nickname, and Mark was Papa Mark. We both loved Rachael a lot. She and our babies spent many hours lined up in their infant seats as we compared their size. Rachael was always the biggest even though she was two months younger. When Rachel started trying to say words, I somehow became Inny, Its funny how nicknames are made sometimes.

In late September, we had a very bad fight. Mark, once again, showed me some of the craziness he was capable of when he was angry. I'd just met this lady who had a daughter Becky's age. She'd been to the barn a few times, and for some reason, Mark just couldn't stand her. One day after she left, we got into a huge argument and he told me that he didn't want her coming over again. "If I see her again or if you let Becky go there again, you will be so damn sorry!" he screamed, shaking his fist, and I came unglued. "Who do you think you are? You can't control everything! You are such an ass," I responded angrily, teeth clenched, shaking my head in disbelief. The woman hadn't done anything wrong; he just didn't like her and didn't even know why.

One thing led to another, and before you know it, it was a full-fledged, scary fight. "You bitch!" he screamed as he got right in my face. Knowing he would never really hurt me, I did not back down.

"This is bull, and you know it! Just get away from me and quit trying to control everything!" I screamed as I backed away from his charge.

Whap!

I could not believe that he had hit me. "Get out and don't ever come back. I hate you!" I was hysterical as I felt the pain below my eye. The babies were screaming, and Becky could not believe what was happening.

"Are you all right, Mom?" my young daughter was pleading as she ran toward me, tears glistening down her cheeks. In an instant, Mark had left.

Thank God that he was gone, I kept my thoughts to myself.

"I'm okay, baby," I sobbed as I sat down to hold my baby girl, comforting her until she calmed down, a baby crawling into each of our laps.

"Oh, Mommy, look at your eye." Her eyes were as big as saucers, tears threatening again. I went to the mirror to analyze the damage, seeing that my eye was already swelling and bright red. Eventually, I developed a very black eye. After we calmed the babies down, I held my Becky and we cried together, all the while I assured her that I would never go back with him and that I would never cause her to be frightened like that again. The fight had scared her badly, and she had been very worried about her mommy.

Later on in the day, I realized that I had to go to the store. I went to get in my car. Much to my shock, there was my car with the rear end jacked up. There were no tires to be found anywhere. He had taken both of my tires with him so that I couldn't leave. I couldn't believe it! What an idiot he could be! What a crazy idiot, I thought to myself.

At this time, Jimmy lived with Rory in a small trailer behind the tire shop, where Rory worked. I called up frantically. I was so mad and having a mini rage. What right did he have doing that? "He hasn't been gone very long, and he was heading for town. Please find him and get my tires back for me," I pleaded.

"He is crazy, Mom. I can't believe you stay with him. Someday he is going to hurt you real bad," my son said in a disgusted voice. Mark scared him so much when he acted crazy like this.

Rory, always the hero, said, "Okay, we'll see if we can find him."

Since it was such a small town; if Mark was anywhere in town, they'd find him. It wasn't long before I got a call from Jimmy. They had found him at our small town market. When they told him to give back the tires, he said, "No way. You just get the hell out of here before there's a big problem."

They called to tell me he was very drunk, but I already knew that.

"What did you say to him?" I demanded, still very upset about the whole thing.

"We said okay."

I knew how Jimmy feared Mark when he was like that. Rory, who did not fear anyone, just didn't want a problem, and I knew that Mark had said it in such a crazy frame of mind that they didn't bother to ask twice. "What do you need from the store? We will bring it up to you, Mom," Jimmy asked, still sounding very disgusted about the entire incident.

I was mad because I didn't get my tires back, but I did understand. There was nothing worse than dealing with Mark when he was acting crazy like that, and I didn't blame them a bit.

You didn't go against Mark when he was acting like that—he was just too scary. Just the way he could look at me would scare me so badly.

The next day, he came home so sorry as usual. He was going to really cut down on his drinking and he felt terrible that I had a black eye. He apologized to the kids and me over and over.

"I'm such an ass," he told them, head hanging low. "I never want to hurt your mom. I'm such an ass!" He paused. "Babe, please forgive me. I promise it will never happen again," he pleaded as he held me close. "I can't stand to see your eye like this, babe. I am so sorry," he said in a choked-up voice. I had been right yesterday—my eye was very black today, and it was not a pretty sight.

"I forgive you, honey," I said, melting into his arms, feeling safe once again.

As usual, I totally forgave him, and I was happy that he was home. I knew if I would watch my mouth when he was drunk, it wouldn't happen again. I do have a big mouth, and when I feel strongly about something, I don't drop it until he understands what I am trying to say. We both knew it wouldn't happen again, and it was soon forgotten. After all, it had been mostly my fault, because I couldn't shut up.

As usual, I had shared with the kids how sorry he was and asked them to please forgive him for me. "You want Mommy to be happy, don't you?" I pleaded.

"Of course, we do, Mom, but he scares us sometimes," they shared quietly, as if to tell a secret.

"Well, I promise that it won't happen again, and if it does, he will have to leave forever, okay?"

"Okay," they reluctantly replied in a very confused tone of voice. As usual, I convinced myself that they were really okay with it all and they understood.

A few weeks later, he gloated when I had to tell him he was right about that lady, since she turned out to be a scum. I had become a typical abused woman by now. Taking partial blame, if not all the blame, for his becoming violent. Walking on eggs, trying to keep things peaceful. Trying to learn to keep my big mouth shut. Trying to make sure the kids were nice to him no matter what. I was becoming a terrible mom with no self-esteem, and I didn't even realize it.

It was October. This was the month for Shelley's long-awaited wedding. She and Rudy were going to be married, and my mom was coming to visit us from Georgia. Mom had managed to work it so she'd be here for the wedding. She wanted to help out in every way she could. She was the planner of all planners. With Mana here— that was what the kids called her—everything would turn out great. Thank God for moms.

As I had anticipated, Mom and Mark hit it off immediately. He loved her a lot, and she him. He always joked with her and made her feel special. He'd say things like, "If your daughter had a pair of legs like that, I wouldn't always have to control my desire for you moms." She'd get all embarrassed and tell him what a big tease he was. We all laughed a lot when she was here.

"Babe, you'd better treat me good, or I might just run away with your mom," Mark joked.

Mom laughed and said, "You stop that, Mark. You're always trying to make me feel good." She was right; he thought she was a great lady.

He'd always flatter me whenever he'd tell me, "You got that from your mom."

The wedding was beautiful, thanks mostly to Mom, and the reception at Gene and Linda's was such fun. Mom liked all our friends. She and Leroy had a lot in common, and they got along great. They'd both worked for General Telephone for years. Mom had recently retired and moved to Georgia. Mom even liked our friend TJ, although he did look pretty mean.

I'd always been her different kid, her hippie type. We'd had a few discussions about my smoking pot in the past. Not long discussions, because it was something she rather chose to ignore. In her mind, if you smoked pot, you were just like a heroin addict, so most of our discussions on the subject went absolutely nowhere. It was something she'd had to accept, loving me as she did, but she always made it clear the she would never ever approve. She loved me very much, and she knew I was a good person, so she dealt with it.

Shelley and Rudy came back from their two-day honeymoon in San Diego with devastating news. Shelley was very upset because she'd just found out herself. Surprise! Rudy was moving Shelley and my granddaughter to Vegas, where his family lived. I was crushed. He'd promised me when they first met that he would never take her away. We were very close, my Shelley and I, and we both had brand-new babies. She might as well be moving a million miles away, and I was very angry with Rudy for betraying me.

"How can you do this to me? You promised me!" I screamed through my tears. "I hate you! Get out!" I was hysterical.

"Mom, please! Don't say that! You know how much I love you!" My darling, precious daughter was crying as hard as I was, and my heart was breaking for her.

"Come here, baby," I said as I held her tight. "I love you so much, and I don't want you so far away, honey," I sobbed, tears streaming down both of our cheeks. It was a very sad night, but eventually, I got over it, knowing I couldn't hang on to them forever. Three hours away seemed like a million miles to me on this night of surprising news, and I was glad that mom had been asleep in the small trailer she was staying in, next to the barn, not hearing all the hysterics of the night.

A few days later, it was time for Mom to leave also. Mark and I drove her down to the airport and put her on the plane back to Georgia. It was hard to say goodbye because I knew how much she hated living so far away from her kids. She felt she had an obligation to take care of her elderly aunt Mae.

The cold season was fast approaching. In came the fireplace, our only source of heat.

Getting firewood was a fun adventure for us. We'd found a place up in the hills above us that was covered with dead juniper trees. They were so dead they would break right off. Over and over, Mark said, "If only we had a chain saw, babe, we could get rich selling firewood this winter." The next time my dad and Virginia came to visit, we told them of our plan. My dad was every bit as great as my mom was, and he was always there for me when I needed him. Dad and Virginia decided to help us out again.

"There's always the good old Sears card," Dad said. He took us to Sears and bought us the biggest and best chain saw they had. It was over four hundred dollars, and Dad let us make the payment since we'd already put the generator and vacuum on his card. The chainsaw made us a lot of money that year. The entire winter, we sold at least five cords of wood a week. We had lots of money and lots of fun.

We both loved the outdoors so much that gathering the wood never seemed like a chore. Soon we had a system down that worked very well. It took us two loads in the morning to gather enough wood to make a cord. Then we'd break for lunch, and it would take another two hours or so to cut and load the cord. We'd deliver it and be home by late afternoon, a little exhausted by the end of the day. There was always a waiting list since we only charged a hundred dollars a cord. It was a fun way to make a lot of money and always be together, so we really liked that.

One day, before we had our guns, we came across two big diamondback timber rattlers mating. I though it was so beautiful and romantic, but Mark thought I was silly to think that. They were all coiled together with their heads really high, right together, almost like they were kissing.

We stopped the truck and started walking toward them. They were startled by us and broke apart, the biggest one disappearing in the bushes and the smaller one very stupidly going up the branches of a dead bush.

"Babe, grab a long, thick stick, like this one," he said as he held the one he had just picked up high in the air. Fearing what he wanted to do, I quickly obliged, feeling a little hesitant, more afraid than anything. "What are we going to do, honey?" Hating snakes with a passion, always saying that the only good snake was a dead snake, I eagerly followed his instructions.

With one of us on each side of the bush, we took turns beating it over and over until its head was hanging almost all the way off. Even though it was a bit morbid, it was very exciting. After it fell to the ground, Mark pinned what was left of the snake's head and cut if off. "Good job, babe," he beamed. "Rattlesnake dinner tonight," he said very excitedly.

"Yuck!" I made an awful face. "You and who else?" I teased.

Much to my surprise, we took it home, where Mark showed Danny how to skin it. Then they cooked it and ate the rattlesnake meat. "That's sick" was all Becky and I could say as the two of them smacked their lips, teasing us, saying what a great meal we were missing. Danny said it was quite delicious. We saved the skin, and later I mounted it on a board. It was very beautiful, about five to six feet long. When I look at it, it brings back a fun memory for me of a time I was brave.

November 17 was my birthday. We had a big party at Leroy's house. As usual, Mark got pretty drunk. Someone had been passing around bottles of hard stuff, and Mark knew that drinking this made him meaner than hell. At one point, after way too much drinking, Mark decided that the few people he didn't know who were with some other friends were narcs. We couldn't believe he had taken a tab of acid. He got very weird and tried to fight the guys. He got knocked on his butt because he was so drunk he could barely stand, let alone fight. Mark was really at his worst that night. He was so unreachable that he frightened me terribly.

He had a bone knife that he wore on his belt all the time. It was very special to him because his friend TJ had made it and given it to him. Sometime during the party, he discovered the knife wasn't in its case. The case was empty. He "wigged," thinking that someone had stolen it right off his belt. Someone had taken it, but not to steal it. Linda had heard Mark talking violently. "I'm gonna kill those narcs over there," he'd said, very angrily, eyes brilliant with temper. Linda thought she'd better take the knife for his and everyone else's protection. Naturally, when he discovered it was gone, Mark thought I'd taken it, and he was in a rage.

Trying to figure out how to calm him down, Linda and I worked out a plan. Mark had already fallen into Leroy's rosebush twice because he was so drunk. We tried to convince him that he must have lost it when he fell. "Don't worry, we'll find it tomorrow, when it's daylight," we said. He wasn't falling for it one little bit, hard as we tried to convince him.

"I want my damn knife, and I want it right now!" was all he could say, in a vicious, mean voice, his stare cold and deliberate. "I need it to get those narcs in there. Give it to me now, bitch!" he ordered through clenched teeth. Every time I'd get away from him, he'd find me. "Give it to me, or else, you bitch," he threatened once again as my heart pounded in my throat. I slowly backed away from him, turned, and ran into the bar area, relieved that he had not followed. I didn't have it, so there was nothing I could do.

Finally, I convinced Linda that we should give it back to him. "It's kind of his security," I told her. Since she realized that keeping his knife was not helping matters, she agreed that she should give it back. But how? "Let's pretend that we found it in the rosebush. That'll be perfect." After Mark got his knife back, he still acted crazy, but at least he didn't bother me about it.

He was too concerned with trying to figure out who all the Narcs were. What a night! "Quit being such an idiot," I'd told him over and over every time our paths would cross. I was so embarrassed, and he would have been also if he could have seen the way he was acting. I hate so much what alcohol does to people. I've seen it turn some of the neatest people in the whole world into such idiots. It's so sad. If only they could see themselves, they'd never drink again.

Things seemed to have quieted down a bit when, all of a sudden, I heard Mark's voice. He was standing right in the middle of Leroy's living room, holding the fireplace poker like a weapon. "I'm gonna kill every single person in here!" he screamed, face twisted with evil. He sounded like a crazy man.

My son Richie, who, by now, had had it with the way Mark was acting, yelled from across the room, "Well, you can start with me, you ass!" Heading directly for him, fists clenched. Mark threw a planter across the room, and soon the two of them met in the middle as they wrestled to the ground. In an instant, Richie had him down, hitting him over and over, with Mark too drunk to put up any kind of fight. After what seemed like a long time, Leroy and Rory pulled them apart. In a short time, Mark calmed down, but he was still not at all himself.

What an idiot, was all I could think. "Some fun birthday," I scolded him, being totally disgusted with him. My stomach was churning, and everyone's adrenaline was pumping fiercely as I wondered, once again, if I could stay with him after this kind of behavior.

Sometime later, Mark grabbed the fireplace poker. "If anyone comes near me, I'll kill them!" he screamed in the middle of Leroy's living room.

Leroy, as if he didn't have a nerve in his body, walked straight up to him. "Come on, Mark, you don't want to act like this," he said calmly as he took the poker out of his hand.

Mark sat back on the couch and seemed to slip into a black silence as he gave in to his longtime friend. Even in the uncontrolled state of mind that he was in, the great respect he had for his friend Leroy was still there, and it had really come in handy this night.

I stood with Mark in the kitchen for about three hours, almost until the sun came up, trying to keep him calm. Someone went to find some pot, hoping it would calm him down, which usually worked. Over and over I told him to think about all that he had achieved since we had met.

"Don't destroy it," I said. "Don't lose it all," I pleaded earnestly, my heart pounding in my throat, fearing another outburst at any moment. For hours he went from one extreme to the other. Calm one minute, violent the next.

It would take a few hours, but I finally wore him down. He was calm enough now to go in to Leroy's king-size waterbed with me to watch our beautiful little babies as they lay there asleep.

I knew I won this battle, as I saw calmness engulf him as he proudly, lovingly stroked his babies. Watching Donny and Darla as they slept had always turned him to putty, and it would be no different today as dawn approached. "I am such a lucky man, babe." He stretched and muttered a big yawn. "What makes me be such an ass?" he asked as he kissed me gently and closed his eyes, shaking his head in disbelief.

The next day, after sleeping three or four hours, he couldn't believe it when we had told him the things he had done and the violent way he had acted. Of course, he was very sorry and apologized to everyone. "If I ever act like that again, somebody just knock me out cold," he said, eyebrows narrowed, in a very serious tone. They were words I would not forget, words that would give me comfort in the future. I knew that he had meant what he said.

The next weekend, we were all over at Leroy's, sitting at the bar. Rory, who was now living there, brought a small box and handed it to Mark. "What's this, a present?" Mark joked, acting excited.

"Yep, it's just for you, but it is staying here," Rory said with a smile, but very serious. The laughter was loud when he opened the box to reveal a pair of genuine handcuffs.

He hung the cuffs right above Leroy's bar on a chain that held up the light, and we all knew that they were for Mark, if he ever acted like that again. "What a great idea!" we all agreed, knowing that it truly was a good idea. They hung there as a reminder of that terrible night. We celebrated my birthday the next day, and it was wonderful. Once again, I begged my kids to forgive him.

"I know that you want Mom to be happy," I told them, never paying attention to their real feelings, only being concerned about me. Of course they did, they would answer, wondering what kind of a stupid question that was.

CHAPTER 6

CHRISTMAS, CANCER, AND GUNS

I t was hard to believe that it was almost Christmas already. It would be such a special Christmas, our babies' first. We were still working hard every day, cutting firewood. We had finally gotten the babies used to the loud noise that the chain saw made. It had been Mark's idea. Usually, when we were outside, cutting, we had to bring the babies out with us. The kids were still in school, and there was no one else to watch them up in the barn.

Their playpen was about twenty feet from us so we could keep a good eye on them. Just before Mark would start the chain saw, he'd say very loudly to them, "Here comes Daddy's boom boom," looking toward them, getting their full attention. "Rum rum rum." He'd do it real loud a couple of times so they'd get used to loud noises, and then right away, he'd start the saw. It sounds funny, but it really did work, and as long as we remembered to do that first, they wouldn't get scared. They learned to expect the loud noise as soon as he said, "Rum rum rum"; they were very smart for being only six months old. Still, it would be nice when the kids were out of school for Christmas vacation so we wouldn't have to bundle them up every day and bring them outside in the cold.

The teenage girl across the street, Lily, was a big help. She'd come over and watch them for us. I loved her very much, and she loved us all. She had begun to call me Mom because she thought I was easy to talk to. She had a little brother, Darrell, who was about five years old. He used to have a real hard time saying some of his words right and was hard to understand sometimes. For some reason, Mark could always understand, and I would tease him, saying, "Honey, the only reason you get along so well is that you have the mentality of a child most of the time." I would say it with a squinted face.

"Right on. I'll buy that," he teased back in a childlike voice, laughing all the while. He loved Darryll very much, and soon we all adopted the nickname Mark had given him: Cool Darrell.

With Christmas almost here, we talked about how nice it would be if Mark's daughter, Tanya, could come to spend a couple of weeks with us. Mark and Lily, her mom, hadn't gotten along very well in the past, but with so much time behind them, their relationship had improved. There was no emotion involved now, and Mark was eager to show off his babies.

We made arrangements to pick Tanya up at a motel near the freeway in Victorville. They were coming all the way from Oklahoma, and Lily would be going on to San Diego. On her way back, in a few weeks, she would call and make arrangements to pick her daughter up. Tanya was five years old and hadn't seen her father in about three years.

After a quick hello to Mark, the introductions began. "Tanya, this is your daddy."

With a big smile and a huge bear hug, she said in a sweet, high-pitched, little-girl's voice, "Hi, Daddy! I love you." It seemed they had never been apart, and I could tell that she had melted Mark's heart and put all his nerves to rest. Her behavior gave me an instant respect for her mom, seeing what a sweet, well-adjusted little girl she was, and it was obvious that her mommy loved her very much. I liked Lily, the little time I had with her, and I knew that she had had to deal with the different Mark, the one that hadn't changed so much for the good.

The two weeks that we had Tanya were full of love, and she enjoyed playing little mommy to her new baby brother and sister.

Mason and Randy were with us part of the time, and it was great having them all together. Mark spent a lot of time telling ghost stories and teasing with all the kids. Becky and Mark were famous for speaking in their English accents—the two of them were so funny. They could talk like that back and forth for hours, sounding just like Tiny Tim talked. Whenever Tanya would scratch her rear, which she did frequently, Mark would say, "Tanya's picking her seat for the movies." It would always get a laugh, as would Mark's famous "Yo mama." He said it so funny and always made us laugh very hard.

One of our favorite pastimes was just staying home, playing spades. Mark had learned to play when he was in jail years ago and told me that it was a very popular card game there, with so much time to pass. His family already knew how to play, so he taught all of us also.

We spent many hours playing spades at the barn or at Roy and Nicki's. Mark and I played for days at a time, keeping a running score to a thousand. I got pretty good, I must admit, but most of the time, he was very hard to beat. One time, I remember we were playing guys against the girls, and we girls were losing badly. After a while, we realized something fishy was going on. The guys had been cheating their butts off. They'd been giving signals and everything. Mark and his brothers had no morals when it came to cheating. They didn't care. They'd just laugh and say something like, "Whatever it takes." They thought it was funny that they got away with it for as long as they did.

It was New Year's Eve, party time. Tanya was still here, as were Mason and Randy. We were all together for the holiday. The party was going fine. No major or even minor problems happened with Mark and everyone was having a really good time. The kids were all excited because they knew we played a game where we took a picture when the sun came up on New Year's Day. Whoever stayed awake all night got to be in the picture. It was considered a real honor to be in the picture, we told them. Those poor kids wanted to stay awake more than anything. They wanted to be in the all-night picture. They were all so proud when they made it. I have the picture to prove it. Needless to say, Mark didn't make it. At about three or four, he had gone inside in a good mood. He was feeling a little bit tired and went to lie down with the babies on Leroy's big waterbed. So far, it had been a really nice, fun party, full of love for our family and friends. It was morning, and all of a sudden, everyone in the whole house heard Mark screaming at the top of his lungs. "Linda, get your ass in here right now! Where are my pants? What the hell did you do with my gosh-dang pants?"

I couldn't believe my ears. How should I know where his pants were? What the heck did he take his pants off for, anyway? One thing was for sure: his pants were not to be found. We looked everywhere as he continued to scream at me. The louder he screamed, the harder I looked. Where could they be? They were nowhere to be found. Leroy had one room in his house that no one ever went in. The door to it was always closed. It was just understood that no one went in there. Since we'd all looked everywhere else in the whole house, I finally decided to look in there. I knew it was a long shot, but it was my last hope. Sure enough, just inside the door were Mark's jeans. They were a little wet, but I took them to him. He was still on the bed with the sheet I'd had over the babies on him. He was yelling even louder at me because I had hidden his pants in that room. Wow! Finally, I figured out what must have happened. He was still pretty drunk after having slept for about four hours. I think that sometime after he lay on the bed, he had probably gotten up to go to the bathroom. He must have accidentally wet his jeans a little and just took them off and left them there. It was the only logical explanation I could come up with. Since the boxers he was wearing were still a little damp, in my mind it proved my theory was correct.

He wasn't about to accept that explanation, though, because that meant he had wet his pants. He preferred to blame me. He got up, put his damp jeans on, and started pushing me around, screaming, "Why the hell did you wet my jeans and hide them in that room?"

Me with my big mouth was screaming back just as loudly, defending myself as usual. He wasn't pinning this one on me. "That's why you shouldn't get so damn drunk!" I screamed back.

Just as Tanya walked into the room, he pushed me really hard and I fell into Leroy's closet door. She started screaming at her daddy and chasing him down the hall, yelling, "Don't hit my mama! You're mean! Don't push my mama!" During those two weeks, Tanya had started calling me Mama.

It was a terrible scene. He went out the door and drove off. I don't remember how we all got home, but someone took us right away. I was in shock. I had ended up in trouble because he was embarrassed. Our nice New Year's Day had been ruined. Maybe I should have taken it as an omen of what the New Year had to offer. It would be the worst year of my life.

By noon, Mark was home. He'd stopped and had breakfast and lots of coffee. He said he'd been down at the aqueduct for a couple of hours, thinking of what an ass he had been, again, and trying to figure out how to apologize. He confided in me how hard it was for him to admit that he had to have wet his pants. He'd never done that in his life. He was like a pathetic little puppy dog with his tail between his legs. It almost sounded like he had an attitude that he could do anything he wanted because he knew I would always forgive him. He was probably right, but there were two reasons I always forgave him. The first reason was that I knew that if I didn't forgive him and we were to stay apart, I would give up everything that made me happy. The second reason, and probably the most important, was that I always knew how sorry he really was.

Mark and I were together most of the time. It sounds like we fought a lot, but if you stop and think, it was nothing compared to the happiness we experienced together. We weren't like any other couple I've known. We never had days that we just existed and weren't totally in tune with each other. We loved each other so much, and the smallest things would bring us joy. We flirted and laughed and tickled and wrestled. We could never walk near the other on a hot day without getting totally hosed down if the water was on. We spent hours out on the roof, me playing guitar for him and he praising my talents. It was nothing for us to take off together, blanket in hand, and find a spot in the desert to make love. We had fun in almost everything we did together. When he'd be doing something at night,

I'd be right there with him, holding the flashlight. We were constantly going and getting each other to show something to. Maybe it would be something cute our babies were doing, a new leaf on a tree, a cloud formation, the stars, or one of the million sunsets we watched together. We were truly in love and very happy. No, sir, I didn't care what anyone thought of me for always forgiving him. You know if someone is really sorry or not. I knew he always was, and forgiving him was a must if I was to be able to enjoy all the other perfect, happy days. I wouldn't trade even one of those days for anything. Love is truly blind.

One day, Mark was complaining to me about how his brothers had been teasing him, saying how whipped he was. He said something I'll always remember. He had told me before that compared to what we had, it seemed like everyone else we knew had nothing. His very words that day were, "I don't care what anyone else says. If I lost you, I would lose everything. They would lose nothing." It meant so much to me when he said that.

In August, Mark did something very romantic. That was exactly how he had worded it too. He said, "I'm gonna do something real romantic, babe. I'm gonna write you a love letter." I was in the rocking chair, rocking one of the babies to sleep. He was very careful not to let me peek as he wrote, telling me how romantic this was going to be. He knew I was an incurable romantic. When he was all done, he said, "There's just one problem: you have to fill in the blank, because I don't know how to spell the last word. It's special." I still have the letter. This is what his love letter said: "Babe, I never had anything that I wanted to keep before. Now I do [he put lines there for me to tell him how to spell special]." I knew he couldn't spell it for sure, since he drew in an extra line. Now tell me, could you give up things like these forever just because someone gets drunk at times? You'd be crazy if you could. I'd have to sum up our life together in just two words, I guess. It was either heaven or hell, and heaven far outnumbered the hell. On my last birthday, he had bought me a card that he was so proud of. He had said that what it said was so true. I'll always treasure the words. They were as follows:

Love is measured in beautiful moments. Count
the memories, not the days. Count your dear
one's loving ways. Count the happy times, not
the tears. For love is measured in moments, not
years.

It was the first Saturday in April. For as long as I had been at
the barn, it was a ritual that my mom called almost without fail every
single Saturday. On this particular day, there was nothing out of the
ordinary happening. Mark and I were getting ready to go get wood.
Saturdays were busy for us because we could get a lot more done when
the kids were home from school to help with the babies. Sundays
were usually put aside for some kind of family fun. Sometimes we'd
go to the stream or lake, depending on the weather, or we'd just pack
up and go spend the day at Gene and Linda's or Leroy's. Sometimes
we would go for a ride on the horses and let the kids ride when we
got back. We tried to take Sunday off from work.

Until that very familiar phone call came this morning, everything was quite normal. After the call, my world seemed to stop.
Mom told me that she had finally gone to the doctor about her
continuous cough. There was a problem, but she didn't want me
to worry. "Problem? My god, what's wrong, Mom?" I knew by her
voice that it was serious. Since she knew how emotional I'd always
been, she was trying to break it to me as easily as she could and not
make it sound too serious. The doctors in Georgia had found some
cancer. I couldn't believe it. Not my mom! Mom had never been sick
a day in her life. She'd taught me that cramps were all in your head
and that there was no such thing as menopause, except for a hot flash
now and then. If you didn't feel good or if you had a headache, the
secret was just to keep busy. You'd forget about it, and it would go
away. It had always worked for me. My mom couldn't have cancer! I
was devastated. She was leaving for California to stay with my sister
near Sacramento, where she could receive the best medical care and
be closer to family. There was probably nothing to worry about, she
tried to assure me. There were lots of cures for cancer.

I walked down the barn stairs in sort of a trance and got into the truck, where Mark was waiting. The moment he saw my face, he knew something terrible had happened. "What's the matter, babe? What's wrong?"

While I told him what Mom had said, I fell apart. "Let's get out of here before the kids come ask what's wrong." We drove down to the aqueduct. It had always been a place of peace for us. We had had many long heart-to-heart talks here. We'd discussed and solved a lot of problems just watching the water peacefully flow by. Mark almost always had some pot with him. Thank God he did today. After we smoked a joint, something that I never ever did in the daytime, I had calmed down a little bit.

"This is one time moms would be thankful for marijuana," he tried to joke. I smiled. We sat there for a long time, trying to gather our thoughts. Trying to accept what was happening. Mark was very sad too. He loved Mom very much. He knew what a special relationship we had. He was proud to be able to brag about how much she loved him too. I was feeling numb as I kept remembering her words on the phone. "Now, don't you cry, baby. We all need to think positive. It will make you feel better to be positive, baby." I would always be her baby, and she was very protective of my sensitivity, always knowing I was the emotional one of her children. Her attitude was very optimistic, as always, and I knew that it was all for my benefit.

I couldn't remember hardly ever hearing my mom complain about anything. "Honey, cancer kills people. This is very serious. It must be a mistake," I said softly, hanging my head, trying to hide the tears that had slowly filled my eyes. My brother-in-law, whom I loved so much, one of the neatest guys in the whole world, had died of cancer. He was only thirty-four when he died six months after they had done brain surgery to remove a cancerous tumor. It had torn me apart when it had happened. Now it was happening again, and to my mom, of all people.

"It's a game," I told Mark. "She's trying so hard to be brave for me. She knows I couldn't handle it if anything happened to her."

He tried his best to console me. He used all her same arguments. Nothing could ease my mind. "You said your mom has always been very healthy, and you know how strong she is, babe," he said in a soft, loving, reassuring voice, never letting go of my hand. "She is not very strong anymore. I just know that she's going to die real soon." I sobbed. "I'm not going have my mom anymore. Honey, I just can't imagine not having my mom!"

"Babe, there's always hope," Mark stressed. "Where's my eternal optimist? If anyone can beat cancer, it's your mom, and she raised you to always be optimistic, so don't stop now when you need it the most."

Even though I had always tried to be an optimist my whole life, I knew that I was also a realist. Mark knew that, so he didn't waste too much time with bullshit, thank God. I was not in any mood for bull, and it was on this day that I acquired this terrible gut feeling that I couldn't explain, even to myself. Trying to explain it to him, all I could say was, "I have a feeling that this year, is going to be the worst year of my life. I'd give anything if I could just stop time right now."

His only reply was, "Your mom wouldn't want us to miss all the good that's ahead for us because of her, babe." Little did I know at that time how really bad would be for my family and friends. If only I had known.

My brother Ronnie was a career army man and was home on leave from Germany. He and his wife, Karen, lived near San Diego. It was a couple of hours' drive. My brother's main interest had always been guns, and he was an expert in the field. Ronnie was excited about coming to see us in our desert, knowing he could bring his guns and shoot them here. He was never much of a city boy.

Ronnie, Karen, and their two-year-old, Margaret (named after my mom), all came for a visit in early April. Even though we'd all just discovered that Mom had cancer, the overall attitude of the situation was optimistic that day. Who was I to ruin things? If they could feel so optimistic about it, more power to them. We went up in the hills in my brother's van, babies and all. It was a lot of fun. Ronnie had a video camera, and it was an exciting thing to us all. He took videos of the babies and me and of Mark and Danny and his friend Monty shooting the guns. They are movies that I treasure. Ronnie couldn't believe it when we told him that we didn't have any guns living in this desert as we did.

"You should have a gun for protection," he insisted. "What about snakes?"

No problem, we laughed. "We just beat them to death with sticks." We told him about our snake incident.

Before Ronnie left the next day, he took us down to the back of his van to show me his artillery collection. He had some really nice guns with him. Much to our surprise, he left two of his guns with us. "No one should live out in this desert without guns," he told us. He left his twelve-gauge Mossberg shotgun for Mark. "It's a fun gun to shoot," he said. "It has a short barrel, just legal." For me, he left a small .22 pistol that he'd bought for his daughter, Margaret. This was the perfect gun to teach someone to shoot with, he'd said. Since Margaret was still too little to learn, it had hardly been fired. We were all excited.

I'd never been around guns but had always wanted to learn to shoot. I'd spent my whole childhood wishing I were Annie Oakley. Ronnie had taught me to shoot BB guns as a kid, and once when I was fifteen, he taught me to shoot a .22 rifle.

Since then, I'd never touched a gun. All he asked was that we take care of them, and we were welcome to use them for a while. I was very touched that he left them because it showed me that he had liked Mark. He would never have left his precious guns if he hadn't. It was important to Mark that my brother like him, and this gesture proved he did. "Wow, babe, that was really nice of your brother. I think he really likes me. Don't you?" He was grinning from ear to ear.

"Yes, honey, he really likes you for him to do that. Besides, who wouldn't like you?" I said proudly, smiling my sweetest smile.

Those guns were to give us much pleasure over the next months. Mark taught me how to shoot, and above all, he taught me to always have the utmost respect for guns. He taught Danny to shoot also. Shooting became one of our most fun things to do. I became obsessed with becoming a good shot, spending hours shooting at targets we set up. At that time, there were no houses near the barn, and we could shoot all we wanted.

I was very proud of what a terrific shot I was becoming. Mark was very proud of his prize student also. I always told him that it wasn't fair that he could shoot off his horse and I couldn't. My Appaloosa mare, Mark's horse, had been a posse horse, and shooting off her back didn't bother her a bit. My Arab went nuts at the sound of gunshots. If I'd ever shot from her back, she would have gone bananas. It was bad enough just being with Mark when he shot. He would always have to warn me so I could get a good hold on Lindy, knowing she would freak from the sound of his gun.

We loved going down to the alfalfa fields. There were a million rabbits there. We'd take turns driving the truck so the other one could stand up in the back and shoot at the rabbits as the truck scared them out. It was like Knott's Berry Farm with moving targets everywhere. At night, there was no one around and the headlights of the truck put off plenty of light. We didn't stop to pick up the rabbits, though, once we learned that most of them were covered with some kind of big ugly ticks. I did feel a little bad just shooting for the sport of it, but I looked at it like we helped put them out of their misery from all those damn ticks.

One day, I got such a scare that I shook for hours afterward. It was the middle of the day. It was my turn to ride in the back of the truck and shoot. Way up ahead in the middle of nowhere was an old beat-up car. It looked so old and rusty that my guess was that it had been dumped there a long time ago. We saw cars like this all the time, and we liked shooting at them. I went in the back with my .22. I didn't shoot the shotgun very often because it always hurt my shoulder. I just couldn't do it right, I guess. Mark usually shot it off his hip, but I'd always been afraid to try that. My .22 worked just fine for me. I didn't get many moving rabbits like Mark did with the shotgun, but I still had a lot of fun.

Anyway, this day, when we started getting closer to that old abandoned car, I was busy setting my sights for the rearview mirror on the door of the driver's side. We were still pretty far from it. I knew it was a difficult shot, but I had lots of confidence in my shooting. Pow! I hit it! I was so excited, knowing how proud Mark always was of my shooting. Wham. He stopped the truck on a dime, jumped out, and started yelling at the top of his lungs.

"What the hell is the matter with you? Don't you have a brain in your freaking head? You don't ever shoot at a car like that. You've got to make sure there's no one in it, you idiot!"

I couldn't believe it. I'd made one of the hardest shots I had ever tried, and all he could do was yell at me. You can't imagine how I felt when we both looked ahead toward the car and there was a guy sitting up in the front seat, starting to get out. My shot had awakened him. Thank God he never realized that my bullet had hit the chrome on the side of his minor.

It seemed that he and his friend had run out of gas and his friend had gone to find help. He had fallen asleep. I couldn't believe that the car actually ran, let alone that anyone would drive it on the streets. I've had some ugly cars in my life, but this car was outrageous. Thank God, when we saw the guy, Mark quit yelling at me. He realized the guy didn't even know what had happened.

By the time Mark siphoned gas for him and got him on his way, he had calmed down. He even managed a little apology for yelling at me so much, realizing how many times we had shot old cars in the desert. The only difference was that we had always walked up them first and knew they were uninhabited. He hadn't covered that rule, he admitted; he'd just assumed it was common sense. He was right, I told him. I hadn't used common sense. I felt so bad and irresponsible. I thought of how easily I could have killed someone just because of my stupidity.

Mark let me suffer for a while, and then seeing how badly I felt, he broke the ice. He said, "Thank God there was no trim on the side of the door. I could just see you aiming for the chrome strip in the middle of the door and killing the poor guy." We both smiled. I knew we both secretly and thoroughly examined where my bullet hit as we were helping the guy, being careful not to let on to what had happened. "By the way, babe, it really was an excellent shot, especially from that distance."

All I could say, feeling as badly as I did, was "Thanks." We talked later about how that guy was going to feel when he found the big dent my bullet put in the chrome of his mirror. As far as he was concerned, we were just two really nice people who were helping him out. Mark's next mission was to defang the snake. He was trying to appease my fears of a deadly snake being in the house with babies. I had to be there just in case. Mark had no fear, and the whole thing turned out to be very funny, at least to everyone but Mark.

The plan was that he would get the snake to open its mouth and try to pull its fangs out with pliers. Mark grabbed it right behind its head so there was no way it could strike. As he did this, the rest of the snake wrapped itself around his arm. The snake was so upset because of the way Mark was holding that him he automatically opened his mouth. Mark reached in with his pliers and pulled one fang out. Immediately the snake pooped all over his arm, and I never saw anyone move so fast in all my life. He threw the snake on the ground and pinned his head. Then he pulled out his bone knife and cut the snake's head off. "No snake's gonna crap on me and get away with it." He was very angry. He skinned it, ate the meat, and TJ made a real neat headband out of it. Mark gave it to me for our second anniversary together.

"That's one way to get rid of a snake, I guess," I boasted, happy that it was dead.

Soon it was Easter and we had a barbecue at our place. Besides our family, Leroy and Mark's dad, his dad, were there. It was a nice day except for Bill getting thrown from my horse, Lindy. He'd been bragging about how he could ride anything, so Mark gave him the chance to show us. It was really more like a trick, because of the way Lindy was trained. She didn't like any pressure in her mouth at all, and she had been almost totally trained off my legs. The minute Bill mounted her, he put pressure on her mouth and gripped with his legs. This would have been a perfectly normal thing to do on another horse, but not Lindy. She immediately started backing up real fast, and when she'd backed up as far as she wanted to go, she showed her confusion by rearing up pretty high. In an instant, Bill was on his butt. After realizing that he was okay, we all laughed very hard.

He was a good sport and tough to boot. I was glad he hadn't been hurt. Even though it turned out harmless, I told Mark I thought it was a dirty trick to play on his dad. He had known that his dad would be a good sport no matter what happened, and he was right. I really loved his dad, and I knew that he was very proud of his eldest son for the way he had turned his life around.

CHAPTER 7

ONE MORE CHANCE

In two days, it would be Mother's Day. We had been working extra hard cutting firewood, knowing that the cold weather would soon be over. We wanted to take care of anyone who had been waiting a few days. We didn't want any cancellations because of the heat. We were both at the point where if we never saw another piece of wood, it would be too soon. We were just plain burned out. On this particular day, we were both very cranky.

It was late afternoon. We'd finished cutting the last cord, or thought we had, but came up quite a bit short. A cord of wood should be stacked real tight and measure eight feet long by four feet high by four feet wide. In my opinion, this stack was only about three-quarters of a cord. It was really short. The man that it was for had been a good customer of ours, having ordered wood from us three times that winter. We had to cut some more—that was all there was to it. Mark didn't agree, tired and cranky as he was. "No way," he said.

"Yes way," I insisted. "We aren't going to cheat that nice man. This cord is way too short."

"Bullshit! It's not that short, so quit acting like a bitch about it. I'm done for the day."

No matter how hard I pleaded, Mark wouldn't even consider cutting more wood. "I am not going to let you do this. It is not

132

right," I kept at him, because I was right, and that was all there was to it. He wasn't being fair.

"Shut up! I don't want to hear another word about it!" he yelled loudly as he walked toward the truck. He started it and backed up to the wood. I could not believe what I was seeing.

"Mark! Don't do this, please!" I begged, my voice sounding desperate.

After warning me to shut up a few times, he started loading the wood in the truck and I finally came unglued, since there was no way to measure the cord now. I put myself between the wood and the truck, trying to keep him from loading it.

"You're gonna get hit, bitch. You better move!" he screamed at me as he started throwing the wood over my head into the truck. It didn't take but a minute, and we were into a full-fledged knockdown, drag-out screaming match.

"What an ass you are! I can't believe you could be such a cheat! This guy pays good money for this wood. How could you screw him over like this? I don't believe you can be such an idiot!" I screamed, trying to avoid the wood that he carelessly tossed over my head. "I don't believe you, you bastard! Every time I think you are the neatest guy in the whole world, you have to do something like this. You always ruin everything. All the good about you means nothing when I see you like this! I hate it!" Tears streaming down my face, I just wanted away from him, but I knew if I left, he would deliver this wood just how it was.

"F you, Ms. Perfect! You always gotta be so damn righteous. Shut up and go in the barn before I knock the crap out of you, you stupid bitch!"

Lily was up in the barn with the babies, and she had heard us. "Are you all right, Linda? Are you all right? Where are you?" She could hear us but couldn't see me because I was underneath one of the stall roofs. When we were screaming at each other, it could scare anyone. We could sound very violent without having any physical contact at all.

"We're not taking this wood to that guy!" I screamed, sounding as tough as I could. I jumped up in the back of the truck and started throwing all the wood that Mark had just loaded out onto the ground. That turned out to be a big mistake.

"Get down from there, you crazy bitch!" he screamed with clenched teeth as he grabbed at my sweatshirt.

"Make me, asshole! I'm not having any part in your screwing someone over. This wood isn't leaving here till it's a real cord!" Mark jumped up in the back of the truck with a piece of wood in his hand and held it up as if he were about to hit me. "Wow, aren't you tough? Go ahead, tough guy, hit me if you want, but this truck isn't going out of here without a full cord in it."

"Get down now, or I'm gonna knock you down, so help me."

"Aren't you—"

Before I could say tough, I was on the ground. I couldn't believe it. I'd known for sure that he was never going to hit me again, so it was such a shock to me when he did. He was the one that would always convince me that no matter what I did, he'd never hit me again. I was always such a good girl to trust and believe him. Realizing what he had done, he jumped down immediately to help me up. I thought he was coming after me again, and I jumped up, screaming, "Leave me alone! Just leave me alone. You're such an ass. A big, tough ass! I hate you when you act like this. Just leave me alone!" I leaped up the barn stairs two at a time, angrier than I had been in a long time and crying very hard.

"Are you okay, Linda?" Lily was very shaken, having witnessed the violence.

"Yes, honey, I'm okay. Don't worry, sweetie," I assured her, giving her a nice, comforting hug. "You need to go now, honey. It will just embarrass him if you are here and he won't come inside." What was wrong with me? I wondered. Why on earth would I want him to come inside after what he had done? I was happy that she went home and sorry that she had to go through that.

I went to the mirror to check the damage. To my surprise, the side of my face where he'd slapped me was just a little red. I was glad it wasn't closer to my eye.

Mark continued to load the rest of the truck, and when he'd finished, he just took off. Wow, he was really going to do it, I thought to myself. I knew he was still angry, or he'd never leave like that without coming up to tell me what was happening and to give me a goodbye kiss. It had taken about a year to perfect that one, but he had perfected it. Yep, he was still furious.

"What a jerk your daddy is sometimes," I said to the babies as I picked them up, one in each arm, as I had done a thousand times. Holding them both at once was the best feeling in the world, and I needed that at that moment. "He loves you so so much, though, and nothing will ever change that," I told them in my best mommy voice. I was already remembering the good in him, and I didn't understand myself at times like this.

I wondered if we would still be able to go over to Leroy's tonight as we had planned. I wasn't going to go if he was still acting like such an idiot. Assuming that he'd come home in a better mood, I went ahead and got the babies ready, as if we were going, just in case. Nine times out of ten, when things like this happened, he'd come back all calmed down and really sorry, begging me to forgive him and making me feel as if I were his treasure.

When Mark got back from making the delivery, he came in and gave me a hug. It was one of those "I know I'd better do it" kind of hugs. We've all gotten those at some time in our lives. There was no "I'm sorry," no explanation, just that "I know I'd better do it," worthless, waste-of-time hug. I wasn't falling for this one. I was still upset and very surprised that he'd actually delivered the wood.

It was Friday night, and I really needed to get out of the barn, so I managed somehow to keep my big mouth shut, just to avoid another fight. It was really rare for me to do that, but for some weird reason, I was doing it tonight. Usually, if there was the slightest problem, it would get hashed around until we felt it had been solved.

Sometimes we could go at it all day, or all night, but when we were done, the problem was over. We'd put it in the past and would have learned a good lesson from it. Tonight was different, though; you could cut the tension in the air with a knife. We only talked when necessary, and everything was short and to the point. I hated times like this, and I was to hate them even more later tonight. We definitely should have stayed home.

On the way to Leroy's house, Mark was still being very touchy and irritable.

Becky was sitting right behind him. I could not believe that he was yelling at her again because he could feel her knees hit the back of his seat once in a while. He yelled at the poor little girl, and she had the saddest look on her face. Thinking that we had overcome this problem a long time ago, I was shocked he was getting so upset about it again. Any other time, this wouldn't have bothered him. A few minutes later, he yelled again, cussing at her this time, which always made me very angry. I knew that she was trying really hard not to do it again. She never wanted to cause a problem about anything. It was hard for the kids not to do this because of how far back Mark always put the seat. They hardly had any room at all for their legs. That was it. I couldn't shut up for another minute.

"You could've reminded her once, don't you think? You know she doesn't do it on purpose. She just forgets. You didn't have to yell and cuss at her like that. I can't believe you're being such an idiot. We need to go home. I really want to go home. You will just embarrass me at Leroy's." We were just turning the corner at the far end of Leroy's street when I said, "Mark, we're almost there. Would you please turn around and take me home? I'm not going to be around you when you're acting like this. It's the old you. The guy I would have never loved."

He was still heading down to Leroy's. "Why don't you just shut up? You just don't know when to stop, do you? We're going to Leroy's."

"I'm not. I'll just drop you off and go home," I said. "It'll be impossible for me to keep my mouth shut about how you cheated a wood customer today and you don't even feel bad about it." I hadn't meant to bring that subject up again, and I was immediately sorry.

"I'll show you what feeling bad is!" Mark yelled as he reached over the baby in the front and tried to grab me. We were just coming to Leroy's driveway, getting ready to turn in, when he stomped on the brakes. Before the car had come to a complete stop, I was out of there. I ran down the driveway as fast as I could, screaming loudly for Leroy. Mark was right behind me.

I guess I thought I was invisible or something. I had my hand on the doorknob and started to turn it. I think I went through the door without opening it, or at least that was how it felt. I couldn't figure out if I'd stopped that fast because I'd hit the door or if it was because Mark had caught up to me just as I'd gotten to the door and had grabbed my hair. The next thing I remember was being on the ground, getting kicked in the head. By now, Leroy had joined us. I was screaming and crying, an impossible combination for anyone to have to deal with. Mark was still screaming at me, and poor Leroy didn't know what the heck was going on. Mark headed back toward the car, which was still parked in the road. The babies were screaming. As Leroy pulled me to my feet, Mark pulled the car into the driveway. The side of my head felt like it was going to explode.

"Give me some money. Right now, you bitch!" Mark demanded. "I'm getting out of here!"

"No," I said, trying very hard to stop my hysterical sobbing. "You're not going to kick me in the head and then take off with all our money. You can't have any!"

"I said give me some damn money!" With Leroy standing right there and because we were now inside Leroy's house, Mark wasn't about to cause any more of a problem. He had a lot of respect for Leroy.

"Fine! You won't give me any money? I'll just go home and get our guns and sell them." As he turned to leave, he said, "You'll be sorry that you didn't give me no money, bitch!"

In just a few minutes, after what Mark said had sunk in, I got myself together enough to think what I should do. "I'm going to call Jimmy and Rory and have them go down to the barn and get the guns before Mark has a chance to get there." He'd never been this violent, and I was scared. He seemed capable of anything, the way he had kicked me. They would have plenty of time to get down to the barn, get the guns, and be out of there before Mark ever got near there. I knew I couldn't let anything happen to my brother's guns. What an idiot Mark was being. I was so mad. Jimmy and Rory said they'd get down there right away.

Leroy had gotten me some ice for the side of my head, and I was finally starting to calm down a little when the phone rang.

"You bitch! Where are the guns? You called Jimmy and Rory, didn't you? You're gonna be sorry for this." He slammed the phone down.

I tried calling Jimmy's, but there was no answer. I was worried that Mark would go after them. He'd been so drunk earlier. I remember wondering why he hadn't asked me to drive. It was because of our fight. He wasn't himself. He knew what an idiot he had been, and he was mad at himself. Whenever this happened, he'd take it out on me. The next day, he had almost always admitted it. He would say, "Sometimes I do or say something really dumb or stupid or downright mean and I get so deep into it I don't know how to get out. Once I go too far, it's really hard to get ahold of myself. I just have to act meaner and meaner."

Not too much later, Leroy's phone rang. It was Jimmy. They had gotten the guns, and just to be safe, they had taken the generator too. They tried to assure me not to worry. Mark wasn't stupid enough to come down there and try to take the guns away from them. I knew this was the voice of Rory talking, not my Jimmy. Jimmy never liked problems. He hated violence. His first instinct whenever there was a big problem would be to get out of there. He just didn't like being around violent, unpredictable people. When Mark acted like this, it would really upset him. He could be very scary.

Somehow I ended up at Gene and Linda's later that night. It was probably because I was so upset and I needed help with the babies. I knew my head sure was hurting. We hadn't been there too long when the phone rang. It was Mark, wanting to talk to me. "You don't have a house anymore, bitch. I've totally destroyed it." He hung up, and we tried to call him right back but got no answer. I thought he'd only been trying to scare me. Where was he? A few minutes later, the phone rang again. "Thought I was lying, didn't you? Just listen." The next sound I heard was glass breaking, and next was a really loud crash of some kind.

"Oh my god, Mark, stop this! Please just stop this. Why are you doing this to me? You know how much my knickknacks mean to me. Why are you doing this? Stop! Please, just stop."

Click.

Mark hung up on me.

The phone calls continued late into the night. Mark always made sure I heard something else break. I didn't know what to do. I had no car. At one time, Gene said he'd come with me because Mark had been calm on this one particular phone call. He was begging us to help him. He was begging us to come and get him and take him to the hospital, but for some reason, he wanted me to come alone. I was way too scared. Right about the time Gene and I had seriously thought of going, we got another very vicious call. No, sir, his mood change had been just a little too drastic for us. No one else was about to go home with me the way Mark was acting. I really couldn't blame them. Ring ring. Once again, it was Mark. "I just broke your guitar into a thousand pieces, bitch. Are you happy now? Don't you wish you'd given me some money now? Bye-bye."

"He's lost his mind. He's gone crazy. He knows how much that guitar means to me. He'd never break my guitar if he were in his right mind. I'm so scared!" Again, we tried calling the barn. Again, no answer. Almost immediately after we'd hung up, Gene's phone rang.

"Still wondering if I'm really here?" I heard a crash. "I am," he said in a frightening voice.

"Mark, don't do this. You know how sorry you always are. You hate yourself when you act like this. Please stop. Just go lie down and go to sleep. In the morning, you can come get me and everything will be okay. You'll see."

"Not this time, it won't. You won't have any stuff by morning!"

"Mark, if you don't stop this right now, I will call the cops. Please, I don't want to do that. They'll take you to jail. Please stop."

"Call them, bitch. You might as well. When you see this house tomorrow, you'll have me put in jail anyway. Go ahead! Call them! I dare you! Bye-bye." He slammed the phone down.

I was hysterical. I was totally exhausted, both physically from working all day and emotionally. I just lay there on the couch and cried myself to sleep, knowing that the babies were being taken care of. It was always so nice being able to depend on Gene and Linda to take the best possible care of those babies.

The next thing I remember, it was morning—late morning, in fact. They had somehow even managed to let me sleep in a little. "Mark," I questioned, "has he called again?" It was the first thing that came to my mind after what had happened last night.

"No, he hasn't. In fact, we tried to call there a few times, but the phone has been busy. I think it's off the hook," Gene said.

I'll bet he's sleeping was all I could think. When he got that drunk and was an ass, he'd sleep late, not wanting to face up to the way he'd acted.

"I have to get home. Who will take me home? I don't have my car."

By now Leroy had arrived at Gene and Linda's, and the four of us were trying to figure out what to do. I wanted to go home, but I was too scared to go alone. No one else really wanted to go with me, not being sure of Mark's condition. I didn't blame them. It was my problem. What a big problem this firewood fight had become. I couldn't believe it.

By the time we all got cleaned up and had something to eat, Mark called. He still had his badass personality going strong, and of course, he made sure I heard more glass breaking.

"When are you coming home, bitch? It's not much of a home anymore, bitch. How come you didn't call the cops on me? You afraid I'd kill you when I got out of jail? Ha, ha," he said and then hung up.

"What am I going to do? He's crazy. Oh my god! What am I going to do?" He was still acting the same as last night. This wasn't like Mark. He'd always come to his senses by now and would be so, so sorry. "He really has me scared." All I could think of was that I didn't know what to do. No one else did either.

After a few more hours passed and Mark hadn't called again, we figured out a plan. We'd get enough of us together and all go to the barn at once. Mark wouldn't do anything crazy with all of us there. Or would he? It was a chance we would have to take. Linda stayed home with the babies. We didn't want them around if there was going to be any trouble. Leroy, Gene, Jimmy, Rory, and I planned to all arrive at the barn at the same time.

We had called Jim and Iona, who lived right across the street from the barn, and they had confirmed what Mark said was true. From their two-story bedroom window, they had seen Mark throwing things down the stairs. Jim agreed to meet us at the barn. All I could think of was, the more people with me, the safer I'd be.

When we all arrived at the barn, we realized almost immediately that we had made a mistake. Our perfectly timed arrivals made it appear to Mark that a whole damn army had come after him. He began screaming at me and being very defensive. What an idiot I was for not listening to him. He had said for me to come alone. Mark stood at the top of the barn stairs, probably feeling like a total asshole, but because this army had shown up, he had to maintain his tough-guy attitude. He was getting himself deeper and deeper into a real mess. Then he grabbed one of my favorite oil lamps and threw it down the stairs. It lay in pieces at the bottom of the steps, along with piles of other broken glass, plants, and a broken barstool. There were also some pots and pans and even curtains that he'd ripped to shreds. He had definitely been telling the truth last night. How would he ever get out of this one?

After a while, Mark convinced me to come up the stairs to talk. Frightened as I was, I knew I had to do something. Nothing else had worked. Everyone had tried to reason with him. I couldn't believe my eyes when I saw the damage upstairs. He had even dumped out all my sugar, flour, and coffee. There was broken glass everywhere you looked. My house would never be the same again. After I had seen the mess, my fear vanished and I could no longer hide my shock and anger.

"Oh my god, you really did it. You really did it! I don't believe it. You're crazy, Mark. You've gone crazy!" I screamed, calling for someone to come up and help me. Mark rushed out on the deck. He had everyone else at a definite disadvantage down there on the ground. What had I done? Now I was stuck up here alone with him. All of a sudden, I looked up and saw our good friend Mabel walking right in the door. This girl had been around, and there was not much she was afraid of, including Mark. She was the type, like me, that thinks she can probably figure out how to solve almost any problem that could come up, and she has a heart of gold as well. The way I looked at her arrival seemed very logical to me. She had "backup" written all over her forehead. "Linda's back up." It was easy to feel protected by Mabel. She always had the attitude of "Don't mess with me," and believe me, you wouldn't want to either.

Naturally, feeling very safe since I had come back up, I started getting quite mouthy. I could say whatever I wanted. There was just one small problem. I couldn't figure out why Mabel was trying to get me to shut up. After about five minutes of my very brave statements, she was finally able to convince me to shut my big mouth. Mark had gone after me two or three times already. I would run, and she'd try to get between us and calm him down. So far, it had worked. This was great. It was neat having someone back me up like this. All of a sudden, I didn't feel as brave as I had. I realized that Mabel was desperately trying to make me shut my mouth. I could see the importance of her request written all over her face. There was definitely no question about it. When Mabel gave you an order accompanied by that look, you did whatever she said.

Later, she would tell me that she had thought things were going to get hairy. She couldn't believe that Mark was acting like he was. "Crazy," she had repeated over and over. At one time, Mark tore our screen door right off its hinges and hit her with it. It was impossible to tell if it had been an accident or intentional. At times like that, it was safest to assume the worst. He had scared her, and Mabel didn't scare easily. I didn't blame her for trying to shut me up. She had seen how mad Mark was becoming, so after I got her message, I began to keep my thoughts to myself.

While all this was going on upstairs with the three of us, Mark had been continuously going out on the deck, yelling things at everyone below. He wanted to make sure that no one else tried to come up. He needn't have worried. The way he was acting, no one wanted to come up anyway. In fact, Jim had gone home and called the cops because the situation was so bad. Before the police arrived, Mark had thrown oil lamps at both Leroy and Jimmy as they stood at the bottom of the stairs. It shook both of them up because that was the first time Mark had ever shown any aggression toward them.

This action was only another indication that Mark had definitely lost it. By the time the police had arrived, Mark had calmed down quite a bit. Now it was up to one of us to press charges. I knew that I couldn't, so I let Leroy and Jimmy know that it was totally up to them. Whatever they did, I would understand. The cops were disappointed when it was decided that no charges would be filed if Mark would just leave the property peacefully. Naturally, Mark agreed, but he couldn't resist talking like a smart-ass as he walked down the stairs, his head hung low. I knew he was in control again. Then he did something that tore at my heart. He walked over to the back of his truck, opened up the camper, took my guitar out, and set it against the rockwork. I couldn't believe it. Mark glanced up at me, looking over the deck railing. I had tears in my eyes.

"I'm so sorry, babe. You see this? I didn't really bust up your guitar. I love you," he said with his eyes, never having to open his mouth. I'll never forget the way he spoke to me with his eyes that afternoon. He drove off toward town, where he would clean up at his mom's. We'd had an agreement about my guitar ever since our first fight.

Mark had picked it up, threatening to break it, and I had panicked. I was solely in his command from that moment on. Later, when we had talked about it, I explained to him that I knew if he could ever do something that cruel to me, I know I'd probably never be able to forgive him, no matter how sorry he was. He knew how much my guitar meant to me. It was a nice Yamaha twelve-string. He might as well have yelled, "See how much I love you? I didn't break your guitar." How sick I was that I could find any good in him after what he had done.

After that day, I knew that Leroy and Jimmy understood a little better why I couldn't ever press charges. It's a very hard thing to do to someone you care a lot about. Needless to say, the cops thought we were all nuts. They didn't know the other Mark very well. The really neat Mark that would do anything in the world for us. That Mark had a heart of gold.

I was still in a daze from all that had just happened, and I couldn't get Mark's last gesture off my mind. However, I had to start cleaning the house. It was such a disaster that there was no way I could bring the babies home until it was cleaned. Mabel stayed to help me for a while, but it was definitely more than a one-day job. It was almost dark when we decided to call it a day. I went back to Gene and Linda's to be with my babies, and we spent the night there.

The next day, Mark called me, begging for one more chance. Over and over he told me how much he loved me and how terribly sorry he was. He would do anything if I would give him one more chance. "I'll even go to a counselor of some kind," he said. "I'll quit drinking, and I'll do anything else you want."

I knew he was really serious when he said he'd quit drinking and whatever else I wanted. Mark had always been a drinker. It was settled. It was Mother's Day, and he came to be with us, heart in hand as usual. The next day, we spent hours on the telephone finding a counselor who could help us with Mark's violence.

Mark told me that he never had anything mean so much to him where a friend was concerned as it did when Jimmy and Leroy had refused to press charges against him. He realized how special we all really were to him at that moment. He had been absolutely sure that he was going to jail that day. It was like a new lease on life. All he had to do now was convince me to give him one more chance, and of course, he did.

Once again, he was able to convince me that it would never happen again. I truly believed that.

CHAPTER 8

HOPE, SADNESS, AND CONFUSION

When Mark had said that he would do anything to keep us, he'd meant it. He was very upset that I was having a hard time finding a counselor that would take us immediately, and he made one suggestion after another. When we finally found one right near, he was very relieved. I was absolutely convinced that Mark desperately wanted to learn to control his violent temper, because for the first time, he had a terrible fear of really hurting me someday.

Mary, our counselor, was excellent. She recognized immediately that Mark really did have a serious problem. She had him see a doctor, who prescribed medicine to help keep him calm. This was a potent drug that acted directly on the brain. The best part about it was that you could not drink alcohol at all while you were on this medication, and I hoped it would be just the extra help Mark needed to help him stop drinking. "Babe, I'm gonna be like a normal person soon, and you will be so proud of me," he exclaimed with a very serious look.

"I already am proud of you, honey. This is a big step for you, and you are doing so well," I said with a cute little flirting smile.

He looked very happy and pleased with himself. "Damn, I'm good," he half-whispered, bragging to himself, and his expression told me that he was feeling good about himself. I knew that seeing

Mary and the medicine was a very good thing, and we continued to see her every week without fail.

The following eight weeks were like heaven as I slowly, happily witnessed this man that I loved with all my heart become very mellow. I had always known that there was a terrific, practically perfect guy underneath all that alcohol and violence. Hardly anything ever upset him, and we had so much fun that summer. The babies were getting big enough to take to places without much trouble. They were priceless to us, and we were on top of the world, watching our precious two little miracles grow and develop new skills almost daily. I had never seen a man prouder of his children than Mark was, and I loved watching him with his babies.

"Babe! Hurry! Come watch us!" he called to me, laughing excitedly.

Never wanting to miss one special thing that those babies did, I stopped folding laundry in the back and hurried into the front room, wide-eyed and very interested in what I was about to see. The three of them lay in the middle of the floor, squealing and laughing as they pushed and threw tiny Hot Wheels cars all over and around them. "Rum rum rum!" Making the sound of engines, and "Screeeeeeeeeech!" sounding very funny as he tried to imitate the sound of skidding tires. Darla's blue eyes would be as big as saucers, never taking them off her silly daddy and intermittently reaching for him to cuddle her.

Donny was always giggling as he would try his best to imitate Mark, and these were scenes that filled my heart with love and joy. "I love you guys!" I said with a loving smile as I returned to my laundry.

Mark loved to wrestle on the floor with both of them at once, never ignoring one for the other. He would always give them equal attention. "Grrrrr," he would say over and over as he rolled on the floor, always acting like they totally understood what he was saying. They loved for him to whistle at them, and it was very funny to watch them pooch out their lips, trying to imitate their daddy. Mark had definitely come a long way for a man that didn't ever want more kids. He was such a big help with the babies, and it seemed like he always had one or the other with him.

Mark was an excellent cook, and after the babies were born, he did quite a bit of the cooking if he wasn't working. We loved his cooking and the way he sometimes went about it. He'd tell Danny and Becky, "Let's make a cake." With widened eyes and hair tousled around her beautiful face, she'd jumped up and down. "Yay! Oh, boy!" She looked out over the edge of the deck for Danny, knowing the great treat that was in store. "Danny, hurry! Come up and help! We are going to make a cake!" she yelled down at her brother. Hearing him leap up our fourteen stairs, two at a time, I just shook my head as I chuckled quietly to myself. I knew that they were excited because Mark would always let them eat a large portion of the cake mix before they cooked it.

"You are all going to be sick," I said firmly but with an approving smile.

When he was ready, Mark would proceed with the instructions, never leaving the couch. "You get the eggs, and you get the bowl. You get the spoon, and you get the beater." It was so funny to watch as he carefully orchestrated the entire task. "Okay, Mark," the kids would respond anxiously, hurrying about their duties, feeling very important. Eventually, he'd have everything he needed, and he'd make the cake from the couch. As they dipped their spoons eagerly, I had to laugh, their lips becoming chocolate colored. When they had had enough, he would have one of the kids put the undersized cake in the oven. It always amazed me how much fun he could make simple things for the kids.

Where his babies were concerned, Mark always wanted to make sure he didn't do anything wrong. He worried a lot about things that most people would never think about. One day, I was trying some dresses on Darla that Rachael had just handed down since she was a size ahead of my tiny Darla, even though she was born two months later. There was a big pile of them, and at that time, the twins weren't quite a year old. Darla was having so much fun, laughing and covering her eyes with the skirt by lifting it up. I noticed that Donny was acting sad and frustrated, grabbing at the dresses that had held so much fun for his sister and trying his best to hide his face, but it was impossible since he didn't have on a dress. "Come here, baby!"

I reached out for my baby boy as he leaped into my arms. "You can wear one too, sweetie," I said, not thinking a thing about it. He just wants to be able to do what Darla is doing, I thought to myself as I picked a dress with lots of frills and dressed him in it.

As he looked up from the newspaper, I could not believe the shocked look on Mark's face. My pulse went sky-high as I prepared myself for a real problem, seeing the anger in his eyes. "Babe, take that off him right now! You can't put a dress on my son," Mark said angrily, glaring with gritted teeth as he threw the paper down. He sighed softly. "Please!" he pleaded in a much-calmer voice. "Maybe it could make him grow up to be gay or something." He had managed to get ahold of his anger immediately, and for that, I was very grateful, but I could tell that he was really upset. Without his medication, and if he'd been drinking, I know this could have turned into a big fight.

"Oh, honey! He doesn't even know they are for girls," I said in a relieved voice, "but if it bothers you that much, I will take it off." I took the dress off immediately to ease his mind. "I'm sorry! We were just being silly," I apologized as I gave him a big, loving hug. How cool, I thought to myself. That was really nice, the way he calmed down before the situation had escalated.

It was a bright, beautiful day, and the temperature was perfect, being in the seventies, with a soft, comfortable breeze. I'd been working the horses a couple of hours with the comfort of knowing that Mark was upstairs with the babies, as he did so many times, so I could take care of my business. "Babe!" he yelled in a soft voice, as if he were trying not to be too loud. I had just walked right beneath him in the breezeway below, and I was sure he had heard me with my mare as I secured her to the ties. He'd been trying to get Donny asleep for me about an hour earlier when I had gone up for a drink. Mark had been lying flat on his back on the couch, with Donny on his chest, and they had both fallen asleep while Darla was playing safely in her crib. Mark had awakened and realized how long they had been sleeping like that, and it worried him.

When I came up the stairs, he said very quietly so that he wouldn't wake Donny, "Is it okay that he's been lying here on me for

148

so long like this? It would seem okay if it were Darla, 'cause she's a girl." His tone was serious. "Is this okay, babe?" he urged insistently.

"Honey," I said, blinking noticeably and taking a deep breath, "if you ever treat those two babies differently, as young as they are, I'll really be upset with you. Little boy babies need just as much love as little girl babies. Trust me, honey, it won't make your son weird." I smiled my most intelligent smile. "I love you so much." He managed to release an embarrassed chuckle as he dipped his head, feeling a little silly.

We had a lot of fun that summer. We'd go to the lake or a nearby stream and take food and a bunch of friends. We'd often spend a whole day there, playing horseshoes and relaxing. At first, I was worried when Mark would be around anyone that was drinking, but he soon proved to me that he was fine. He was doing too good to blow it now.

Mason and Randy spent a lot of time with us during the summer. They were really enjoying their dad in his new, calmer state of mind. Mark continued to fill their heads with funny stories. There were scary stories about the bad guys in our desert that he had invented. Their names were Chain Saw Charley and Desert Jim. He could make up a scary story at the drop of a hat, mesmerizing the kids, always leaving them begging for more.

One day, Mark told us all about a giant chicken he had just seen running loose down near town. He said he'd show us, so like a bunch of idiots, we all jumped in the truck to go see this giant chicken. It turned out to be a big, giant fake chicken in someone's backyard. We sure felt stupid.

We had a big black Labrador dog that Danny had named Motley after the rock group Mötley Crüe. Mark wanted him to be protective and to attack on command, which was totally out of character for a Lab, but he was determined. He would feed the dog Tabasco sauce, saying it would make him mean. It was funny. I never saw that dog be mean once. Mark would tell people that if he wanted him to, Motley could tear someone up in a minute. One day, Mark was riding his bike around the driveway, and Motley ran right out in front of him and he could not avoid hitting him. The bike got away from him enough that the throttle stuck as his feet were on the ground and the front end came way up. He hurt his ankle pretty good, dropped the bike after holding on as long as he could, and fell down because of the pain in his ankle. Furious by now, he jumped up, limping, as he chased that dog, calling him every name in the book. Mark said he was going to get rid of Motley for sure, and we all just laughed, knowing that he wouldn't, because he loved him a lot. It had been a funny scene to witness, and we tried not to joke about it too much.

Motley was quite a character. Danny used to make him pull him all over the desert in thick sand, on his bicycle. We told him that someday he was going to get hurt, the way he always tied the rope directly to the bike. One day, he came in the barn a mess, covered with cuts and scrapes. Motley had seen Mark on the motorcycle and gone after him, pulling Danny through a whole bunch of greasewood trees. We laughed so hard, seeing that he was okay. "Why didn't you just let go of the bike?" I asked in a puzzled tone, trying to hold back the laughter.

"I don't know why," he answered, a little embarrassed. "It happened so fast that I couldn't think right."

I hugged my embarrassed young son and turned my tone to one of concern. "Are you okay, honey? Do you hurt anywhere, baby?"

He smiled his sweet smile. "Naw, I'm okay, Mom," he responded, dipping his head.

"You are so tough, Dan Dan." I gave him a quick kiss, and all was well.

Motley was often a pest, like the time Mark had a gopher eating all the roots of his baby trees. It was before we got our guns from my brother, and he had decided one day that he had had enough. If he didn't do anything else that day, he was going to get that sucker. I'll never forget looking over the deck rail, seeing the method he was using to catch the gopher. He was kneeling down over a hole and was as still as a person could be. His right hand was in a raised position, and he had a large bacon fork in it. "When that sucker pops his head out again, I'm gonna nail him. He'll never know what hit him, and I am not coming in until I get him."

"See you in about a month, honey," I said. I was laughing very hard by this time.

You'd never believe that about two hours later, I heard Mark coming up the stairs, so I walked out on the deck and saw that damn gopher hanging from the bacon fork. When he was almost to the top of the stairs, Motley grabbed it right off the fork and ran away and ate it. "What a lazy dog! He wants me to do his hunting for him. Why didn't he catch that sucker for me?" We laughed so hard about it. I had never seen anyone be so still for so long, but Mark had been determined.

"Honey! That is very sadistic! I can't believe you did that," I said, shaking my head and making a terrible face as I walked away in disgust.

"I sure am quick, though," he said, chuckling. "Damn, I'm quick!"

The end of June was a very sad time for me. Mark and I were going to take a trip to see my mom in Grass Valley. She was still able to have her own little place, so we would have a lot of time alone with her, but I knew that it would not be a fun vacation. She wanted to give me all the things that she wanted me to have, since she knew her time would be over soon.

In the three months since her cancer had been diagnosed, it had begun to spread throughout her body. She refused chemotherapy, wanting her short time left to be as good as possible, and we knew that she would leave us soon. All my fears had become a reality, and I could not believe that I would lose my mom soon. I am glad I didn't know just how soon it would be. She wouldn't even last six months after her diagnosis.

"I don't want your things," I had told her firmly with love. "I just want my mom! I'm too young to lose you, and I don't know what I will do without you," I sobbed on the telephone. I knew I wouldn't have her for very much longer, and I was afraid that this could very well be the last time I would ever see my mom.

Trying to be excited about our little trip wasn't easy. I couldn't get the purpose for it out of my mind. Jimmy let us borrow his Chevy Luv pickup truck, knowing what good gas mileage it got. With us knowing Mom would die soon, death had become a common topic of conversation with Mark and me lately. We talked in depth about how we felt and the things we wanted done if one of us died. There wasn't much we didn't cover about how we felt about death and dying. Mark had always told me that his whole life, he felt he was going to die young. "It never bothered me before I had you and the babies, but now it does, because I really want to live. I have so much to live for now," he said in a very serious tone.

It bothered him that even with all that he had now, he still couldn't shake this feeling he had. Every time the subject came up, I'd tell him, "Honey, you don't have to worry about that anymore, 'cause you have me now. God knows I couldn't handle it if I lost you. God would never do that to me. He'd never take you away from those babies and me." This was something that I really felt was true. I always knew in my heart that God would never do anything like that to me. He knew I wasn't strong enough. He knew I couldn't handle it.

Our visit with Mom was as perfect as it could be under the circumstances. She and Mark grew even closer than before. There was always a lot of laughter, just the way Mom wanted it. When she would see my tears, she would always try to comfort me, saying something that was supposed to lift my spirits, like, "I'll be so much better off" or "I'm not afraid of dying, baby." I'd tell her that my sadness was for myself, because I wouldn't have her anymore. The sadness came and went the entire time we were with her. We got to spend a little time with my sister, her husband, and their six girls. It was a pretty normal vacation, except that the thought of my mom dying soon never really left my mind. Before I knew it, it was time to say goodbye.

I remember it so clearly. Mark had already loaded the truck, and all that was left to do was say goodbye. I felt like I was going to pass out, and I held on to my mom tighter than I ever had in my life. "How do you say goodbye to your mom when you don't know if you'll ever see her again?" I sobbed uncontrollably in her arms, the arms that had always been there for me.

"I love you so much, baby. You be strong for me now," she whispered as she softly began to cry. "You are the only thing I am worried about, honey. Help me not to worry so much about you, baby," she pleaded, stroking my hair gently.

Voice quivering and body trembling, I somehow managed to say, "I love you so much, Mom. You know that." Tears were streaming down my cheeks. "You've always been such a good mom, and I am so sad that this is happening. I can't believe this is happening," I said as I pulled away from her for the very last time. I couldn't even say goodbye. I didn't want to say goodbye. Walking away from her was one of the hardest things I ever had to do.

I'll never forget what she said to Mark when he hugged her goodbye.

"I love you, Mark. I'm so glad I have you to take care of my baby girl."

Mark's eyes filled with tears when he got into the truck with me. He knew it was our last goodbye, and he knew I was not handling it very well.

We had been driving for about an hour, and no matter how hard I had tried, I could not stop crying. He'd been holding my hand the entire time, and I don't think either of us had said a word. I'd been crying as hard as a person could without making much of a sound, and finally, Mark pulled off the road. "Babe, you're tearing me apart. I'll take you back to your mom's. Do you want me to take you back so you can say goodbye one more time? Will that help you? Will you feel better?" he pleaded. "Please, babe, tell me what to do. I can't stand seeing you hurt this way." Later, he told me that he'd never felt so helpless in his entire life and he did not know what to say or do.

I convinced him that going back would only make things worse, and somehow, I managed to pull myself together. I couldn't stand the fact that because I was hurting so badly that I was making him hurt just as much. Mark's gesture was one of the nicest things anyone had ever offered me in my whole life. It was just one more example of the enormous loving heart he had.

We arrived home the morning of the Fourth of July, and in just two days, our babies would celebrate their first birthday. Mark had wanted to make them something out of wood for their presents. He wanted to start a tradition of making them something every year on their birthday. It was really important for him to do it. The night before their birthday, he and Gene had stayed up almost all night in Gene's garage, making rocking horses and a little car with wooden wheels. Mark painted one brown and the other black. He put yarn tails and manes on them and painted the twins' names on them. They were beautiful.

Mark had always liked to sing, goofing around mostly, but he had fun. He was always coming home after hearing a song on the radio that he could relate to us, trying to sing songs to me. One day, he came home and said, "Babe, I heard the perfect song from me to you. It's old, but it's just how I feel about you." I wanted to know what it was, but he couldn't remember the name of it. He knew that it just kept saying over and over, "I love you, I love you, I love you," louder and louder. It turned out to be "Nights in White Satin" by the Moody Blues. When I found it and listened to it, I didn't understand how he related it to us. Mark said after listening to the words very carefully that he couldn't really relate it to us either, except for the part that said over and over, "I love you." I thought he'd been very romantic.

One of our songs that meant the very most to me was a Bob Seger's song called "Understanding." Mark always said that he meant every word of that song to me. It's a beautiful song. "Leather and Lace" was ours because of the part that says when he walked into her house, he knew he'd never leave. That was because on our first date, when he walked into the barn, he never left. Another was the one that says, "I've been waiting for a girl like you to come into my life." "We've Got Tonight" by Bob Seger was special to us too. He liked to lip-synch that one to me, acting all romantic and all at the same time.

That summer, we spent a lot of time shooting and riding the horses. It was very different for Mark because he wasn't drinking and we no longer took six-packs on our rides together. Once he told me that he looked at almost everything differently now that he was always sober. "Everything is so much clearer," he said.

"I guess there would be a difference." Having rarely been drunk myself, it was hard for me to relate.

One night, a guy who lived down the road stopped by the barn. He wasn't a close friend. We hadn't known him very long, so I'd say he was a casual acquaintance. He was a rough kind of guy that I didn't really care for at all, always trying to act tough. He was pretty drunk on this particular night, and somehow, the subject got onto guns. All of a sudden, this guy pulled out a handgun and was waiving it around like a toy. He'd had it in the inside pocket of his jacket. What an idiot he was. Both babies were right there, playing in their Johnny Jump-Ups, and I couldn't believe how upset Mark got. He wasn't drunk, of course, and had been faithfully taking his medication, but it sure didn't keep him mellow in this situation. He jumped up so fast that he scared the guy to death. Mark grabbed him by the shirt under his neck and spoke in a tone of voice that no one would ever question.

"You idiot! Who the hell do you think you are, coming over here with a gun? Get out of here right now and don't ever come back again with a gun." The guy, seeing how upset Mark was, started trying to explain, but Mark cut him off immediately. "I said now!" He was furious. That was enough for that guy. He was history. It took me quite a while to calm Mark down that night.

For a few days, all I heard was how that guy had no respect for guns. Mark had been through with that kind of life. He had lived it long enough. He was so thankful that he didn't have to live that way anymore. There was a time that he had had so many enemies or people trying to "screw him over" that he wouldn't go anywhere without a gun. Since he'd been with us, it was hard for him to believe that he'd ever had to live that way. He was ashamed of the times that he had pulled a gun on someone, threatening them. He realized what an idiot he had been. The kind of people he'd hung around with in his past didn't have much respect for guns, he had said. He preached to me over and over how important it was to have the utmost respect for a gun. "You never pull a gun on someone unless you intend to use it," he'd said repeatedly, and I knew that he really believed that now.

One day, we got a call that Mark's mom was in the hospital. I can't remember what it was that was wrong with her, but it turned out that it wasn't nearly as serious as we had been told. Mark was really worried since he loved his mom a lot. She had so many little ways to show her boys how much she loved them. She always seemed a little tough on the outside, but Mark would joke about it, saying she was really just an old softie underneath. He always came home so proud when he'd stopped by there and she had bought him something new, and she always knew just what he liked. Naturally, after hearing that she was in the hospital, he called her right away, and it would be a call that would touch my heart forever.

After finding out that the problem wasn't nearly as serious as he had been told, Mark was very relieved. They talked for a while, and right before he hung up, he said something very special to her. "Take care of yourself now. I love you."

Hearing this gentle, loving comment come from Mark to his mom filled my eyes with very proud tears. "Honey, I'm so proud of you for saying that. I know how much it meant to her," I said immediately after he'd hung up the phone.

"Damn, babe, I can't remember ever telling her that, at least not for a long time. It's all because of you that it's easier for me to tell my true feelings. Saying I love you around here is like saying good morning."

"I'm so glad when you let your family see the side of you that I love so much."

Sometimes it meant Mark had to take a lot of kidding from his brothers with comments like, "You're so pussy-whipped." It had bothered him at first, but after a while, he got to where he didn't care. Some of his family used to tell me that I was the best thing that ever happened to Mark. We both knew how true it was, but it made me feel so good to know that they thought so too.

We used to play spades with Nori and Ray. Ray and Mark had been the closest of the five brothers in their rowdy days. Those two could really tell some stories. It always amazed me when they got together and talked about something they had done, and I learned that the story Mark had told me had been exactly the truth. Some of the things they had done were downright unbelievable, and often I would chalk it up as nothing but a bullshit story. Mark always loved it when I was able to check out his wild stories and found them to be true, then he would gloat.

One day, when they were at the barn and we were playing spades, Nori and Ray got into a big argument. It was during Mark's sober days, when he was always logical and calm. Nori had gone downstairs for a walk, embarrassed because of the way Ray had talked to her. Mark took the opportunity to give his brother a little advice. Mark told him that he shouldn't treat her so badly, and then she wouldn't act like such a bitch. I'll never know how Ray took it, but they did make up when she came back. Once again, I was glad that Ray had a chance to see the gentle, caring side of Mark that was usually reserved for just me. Later, when I told Nori how Mark had stood up for her, she was so happy. She loved Mark very much.

Mark really loved his youngest brother, Kyle. When Kyle and his wife, Brenda, were having problems, Kyle would come over to the barn so he could get away from her. He was so much fun. He and Mark would sing together and act silly, pretending they were the Beatles. Mark felt sorry for Kyle because his marriage was becoming very unhappy all of a sudden. We would cheer him up. Mark thought Kyle had always idolized him and his old lifestyle of being wild and free. Kyle had been with Brenda since he was about fifteen and had never been "free" to grow up on his own.

During Mark's extra-calm period of not drinking, he became obsessed with wanting to get married. It was just something we had never been able to do because of the fact that we were both still legally married to other people. I'd always told Mark that my divorce would be no problem and that I wasn't going to hassle with him until he did something about his. I knew how unlikely that would be since he had already brought it up to his wife quite a few times and it just wasn't getting anywhere. One day, he finally told her that he would take care of it himself and have her served.

He wanted us all to have the same last name so badly. The babies had his name, but of course, I didn't. He was always sending away for things in the mail, mostly free giveaways. He'd put the return address. Whenever it would arrive, he'd smile and say, "Aren't I romantic?" He knew it always made me happy to get something addressed that way. Even during those weeks when he was staying at Moms and Pops, he sent away for things. For months afterward, I received mail with his last name instead of mine.

Nori's Special Poem

Our lives are albums written through,
With good or ill, with false or true,
And as the blessed angels turn
The pages of our years,
God grant they rode the good with smiles
And blot the ill with tears.

—Author unknown

CHAPTER 9

FINAL SEPARATION

It was August, and Mark had no longer been able to control his urge to drink. He'd started off slowly, trying to prove to me that he'd be okay with just one or two. At first, he made absolutely sure that he never lost his temper, and it seemed to work, so I, always wanting to please him, didn't make a big fuss about it. He'd been so perfect lately that I had honestly forgotten what alcohol could do to him.

It was at this same time he'd stopped taking his medication, knowing that it could not be taken with any alcohol. This combination of actions proved to be too much for Mark to handle. Soon he was having problems controlling his temper, and just as before, it could happen without warning and at the most unsuspecting times. In an instant, he could become a raging alcoholic.

Because it frustrated Mark so much that it was happening again, he had become worse than ever. One day, we had decided to go to Gene and Linda's to spend the day and have a barbecue and watch movies. We hadn't been there a half hour before there was a problem. Naturally, Mark had already had quite a bit to drink from noon to four. Since he'd stopped drinking, it didn't take much now before it hit him really hard. He was in the garage with Gene, and I went out to see what he was doing. I casually said something to him; I have no idea what it was. "F you!" he replied.

I couldn't believe he'd said it. This was a problem we had straightened out the first few months we'd been together. No man was ever going to talk to me that way, I had told him. I couldn't be with a man that could say that to me. Quickly he learned the few times it had happened that there would be an all-out war about it, and soon he learned not to say it. Once in a while, if he'd slip, he would catch himself immediately and apologize. This time, there was no apology.

"Excuse me?" I said in total disbelief.

"F you, bitch," he said.

That was it for me. I loaded up the truck as fast as I could, explaining that there was no way I was going to stay. He had embarrassed me so badly in front of our friends. Within five minutes, we were all in the truck with our belongings, ready to go home.

"I'm leaving right now. Are you coming or going to stay here?"

There was no way I could stay after the way he'd talked to me. He ended up coming with us, but I had to drive because Mark was so drunk. I was prepared for a knockdown, drag-out fight when we got home. It never happened, though. In a few minutes, he was sound asleep. He hadn't said a word all the way home, thank God. He knew he was wrong and didn't have an argument.

The next morning, all he could do was apologize over and over about ruining our fun time.

The man who is mean
Is meaner to himself
Than anyone else.

After our little problem with the F-word, Mark was fine for a while. He was pretty good about catching himself when he messed up, and as usual, the good was so good that it was okay. When there was a little bad, he was worth it. We loved each other so much. All that we had been through had made us feel closer than ever before. We knew by now that we could handle anything. We had no doubts that we would always be together.

Our babies were the most important things in our lives. The joy and happiness they gave us was unbelievable. We were constantly going to get each other to show something cute they were doing. If he was all the way across the property, he would never hesitate to come see the special thing that I had to show him. He knew that the walk would always be worth what he was about to see.

Mark had cut his drinking way down after what had happened at Gene and Linda's. Mostly, he drank only on the weekends. He was feeling proud of himself about almost everything. We were still seeing our counselor, Mary, and she was helping him. The only problem we really had to deal with was the fact that we both knew how much worse my mom was getting. It was happening way too fast for us to deal with it. Mark did his best to comfort me during my hardest times. I would never have believed that a man could develop so much compassion in just two short years.

We spent lots of time at the lake and stream, trying to stay cool. We liked packing up all the kids and going to the drive-in movie. It was cool in the evenings, and we would take the truck and lounge chairs. It was always fun going to the "outdoor theater," as Mark called it. His boys came up a couple of times, and Little Mason told us how badly he wanted to move in with us again before school started. He knew it was fine with us, but he couldn't get his mom to agree. He was really upset about it, but our hands were tied.

One day, when Mason and Randy were up, we had a major fight. Mark was having a bad day; he'd been real irritable and edgy for some reason. He had been jumping on the kids for every little thing, things that normally wouldn't have bothered him. Finally, I had heard enough. Mark just wasn't being fair to the kids, and my motherly, protective instincts kicked in. I started in on him to lay off the kids. "You're being a bastard." One thing led to another, and before you knew it, we were going at it real good.

We had made plans to go to the drive-in, and it was almost time to go. Mark's macho guy was out now, in full swing. He was leaving and wasn't taking any of us to the show. "You can stay home and rot for all I care!" he yelled. Realizing how disappointed the kids would be, I tried to put a halt to things and tried to calm him down, but he had already passed the point of no return. Mark was screaming at his boys to get in the truck, but of course, they didn't want any part of going with him when he was acting that way. He kept telling them to get in, and they kept saying no, which only made him madder. "Screw all of you! I'll go by myself!" he screamed as he was going out the door. Like an idiot, I tried to stop him by grabbing his arm. "Don't do this, honey, don't do this to the kids," I pleaded, hanging on tight.

"Let go now, or I'm gonna knock the crap out of you!" he warned, clenching his teeth tightly.

Naturally, I was sure that Mark would never hit me again, so I didn't take his words seriously. "No, honey! Please settle down and think about what you are doing," I begged again with tear-filled eyes. By this time, we were out the door on the deck, and suddenly, he pushed me real hard, trying to break away from my tight grasp. I fell into the window so hard that it broke. "Oh my god, you are crazy! Get out of here, you bastard!" I screamed hysterically.

The kids inside were so scared and worried seeing me fall into the small window, glass flying everywhere. Immediately Mark was down the stairs, in the truck, and gone. I was okay except for the shock that he had done it again. While we were boarding up the window, Randy said something that would later come back to haunt me forever.

"You know what, Linda? When my dad acts like that, you should just shoot him."

"Randy, don't talk like that, ever. I love your dad. You know that. And he loves me. You can't shoot someone just because they push you. Don't ever say anything like that again."

"I don't know. If it were me, I think I'd just shoot him when he acts like that."

The next day, Mark came home, heart in hand, as usual, and all was forgiven. The night before hadn't been a total disaster. I had managed to get myself together enough to take the kids to the drive-in. They had managed to scare me half to death with their choice of movies, Friday the Thirteenth. I've always hated scary movies because I've always been afraid of the dark. Coming home that night with just the kids had been a nerve-racking experience. We couldn't just flick on a light switch when we unlocked the door like most people. We had to go way inside and light a lamp before we could see anything. I've never been afraid of the outside dark, only the inside dark. Robert Frost understood my fear.

House Fear

Always—I tell you this they learned—
Always at night when they returned
To the lonely house from far away,
To lamps unlighted and fire gone gray,
They learned to rattle the lock and key
To give whatever might chance to be,
Warning and time to be off in flight;
And preferring the out- to the in-door night,
They learned to leave the house-door wide
Until they had lit the lamp inside.

—Robert Frost

Money was getting a little tight all of a sudden, so we knew we had to do something. We had done so well with our firewood that we were having a hard time adjusting to not having that money, and Mark wanted to work. His brother Stan was an established electrician, and Mark was hoping to work for him. But a few years before, Mark had let him down and his brother wasn't sure he was reliable enough to hire. Stan and his wife, Lonnie, were the only brother and wife that we never socialized with, so they had no way of knowing how much Mark had changed. Stan was the religious one of the family, and so they were very involved with their church.

Mark let Stan know how eager he was to learn to be an electrician and asked if he needed anyone at work. My son Jimmy had been working for Stan for quite some time now. It had been a big decision for me to make since Jimmy was just sixteen at that time, but Mark had convinced me to let Jimmy try it. Learning to be an electrician was an opportunity he thought my young son shouldn't pass up. Since I had been having a hard time getting him to go to school, I reluctantly gave in. It had been hard for Mark to accept the fact that his own brother had wanted to hire a sixteen-year-old kid instead of him, but he had handled it really well. I'm sure the only person that knew how sad it had made him was me. Besides, Mark understood why Stan had been leery of hiring him. Mark was paying for his "fup."

Quite a bit of time had passed since then, and Jimmy had done real well because he was a very fast learner. The whole crew consisted of Mark's 4 brothers Roy and my Jimmy. Mark wanted to work with them so badly since Jimmy had been telling him that they might need someone else, but still there was no call from Stan. It was hard for Mark to do, fearing that Stan would turn him down, but he called Stan anyway. It turned out that Stan didn't really need anyone right now, or so he told Mark, but he had some landscaping work he needed done if Mark was interested. Needing the money and hoping this would be a chance for Mark to prove to his brother how much he had changed, he was glad to have chance. Besides, he loved landscaping. Stan had been happy with Mark's work, but there still had been no job offer, so soon he gave up hope and looked for another job.

By the last week in August, Mark had found a job. It would be the first time he would work under payroll in years. He would be building apartments in town, and he was really excited. This job turned out to be the beginning of our final problems.

Mark met a guy, named Fred, with a scooter. It was a real nice Harley, something Mark had been wanting for a long time. The guy was single and had no one to answer to. He and Mark hit it off right away. The first time I met Fred, I knew it meant trouble. I realized immediately that when Mark was around him, he took on his hard, bad-guy attitude. This was the side of him that I couldn't stand to be around with. It made me sick to my stomach to see how easily Mark could go back to his old personality. They were awful when they were together, and Fred was the beginning of many major problems for Mark and me.

Mark had been working for four days, and I'd watched his personality change for the worse as the week progressed. He was starting to have a hard time leaving the badass personality at work, and I was very worried. Whenever I'd bring it up, he'd just get upset and tell me things like "You're just jealous that I have a buddy that's a bachelor and has a scooter." In a way, he was right. Hadn't we both always agreed that it was best to surround ourselves with couples for friends? He would never have allowed me to go off with a single girlfriend, and I felt the same way. We had done everything together; that was why we were so close. Except for Leroy, all our friends were couples. We had both always been very possessive of each other. We were each other's favorite people to be with, and that was all there was to it. There had never been a problem, because we had both always felt the same way, but now, all of a sudden, things seemed different.

There were certain things that I could always depend on where Mark was concerned. One of those things was calling if he was going to be late or if his plans had changed in any way. We always prided ourselves on the way we communicated. There was never any guessing to be done. We saved a lot of problems because we always knew what was going on with each other. I knew what was going on with each other. I knew that if Mark was ever going to be late, I could depend on a phone call. I always let him know how much I appreciated it and how much I'd worry about him, so he spared me that.

It was Friday, his first payday. All week we had planned to go out and celebrate with dinner at the Sizzler. He had told me to be ready around five o'clock. I was very excited and had been ready early, anxiously waiting for our "big date." Five o'clock came and went. Six o'clock came and went. By now, I was frantic. What could be wrong? I was sure something was wrong. Mark had always called when he was going to be late. At almost seven o'clock, he came strolling in as if nothing was wrong, and he seemed very drunk. I was furious but somehow managed to stay calm, being thankful that he was okay.

"How are my babies? Come see your daddy." He held out his arms for them, acting as if nothing was wrong. They eagerly climbed onto his lap as he sat down on the couch.

"Where have you been? I have been worried sick! Did you forget that we were going out to celebrate? Why didn't you call? You always call when you are going to be late." I was so mad.

I couldn't believe he interrupted me with "Shut your damn mouth for a minute and I will tell you! I've been at Leroy's. Jimmy and Roy were there, so I stayed and had a few beers with them."

Now I was furious. "All this time I have been worried sick about you, and you have been sitting at Leroy's bar, right next to a telephone. Did it ever enter your mind to just give me a quick call so I wouldn't worry? I can't believe you could do that to me. You always call, you know that!" Voice quivering and feeling my whole body shake. "I was so worried I threw up! What a mean thing to do to me!" I was so mad, and there were no tears this time because I hardly ever cry when I am really mad.

Mark went into a rage. Moving both babies, much to their regret, he jumped off the couch and got right in my face. "That's it! I have had it! You're nothing but a bitch. No one is gonna have me so whipped that I have to call her up just because I am going to be a little late!" He had a crazy look on his face. One that I was beginning to be very familiar with lately.

I couldn't believe what I had just heard. He was heading for his drawers, throwing all his stuff into a pillowcase. By now I was screaming and crying, my anger having turned to sadness, not wanting him to leave us again. "You always call me!" I screamed in a high-pitched voice as the tears wet my face. "Honey, I was so worried! You know how I worry, babe," I said, desperately trying to explain to him why I was so upset. I tried to get him to admit that he had always called me. "Don't do this, Mark," I begged. "Don't throw away all that we have." My desperate pleads were useless. He wasn't even hearing me.

"Shut up! I'm sick of being tied down, and I want out. No friggin' broad is gonna tell me what to do!" he yelled.

I grabbed his arm as he was heading toward the door. This time, he was too macho; there was no warning as he grabbed me by the hair and threw me to the ground and kicked me near on my cheek. The babies were screaming like crazy, and I was crying uncontrollably. By now Mark had reached the door but hadn't opened it, standing very still, looking down at the floor. Suddenly, he threw down the pillowcase and ran back to me. He picked me up and held me so tightly that I thought I'd break in two. He walked me back to the bed, where we sat down, his arms still wrapped around me. While I was trying with all my might to stop crying, he rocked me like a baby for at least ten minutes, saying over and over, "I'm so sorry, babe, I'm so sorry. I love you so much. I don't ever want to lose you. Please forgive me." He was crying very hard, never losing the rhythm as he held me close and rocked me.

The babies were okay now. Seeing us hugging each other, they pressed close against us, wanting to be held also. Meanwhile, the minute the fight had started, Danny had called the cops from the phone down below, and they were here. I didn't know what to do. It was the same cop that had been here when Mark tore up the house. Officer Jones was pissed as I was busy trying to explain to him that everything was okay and that I had had no idea that my son had called the cops. He didn't want to hear a thing I was saying.

"Look at you. Just look at your head," he said and then turned to Mark. "Don't you know that people die from blows to the head? Look what you did to her. An inch closer and she'd be dead right now!" He turned back to me. "And I bet you don't want to press charges again. What, do you have a death wish? Do you want this guy to end up killing you?"

I looked in the mirror and couldn't believe what I saw through my swollen eyes as I brushed my hair away from my face. It looked like someone had put an egg under my skin right by my temple. I thought Mark was going to throw up when he saw it, becoming very pale. With eyebrows raised in disbelief, he had already decided what he was going to do. "Don't worry," he said in the saddest voice I had ever heard. "I'll leave with no problem. I don't ever want to hurt her again." He held me close, as if it would be the last time we would ever embrace. "I'm so sorry, babe!" His voice was trembling. "I love you way too much for this."

"I can't insist that you press charges, but I've seen what he did this time, and if it happens again, I won't need anyone to press charges. I can do it myself."

Mark was leaving, and as it had always done in the past, I became a desperate, irrational woman without an ounce of pride. I couldn't believe what was happening. Crying and pleading with all my heart, I somehow found the words. "Mark, what are you doing? Don't leave me, please!" I sobbed uncontrollably. "Honey, we love each other so much! Please, Mark, please!"

I'll never forget the look he gave me through eyes filled with tears.

"I have to, babe. I don't ever want to hurt you. I love you too much."

Just like that, he was gone from our lives once again, but somehow, this time, I knew it was for good. Standing on the deck that we had fallen in love on, I held a baby in each arm as I watched him sitting in his truck, looking all around our place, which he loved so much and was so proud of. I knew that his mind was made up and that there was nothing I could say or do to change it.

This was for real, and the empty feeling inside of me cut like a knife. It was the beginning of the worst pain I could ever imagine, and there was something very final about it all. I watched as he started up his truck and drove slowly down our long dirt driveway, wondering if he would ever be back. He could not have been going more that ten miles an hour as he pulled up to the stop sign. I watched him for as long as I could see him, until the tiny dot of his truck finally disappeared down the long highway. "Da-Da! Da-Da!" his precious babies said over and over as I stood there in silence. It was the saddest I had ever been in my entire life.

The next day was Saturday, and Mark came over to give me some money. He had cashed his check and was acting very cold and macho. I assumed he'd been with his new buddy from work, but I didn't bother asking. He played with his babies for a while and told me very matter-of-factly that we couldn't be together anymore. It didn't matter how much we loved each other. He was afraid of himself. He made it very clear that there was no use in discussing it further. Of course, I persisted, and he ended up leaving mad. I didn't see or hear from him for four days. I felt lost. I had this gut feeling, for the first time since we had met, that we would never be together again. I felt like part of me had been ripped away, and I clung to my babies almost constantly.

"Daddy loves us. Daddy will be back," I told them again and again. I felt like as long as I was holding on to them, I still had a part of their daddy with me. I wrote a song for Mark that I called "I Miss You So." When I was finished with it, I realized how tough I'd been trying to be. I'd tried to convince myself that it was the best thing for both of us. In writing the song, I'd been reaching for the bad points of our relationship. I guess that was to try to make myself feel better about not having him anymore.

Making love had always been a sore spot with us. My whole life, I had always related "making love" to love. It was all I'd ever known. I'd never been with anyone that I hadn't loved, of course, but Mark had lived such a totally different kind of life that he couldn't understand why I would get so upset if he didn't want to make love.

He would always say, "Screwing is no big deal. You can screw anyone. What we have is special, babe. We have love. We really love each other. Screwing is just something extra, and anyone can do that, but not everyone can love like we do." What could I say? I had still spent many nights crying myself to sleep because he just wasn't in the mood to make love. It was just one of the things I had to learn to accept, and being rejected had always hurt me very badly. It was not very good for my already-shaken self-esteem. I knew that he was right about one thing, though. Our love was really special.

Looking back, I know that this fight was the one that, for the first time in our relationship, had me thinking that it was really over for good. I was beginning to realize that I was as sick as he was for allowing this violence to continue. It didn't matter. One moment I would convince myself that I didn't need or want him, and the next moment, I would be trying anything I could to get him to come home.

I spent hours out on the roof of the barn, playing my guitar, watching and waiting for the familiar sound of his truck turning the corner to come home. The babies missed him terribly, as did I. I played the song that I wrote for him over and over, "I Miss You So." The words showed that I was trying to convince myself that it was okay that he was gone. The title was the heartbreaker, though, since I really did miss him so. I must be crazy.

I Miss You So

I still live in a barn, you know, and I don't keep house too clean,
But I give my kids the love that they need,
it's the most important thing.
I still lay in our same old bed and look out at the stars,
But you can't reject me anymore, you can't leave no more scars.
I miss you so.
I wonder why I always sit and cry and miss you so.

You always had control of me, now suddenly I'm free.
I love my kids and our babies so, and I'm who I want to be.
But I can't forget the perfect times, and I see you everywhere.
We cause each other so much pain, but our special love is so rare.
I miss you so.
I wonder why I always sit and cry and miss you so.

Did you find out who you really are, and
can you buy your Harley yet?
Is it really so much better now, or do you have some regrets?
You need a girl who wants a dad and doesn't like to love,
Real pretty, with no point of view, and she'll have to be real young.
I miss you so.
I wonder why I always sit and cry and miss you so.

For all the times that you made me cry,
when you told me not to touch,
I'd say please don't turn me away, I love you very much.
I can't believe you could hurt me so, I could easily be gone.
I hope you find what's in your head so we can soon be one.
I miss you so.
I wonder why I always sit and cry and miss you so.
I miss you so.
I wonder why I still sit and cry and miss you so.

About a week later, I played my song for Mark. He liked it so much and couldn't believe I had written him a song. For the next six weeks, Mark and I both played head games with each other. I never knew what to expect since he was definitely unpredictable. One minute he would fall apart on me, telling me what a hard time he was having, and the next minute I was nothing but a bitch that he wanted nothing to do with. When he'd break down and tell me how bad he wanted to get back together, I would act tough and tell him it would never work. The very days that he'd been begging me to take him back, I would hear from someone that he had done nothing but run me down, saying how he never wanted to be with me again. I was so confused.

I couldn't believe the kind of things he was saying to our friends. Most of the time, it was the total opposite of what had really happened. When he'd say he wanted us to go back together and I would say no, we were not ready, he would tell everyone how badly I was begging him to take me back. People would tell me the things he was saying, and when I'd see him again, I'd bring it up and we would fight. He couldn't handle the fact that I caught him showing his tough-guy attitude to everyone. It was a vicious circle.

Since we had separated, we were seeing our counselor once alone each and once together. Nothing was helping by then, though. He had been maintaining his macho, "I don't need or want her" attitude with Mary also. Of course, he'd deny it to me. When we were together, he wasn't admitting to anything in front of her, and soon I realized that the whole thing was a waste of time. Even Mary couldn't help us if he wasn't going to be honest with her.

One day, he started insisting there was something very wrong with him inside his head. To rule this out, the doctor ordered a brain scan at the hospital. It was scheduled for October 9, and I'd promised Mark I'd take him. He said it was his last hope, and he desperately wanted them to find out that there was a reason for his bursts of violence. Because of all the blows he had taken to his head when he used to fight a lot, there was a slim chance there could be some kind of damage. I felt all along that he knew better, and I believed he was just looking for excuses, not wanting to admit that it was just the way he was.

With Mark gone, I had lots of free time on my hands. There were many lonely, sad times, and I always had this pain in my gut, a constant reminder that he was gone. I found myself spending almost every weekend at Leroy's, since I knew that being alone wasn't good for me. I could practically drive myself nuts wondering where Mark was and what he was doing, always wondering if he was okay. We saw each other at least four times a week, and he would usually stay all night at least once a week. Depending on how the day went, he'd either leave happy or mad. Nothing was consistent, as everything had become totally unpredictable where we were concerned. The only thing I could count on was the constant love he always maintained for his babies. He adored them as they did him, and this fact tore at my heart constantly.

At this time, both Jimmy and Rory lived at Leroy's. It was nice to be with all of them on the weekends. We played a lot of music. There was another advantage being at Leroy's. Moms and Pops lived only a short distance away, and since Mark lived with them, there was always the hope that he might stop by. He didn't stop by very often on the weekends.

I had been hearing a lot of talk from different people, Mark included, about a lady that lived down the street from Moms named Claudia. Everyone was telling me that she had a crush on Mark and was always throwing herself at him. I'd heard enough to know that she wasn't his type, but I was still upset about all the talk. I never worried again after I had met her. I was sure that Mark probably "did her," as he would put it, but I was also sure that it wouldn't have meant a thing to him. I knew how much he loved me. It didn't matter what he was telling anyone else. I knew the truth, but why was he acting this way?

One day, he came over in a rage. The bitch, as he always called her, had gone into his room and cleaned it up without his permission. He was so upset that I was afraid he would do something awful to her as he ranted and raved for at least an hour. He couldn't believe that she had the nerve to do that. Wow, he was pissed! I'd always tell myself that I wasn't going to give in to him again, but no matter how hard I tried, all he ever had to do was hold me in his arms. The weeks we were separated, whenever we would make love, it would be the best ever. I'll never forget the way he would quiver and how he wanted to be kissing almost all the time, melting into one. That was how the other song I wrote for him was born, and he loved it very much. It gave him a very positive attitude and a "big head." The last verse still gives me goose bumps every time I play it. Maybe my song was trying to send me a message.

You Can Get Away with Anything

You always seem to know that you can get away with anything,
You always swore to me that we would never be apart.
I put you on a pedestal and worshipped
the ground that you walked,
You always knew for certain that I loved you with all of my heart.

(Chorus)

But you're such a pro at convincing me to forgive you,
You always seem to know just how to handle me.
Just give me a little lovin' and tell me how sorry you are,
I'd swear to everyone that we'd always be together for sure.

I always used to brag about you to our friends,
I convinced myself that they all envied me.
But now I sit and wonder, Could love really be so blind?
And all this time, did they really feel sorry for me?

(Chorus)

When things are going good, you're happy
and you seem so strong to me,

You tell me you'd be lost without me and how much you've grown.
Then out comes your other person, and the violence scares me so,
You tear my heart apart, and I know I ought to let you go.

(Chorus)

Was my song meant to be some kind of an omen? It had always
been so true that he always thought he could get away with anything.
Is that how my story would end? I often wondered.

CHAPTER 10

PARTIES, HORROR, AND SAD GOODBYES

Roy and Nicki decided to have a party, and I was excited, knowing it would be lots of fun doing something different for a change. I was really looking forward to it. "Mom, I am bringing my drums to Rod and Nicki's," my son had told me earlier, knowing how much I loved to watch him work his wonderful magic as he became one with his drums.

He was very talented and had come a long way from the twelve-year-old boy that had been on the verge of tears many times. "Mom," he would say in his saddest and most hopeless voice, "I can't even do two things at the same time and keep a good beat."

My heart would break for him. "Honey, you can do anything you want to do. It just takes practice," I would reassure him over and over.

Roy and Mark had a good friend from down the hill named Bill, and they had told me a lot about him. He played the guitar really well, and they knew that I would have fun playing with him since he wasn't into that crazy, heavy-metal music the kids liked to play all the time, music that I was not talented enough to play very well.

I anxiously waited for evening to come so we could leave, and I was happy that Mark had called earlier in the day to make sure that I'd be there. "Babe, I have a present for you," he boasted in a proud-sounding voice.

"Really! What is it, honey?" I pleaded excitedly.

"You will just have to wait till tonight," he kidded, knowing that I would be going nuts trying to figure out what it was.

I loved him so much when he would show me his kind, loving heart, as he did many times over. I felt like we were getting closer and closer to getting back together; after all, we had seen each other three times in a row without having even one disagreement.

Everything went well for a while. The kids played music, the babies were in a good mood, and Mark was treating me very special. As the evening progressed, Mark got very drunk and decided he wanted to leave long before I was ready.

I had just put the babies to sleep on Rod and Nicki's bed and was finally able to kick back. I still hadn't gotten to play guitar with Bill, and I'd really been looking forward to it. The kids had quit with their loud rock-and-roll. It was getting pretty late, and Mark was insistent. "I want to leave right now!" he said with raised eyebrows and a very stern voice, and it was very obvious that he meant with me.

"Mark, I just got the babies to sleep. I really want to play guitar for a while. Please?" I said, begging permission, forgetting that he wasn't supposed to tell me what to do anymore. I decided to use this separation to my advantage for once. "If you want to come home with me, you're just going to have to wait a while. I never do nothing except go to Leroy's," I said in my sternest, independent voice. "I'm going to have some fun and play guitar. Besides, you can't tell me what to do anymore. Remember?"

Seeing how insistent I was being, and knowing that I was right, he tried a different approach. "Come on, babe, please. I gave you presents and everything. Don't you love me? I just want to go home and make love and hold you." He was making this very hard on me. He had given me a blue plaid Pendleton and a real pretty gold wedding band.

I was tough and stuck to what I had originally said. I was staying, and that was that. When he realized that he wasn't going to change my mind, he left angrily, telling me how unappreciative I was and that I didn't love him anymore. He knew that was a bunch of bull; it was just because he was so drunk. I worried about him driving all the way home to Hesperia.

We hadn't been playing guitar for very long at all when the phone rang. It was Mark, for me, and my first thought was, How did he get to Moms and Pops so fast?

"Where the hell are you? Are you gonna stay there all night?"

"What do you mean where am I? Where are you? At the barn?" I asked, very shocked at his irrational behavior.

"Where do you think I am? I told you how bad I wanted to make love to you." His was voice becoming sad and calm.

"I'll be home soon. Just lie down and rest," I said, wanting to show him just how much rejection can hurt. Needless to say, I was not really eager to rush home to him, as drunk as he was. I was hoping that he would be down and fall asleep while he was waiting for me, but I was wrong about that. When he'd realized that I wasn't coming home soon, he called again.

"You damn bitch! I told you I wanted you home now! You've got ten minutes," he said before slamming the phone down. This time, I knew I'd better go. What was I going to do? I was scared to death. Mark's brother Kyle told me not to worry, that he'd go with me to make sure everything was okay. I was really happy about that, and his other brother said he would come too. We rushed as fast as we could, loading my stuff and the babies in the car. He'd only given me ten minutes, I reminded everyone.

I was surprised but very relieved when we got to the barn and Mark had left. His truck was nowhere in sight. The barn was locked up tight with our combination lock that hung on the outside; it was the only way to lock the door when we left. If we were inside, there was a bolt we slid across.

"We'll help you get the babies and your things upstairs," Kyle offered.

"Thanks! That'll be a big help," I said as I unlocked the door. "Mark must have thought that I wasn't going to come home, so I am sure he probably left mad," I said in a relieved voice. "I'll hear about it tomorrow, I guess."

As I lit a kerosene lamp, the guys put everything down on one of the couches. "Is that everything?" one of them asked.

"Yeah, thanks a lot, you guys. Sorry you came all the way down here for nothing, but I really appreciate it. He was acting real scary on the phone. I hope he made it all the way to Hesperia okay, as drunk as he was. I'll never know why he has to act like this. He always hates himself for it later," I said very apologetically, wondering why I always tried to make excuses for his drunken behavior.

Just as they were saying goodbye, I heard something in the bedroom, and all of a sudden, he was right there. "Mark, what's wrong? What are you doing?" I asked in absolute horror. The look on his face was so evil and vicious I was really afraid. He was walking toward me very slowly with a butcher knife in his right hand. His arm was raised, as if he was going to stab me, and I was terrified. He just kept walking right toward me, but he didn't say a word. He had that Charles Manson crazy look in his eyes. His aim was still raised as I slowly backed away from him, tears of fear filling my eyes. Finally, he spoke.

"You thought I left, didn't you, bitch?" he half-whispered behind clenched teeth. "That was just what I wanted you to think, stupid. You should never underestimate what I am capable of, stupid." He glanced toward his brothers. "And what is this? Did you bring some protection with you? Did you think that would help you?"

Never taking my eyes off him, I slowly continued to back up. Now one of his brothers was between us, trying to talk to him. "It's okay, Mark. She's home now, so calm down. We hurried as fast as we could, and everything's okay now," his younger brother pleaded in a stern but gentle voice. "You don't want to act like this, dude!" I could hardly believe that his brother seemed to be reaching him.

He was trying to take the knife, but Mark wasn't about to let go. He was very smart and wasn't being forceful, not wanting to provoke him or have him feel threatened in any way. He talked some more, still being very calm. He had handled Mark exactly right, knowing all along that his brother would never hurt him. I sighed with relief as he allowed him to gently take the knife from his tightly clenched fingers.

"Thank God," I whispered. Both brothers continued to talk to their very troubled eldest brother, and Mark was beginning to look better. The vicious look he'd had only a moment before, which had scared me so badly, had disappeared, and he was listening to his brothers and starting to act a little embarrassed about his behavior.

I was very grateful to them for making sure he was all right before they left. He was so drunk and very tired, and I watched as he had turned back into the loving, compassionate man I had fallen in love with, and all my previous fears had disappeared. "He'll be okay now," I said. "He'll fall asleep with his babies." By this time, one of them was awake, and Mark was holding the baby very close to him. "What can I say, guys? Thanks a lot."

"No problem." We were all three feeling a huge relief that this had ended peacefully, and they were out the door.

"I'm so sorry, babe. I just needed to be with you tonight, and you didn't even care," he stressed in his most apologetic voice. "You really hurt me. I thought I was going crazy." I hadn't stopped to think of it that way.

"I'm sorry, honey. You know I don't ever want to hurt you. I love you so much." He always had a way of making me feel guilty and believing that it was partly my fault also. He held me tight, and I knew everything was okay, except that he was hungry.

"Babe, would you make me some French toast? Please? I haven't eaten all day. Please?" He knew I could never tell him no since I knew it was my job to take care of him, but I playfully argued back.

"French toast? It's two o'clock in the morning," I said very matter-of-factly in my teasing, pretending-to-be-tough voice. "You're lucky I love you so much. You are spoiled rotten," I joked as I carried the sleeping baby to our big, king-size bed. He got up to go to the bathroom, then lay down on the bed with his pipe. I gently handed him his precious, almost-back-to-sleep baby and dutifully and lovingly went to make him his French toast.

I thanked God that his brothers had come home with me, since I cringed to think of what might have happened if they hadn't been there. "Honey, do you want powdered sugar on your French toast?" I asked quietly from the stove. No answer. I walked back toward the bed, knowing if I yelled, it would wake up the babies. I smiled. "No need for the powdered sugar," I said to myself. "No need for the French toast either." They were all three sound asleep, all cuddled up together. It was a sight that always made me smile. The dog was happy—he got the French toast. "Don't act so excited," I warned him as I held the plate above, teasing him. "You have to eat it dry," I said in my strongest tone. He was not about to get the syrup and powered sugar; after all, I did have control of some things.

I suddenly realized how tired I was. I climbed into our giant bed and cuddled up to my three babies. Mark's whole appearance had changed and now had the look of a very happy and content man. He was always so content when he'd come and stay the night, because he was home, where he really wanted to be all the time.

Would he ever be able to learn to control his violence? I wondered. He had gone to such an extreme tonight to make me think he had left. He'd locked the barn door from the outside, climbed in the window, and hidden in the bedroom. He had parked his truck behind the barn so we couldn't see it. He hadn't been the Mark I loved. He'd been that other man, the one that I would never understand. In the morning, he would tell me the very same thing while apologizing again and again. It was a vicious cycle.

The next day, Mark got up early, so when I woke up, he wasn't in bed. As happened so many mornings before, when I looked out our bedroom window that overlooked the chicken coop, I could see him out, watering his trees. He loved being up early, taking care of the animals and watering.

"Hey, cutie!" I yelled down at him. "Where's my breakfast in bed?"

He looked up and smiled that familiar smile that said how much he loved me. "I'll be right up, babe," he answered as he put down the hose and walked behind a big clump of bamboo to pick up his baby girl. Darla had awakened early, and Mark had fed and dressed her, and the two of them had gone outside. This was something else that he had done many times, knowing how I loved to sleep late. Donny and I were just the same, always lazy in the morning, but Mark and Darla loved getting up with the sun.

Mark didn't stay very long, explaining that he had business to take care of. That had usually meant it had to do with his new friend from work. They were trying to get their own business going on the side. As usual, he was sorry he had scared me last night and explained that incidents like that were the reason we couldn't be with each other. "I don't know what difference it makes. You still do it, and we're not with each other now," I said in a shocked, stern voice, shaking my head.

"I guess you're right. I never thought of that. I'll always think of you as mine, I guess." He gave me a kiss and the babies a kiss and told the three of us how much he loved us, and he was gone. His last statement had left me very confused. Why were we apart, then? It was just head games, and I was getting tired of them.

I hadn't mentioned it to Mark, but Rory had promised that he would come and put the fireplace in today. It was getting colder and colder. Since it was our only source of heat, we needed it in right away. Mark got so upset every time Rory did anything for me because he always wanted to be the one that took care of me. He definitely didn't want Rory doing things for me. He knew how smart Rory was and hated it when I would depend on him for something.

Mark hadn't said that he'd be back later, so I was surprised when he showed up, and naturally, Rory was still there. I could tell that Mark was very irritated about him helping me. "Why didn't you ask me?" he pleaded angrily with raised brow. "I'd have put it in for you."

"I didn't think you'd have time." As usual, I felt like I had to defend myself as I reached for his arm to give him a loving pat, pulling away angrily. "Honey, whenever I ask you to help out lately, you always have something you have to do."

"Well, I'd have done this for you and you know it. It seems like you don't need me for anything anymore." He didn't stay long this time, pouting like he was. "Fred and I will be over sometime next week to get this barn in better shape. It needs a lot of work," he added very sarcastically. It seems he'd been able to get seventeen sheets of plywood the other day for free.

"I don't want that guy around here," I told him right up front in a very stern voice.

"Fine! Fix things yourself, bitch," he said, leaving mad once again. I didn't see or hear from him for a few days after that, nor had I expected to. There was a definite pattern to his behavior lately. He was becoming very predictable. When I finally did see him again, he'd been in his badass attitude. I told him that I had talked to my mom a few days earlier. She'd been so bad that she hadn't made hardly any sense at all. "She said to tell you how much she loves you, honey," I said softly, knowing that would bring out his soft side, and I was convinced that she would not be alive much longer. Upon hearing this news, he instantly became the Mark that I loved so much. He came upstairs and called his friend and told him he wasn't going to make it there today because something had come up. We had such a beautiful night, sad as we were. Thank God we'd had each other to cling to. The next few days, he made sure he called often or came by to see if Mom had gotten any worse. I hadn't heard anything.

It had been much easier for me to avoid calling than worrying about finding out the worst. I knew that my sister would call me when it happened. It was a call I dreaded with all my heart, but I knew it was inevitable. When I had talked to Mark the day before, I'd told him that he'd find me at Leroy's the next day.

As it turned out, that was where I was when I received that very sad phone call from my sister. My mom was gone forever, and even though her death had been a peaceful one, nothing seemed to help the shock of those words. "Mom is gone," my sister had said in her usual soft, calming voice, always the mature sister, totally in control of her emotions. I was in a daze, and the only thing I wanted right now was Mark. I needed him so badly. Where was he? He'd promised he'd be here when I needed him. How could I handle this without him? "He should have been here by now," I whispered quietly as I grimaced from the physical and emotional pain I was feeling.

Without my saying a word, everyone there had realized what the call had meant, and no one knew what to say. There was nothing anyone could say, anyway. My eyes filled with tears as I concentrated on taking a long, deep breath, trying to stay in control of my emotions. I just wanted to scream at the top of my lungs, "My mom is gone, just gone! I don't have my mom anymore! Oh god! I will never have her again." The tears covered my cheeks. I couldn't believe the shock I was in. Why? I'd had months to prepare for this. Why wasn't I more prepared? I didn't understand, and Mark, where was he when I needed him more than I ever had? I was feeling so alone and so lost, and I had never been this sad in my entire life.

In a daze, I found myself heading toward Leroy's bedroom. I knew I would be alone. Is that what I need right now? I wondered, feeling more and more pain as time slowly passed. Sitting on the side of his huge waterbed, head in hands, and starting to sigh in disbelief, I slowly began to rock, trying to comfort myself, the way I always do when I am very sad. After what seemed like forever, I knew that I had to somehow find the will to get up. Slowly rising, feeling very light-headed, I somehow managed to take one step at a time and made it into the bathroom, thinking maybe a shower would help me feel better and to relax a little. My whole body had begun to tense up all of a sudden. I could not believe how weird I was feeling physically as well as emotionally. It seemed like I was in the shower for a very long time. After a few minutes, my whole body started to feel numb, and I could hardly move. "What's happening to me?" I said softly as I cried harder than I had ever cried before, but barely making a sound. I was glad to know the noise of the shower would help hide my pain. Soon afterward, I started having dry heaves. Since I hadn't eaten for a while, there was nothing coming up, but it seemed to go on and on. There I was, in Leroy's shower, crying quietly out of control and having the worse dry heaves I ever had. I felt like I'd better not try to walk, because my whole body did not seem to be cooperating with my brain. How am I going to get out? When would someone realize how long I'd been gone? I wondered. Trying to remember who was at Leroy's, I realized it was all just a blur. Just when I finally came to the conclusion that I was going to have to get out of the shower somehow, I felt his presence. "Mark," I said with great relief. The tears were coming faster than ever, and my voice was so strained I could hardly speak.

"I know, babe, I know. It'll be okay. I'm here now," he said with tear-filled eyes. He gently led me out of the shower, wrapped me up in a towel, and walked me very slowly toward the bed. I knew how sad he was also as I felt his body quivering into mine. "Shh! Shh" he repeated over and over as I tried to explain to him how sick I was and about the numbness throughout my whole body. "It's okay, babe. I'm here now. Shh! Shh!"

"Thank God you are here, honey. I needed you so much," I said, my voice quivering. "Just lie down with me. It's gonna be okay now."

Thank God he was here. Thank God was all I could think. "My mom's gone. I can't believe she's really gone," I sobbed over and over.

"Shh, it's okay, babe. I know, it's okay. You cry all you want, just try to calm down." The poor guy tried so hard to comfort me. He told me later how helpless he had felt. We lay there on Leroy's bed for a very long time. Mark held me close until I finally fell asleep, totally exhausted. My entire body ached, but it was nothing compared to the pain in my heart.

The following week was very hard for me. I was having trouble accepting the fact that Mom was really gone forever. I learned a difficult lesson that week. I learned that death is something you can never really prepare yourself for. Mark was with me almost constantly the entire week, every spare moment that he had. He'd even missed some days at work so he could stay with me, and we talked about how Mom's death had brought us closer than ever before. It had made us stop and think just how final something can be, and we talked in depth about death and dying. I was so glad that we had decided that it wasn't necessary to tell her when we'd split up. She never had to know that she no longer had her priceless Mark to take care of her baby girl.

The funeral would be on Saturday. There was something very important that still had to be done, but I wasn't sure if I could do it. A few years earlier, in a period of about eight months, I had lost three different people that I loved very much through death. It had inspired me to write a song about it. It was a beautiful song, and my mom really loved it. She had made me promise when we were up north, visiting her, that I would make a tape and play it at her service. I had promised her I would, but now I wished I hadn't.

The night before the service, we all went down to Richie and Dawn's house in Riverside to make the tape. He had great equipment to do it with. As it turned out, we stayed up all night, trying for perfection. I played guitar and sang, Richie played guitar, and Jimmy played the spoons. The tape turned out really good. I'm sure no one ever suspected how long it had taken us until we were finally satisfied with it. Rudy and Shelley had come from Vegas, so they were there with us. The whole time we were making the tape, Mark was lying on the couch behind me as I sat on the floor Indian-style. He acted silly at times so I wouldn't be too sad. Every once in a while, he'd say, "Sing my songs." I'd oblige him for a moment every time with "I Still Live in a Barn, You Know" or "You Always Seem to Know that You Can Get Away with Anything." Later on, after I'd brought the tape back home, I'd play the parts that we hadn't been satisfied with. It was neat hearing us all talking, Mark making his musical requests, and me obliging him by singing the first few lines of whatever song he asked for.

The song I had written for those that had died spoke of a very important belief of mine. It was meant to help those of us who were hurting, because we would never have a chance to tell this person again how we felt about them. It sort of relieves all guilt. The main message is, "Now that you're gone, I know you know all the thoughts of those of us who loved you so." It speaks for itself. Whatever it was we wished we could tell them, they know it now that they're gone. It was my last gift for my mom, just from my sons and me, and I was sure of how it would make her smile at us from heaven. I know how much it meant to her. I thanked God that I was able to do it for her.

I Know You Know

Did you ever really know you were so special?
And did you know that everyone loved you so?
I know it's wrong for me to be so angry,
But it seems so soon for you to have to go.

You always helped when others were in trouble,
You were never known to turn a friend away.

That's why you were needed by our Lord now,
And it's selfish for us to wish that you could stay.

(Chorus)

Now that you're gone, I know you know
All the thoughts of those of us who loved you so.
During all the life we shared. did you really know how we cared?
Now that you're gone, I know you know.

Remember all the special times that we shared?
And all those times that we laughed so hard that we cried?
The sadness, fears, and anger that we always handled,
Now there's such an empty feeling down inside.

Now it's time to ask you one last favor.
Will you please go give him a great big hug for me?
Thank him for the time that he let us have you,
And tell him thank you for all the priceless memories.

(Repeat chorus)

Mom's service was beautiful, thanks to my sister Barbara. She was always the great organizer. The entire service was a beautiful tribute to one of the best ladies that had ever lived. She had met her untimely death as bravely as she had lived her life. She had an undying love for her children and her grandchildren. I never knew her to do anything wrong in her whole life. I never knew her to tell a lie, and yet I had watched this wonderful woman endure so much pain during her life after her painful divorce after twenty-five years with my dad. She had been looking forward to finally being at peace with her Joe, a man she had loved for years. She had been looking forward to the time when she wouldn't hurt anymore.

"Accept it, baby," she'd urged me. "Don't wish for me to stay alive not the way I am." She was so worried about me. She knew how emotional I was. She knew how I felt everything so much stronger than most people. Many times she'd told me, "The only thing I'm worried about is you, baby. You be strong for me."

I tried the very hardest that I could. Thank God I had Mark and my kids. I'll never forget how it had touched my heart to see her casket being carried out to her final resting spot beside her precious Joe. Mark, Richie, Jimmy, Rudy, my brother Ronnie, and my brother-in-law John had carried it with love.

My mom was never at a loss for words during her lifetime. Always the friendly and outspoken one, she wasn't about to leave us all without one final message. I'll always feel in my heart that I know her message had mainly been meant for me, her weakest, most emotional child. It truly touched my heart. The words were read very bravely by my sister, who had lovingly and unselfishly cared for Mom until her death. It was found in her wallet after her death, with a note that said, "Read at my funeral." It would serve to remind me for the rest of my life of her incredible strength and her kind, compassionate, optimistic, and loving ways. My wonderful mom's cup was always half-full. With her, there was always forgiveness and always hope. I knew how blessed I had been, and no one could tell me that this poem in her wallet wasn't for me.

When I am called away, my dear,
I wish you wouldn't cry.
Instead, drift into memory
Of happy days gone by.
If we are near when darkness falls,
Touch me with your sweet kiss,
So through eternity I can
Sleep on with endless bliss.
Enfold me closely to your heart
As my life ebbs away,
Remembering that we'll meet again
One bright and sunny day.

Perhaps I ask too much of you,
Yet this is my request.

Try to answer me and I
Will know a tender rest.
And if by chance you should go first,
I'll do the same, my dear.
Ever and ever loving you,
Always staying near.
Now you know the feeling
That lingers in my heart,
Let there be no bitter tears
On the day that I depart.

Mom's death forced us to think about our own death. We tried to cover every detail of the things we wanted done when we died. Mike told me, "Just don't cremate me, babe. I don't know why anyone would ever want to be cremated. And promise me you'll sing your song for me, or at least a tape. I know you could never sing at my funeral."

The long journey home after Mom's funeral seemed to take forever. I was feeling very sad, very tired, and a little numb. All I could think about was going home with Mark to our barn and spending a nice, quiet evening with our babies. Gene and Linda had kept them so we wouldn't have to worry about them at the service. They had always come through when I needed them. They were such good friends. I was missing the babies. I needed to hold them. Death does that to you, I guess. It makes you want to hold on to those you love.

Mark told me he wanted me to go to Pops's birthday party with him. He said he wanted to have a chance to show me off. I immediately said, "No way. I'm not going with you to a party over there." Fred would be there, and so would Claudia, the lady down the street who was always trying to get in his pants. I couldn't stand to be around him when he was with those people. He always took on his badass personality, the one that made me sick to my stomach. He was mad that I wouldn't go, but my decision was final. "Please stay with me tonight, honey?" I pleaded. "I really need you, baby!" I urged.

"No way. I promised I'd be there, and I'm going." He was furious.

Since Mark wouldn't be there, Rudy and Shelley decided to stay. We would play cards or something. We talked Rory into coming too. Mark called about three times after he'd gotten to Hesperia, still trying to talk me into coming. I said no every time. We were all going to play spades tonight. After he got real drunk, he called quite a few more times, making all kinds of stupid threats to me, Rory, and Rudy. We were glad when the calls finally stopped. Just drunk Mark, we all thought. Dealing with him in this state of mind was the last thing I needed on this particular night.

It was at this party that Mark had told our friend Big John, "Maybe I'll just kill us all so we can be together." All of us meaning the babies, himself, and me. Just drunk talk, Big John had thought. If only he'd known. This was also the night that Mark and Claudia had gone into the bedroom alone for a while. After that, Mark would never refer to her again without calling her a slut. For this reason, I figured something had happened. Mark denied it, but surprisingly, it didn't bother me. I knew that if something had happened, it hadn't meant a thing to him. He had just been getting even with me for not going to the party so he could show me off. What a mean thing to do to someone you love.

For Mom and Mark

Some people come into our lives
And quickly go.
Some stay for a while
And leave footprints on our hearts
And we are never the same.

—Unknown

Mother

Since Mother went away, she's nearer than before,
I cannot touch her hand and yet she's with me more and more.
The years have never lessened the longing in my heart,

That came the day I realized that we must dwell apart,
And yet as long as memory lives, my mother cannot die,
For in my heart, she's living still, as passing years go by.

—Helen Steiner Rice

CHAPTER 11

HEAD GAMES AND HOPE

The week to follow was filled with ups and downs and highs and lows. Mark and I were playing head games, and I hate to admit it, but by now I was almost just as bad as he was about it all. These games were messing up our lives. It was especially hard on us because we'd always had such excellent communication in the past. It was very confusing. When Mark would say how much he wanted us to get back together. I would say no and tell him he'd been acting too unpredictable lately, that I couldn't trust him. The way I really felt was that I wanted to be with him more than anything in the world. When I would say maybe it would be okay to try again, he'd act tough and say it would never work.

One of these days, we both stopped the game long enough to say we'd give it a try. We had a nice talk the night before a really honest, no-bull kind of talk. Things seemed really hopeful, until Rory showed up, making Mark very upset as usual. I explained that Rory had come to help me get some firewood. I couldn't believe Mark got so upset. He left very angry, saying I didn't need him, that I had Rory to take care of me. I thought he acted like an idiot. Thank God I had someone to help me do all the important things like getting firewood. Mark never seemed to have time to help me. That ended any chance of getting back together for the time being.

That weekend, as usual, I went to Leroy's. Richie and Dawn were there too. We ended up staying up all night, playing music and talking. Leroy and Danny had gone for the weekend, camping out and riding the ATVs. Around four o'clock in the morning, we decided to go in the hot tub. It was Richie, Dawn, Rory, and myself. I hadn't brought my suit, so I put on one of Leroy's long T-shirts and, of course, leaving my panties on. Around six thirty, Richie and Dawn went inside. Soon afterward, Mark stopped by on his way to work. I was still in the tub with Rory when the sliding glass door opened, and I looked up and saw him. I was happily surprised. "Hi, honey!" I said with pleasure and a very big smile.

"You fucking bitch, I don't believe you! You slut!" he yelled as he left.

"Wow, now what did I do?" I said in complete shock to Rory, eyebrows raised.

I was excited to see him, and I knew he could tell. He was just trying to cause problems again. Feeling very sad and confused, I got out, took a shower, and dressed. Since I had worn one of Leroy's T-shirts in the hot tub, a dark one at that, what I heard later really upset me. Mark had told one of our friends that he caught me in the hot tub with Rory, naked. I couldn't believe it. Why was he trying to make me look bad to people? I know that he could see the shirt very easily. There is a big difference between wearing a shirt and being nude. He must have been in one of his badass moods that day. This was the sort of thing he did to me quite often.

Of course, when I'd question him about it, he'd deny saying anything. I didn't mention what I'd heard to him because I didn't want to cause a problem. I just didn't understand why he did these kinds of things.

At around nine o'clock, he called from work. He needed me right away. "Babe, I cut my finger really bad. I need you to take me to get some stitches. Will you please hurry?" I couldn't believe it. After the way he had talked to me just hours before, he had called acting like we'd never had a problem. He didn't say he was sorry; there was no mention of the way he had acted earlier. It was so weird. In fact, it frightened me. What if it was just a plan to get me alone? He'd been so upset when he'd left earlier that I was just too scared to go.

Since he was working only a few miles away, Rory and Richie decided it would be better if they went. I was a little worried about it since Rory was the one that had been upsetting Mark the most lately. I knew that Rory was not afraid of Mark. They didn't seem worried at all, so I decided it was better them than me if it was a trick of some kind. I was sure that Mark wasn't as apt to try anything with the two of them, but I was still worried.

It seemed like the guys were back home in no time. It was true that Mark really cut his finger. They took him to the urgent-care center for stitches. They couldn't figure out why he hadn't driven himself. At least I was glad to hear he wasn't upset because I didn't show up myself. The guys said he had acted normal, never mentioning his behavior that morning. Afterward, he had them take him back to work and said, "Tell Linda I'll see her after work."

I was really puzzled. It almost seemed like he had no memory of what he'd done earlier. Had he actually gone to the extreme of cutting his finger so he would have a chance to see me? I'll never know, but it was sure weird. He came by after work, as promised, and explained exactly how he'd cut his finger. Since he didn't mention the morning episode, I thought it best not to even bring it up, since he was being so nice and loving, playing with his babies, telling me about work, and talking about our plans to start a nursery with the money my mom left me. It would be about a month or so before I received it, but we already knew what we wanted to do. It would be a new beginning for us.

We had decided that a nursery would be a very good investment with Mark's green thumb. Our barn was on a main street, so it would be easy to advertise. I wasn't getting a large amount, but it would be enough to start out slowly. I knew, the way Mark had with growing things, that our business would do well. He knew by now that I would never accept his starting a business with his new friend, Fred. They had talked about starting a business and calling it M & F Construction. They said it wasn't only their initials but that it also stood for motherfucking. Mark was so immature and hard when he was around this guy, and I was glad he was finally beginning to realize that it was either Fred or me. There was no way I'd ever be with him as long as he spent time with his new friend. During our whole separation, this had been one of the biggest issues. I just couldn't stand the way he acted around this guy.

The kids decided they wanted to have a party at the barn. It would be fun, they said. I feared another incident like what had happened after Roy and Nicki's party. Soon I learned my fears must have been an omen. Our friends across the street, Jim and Iona, had a friend named Mike. Like Jim, he was a truck driver. They had known him for a long time. Jim wanted me to meet him. I assured Jim I wasn't interested in any relationship, that I was still very much in love with Mark. He said he understood, but did I mind if he brought Mike to the party? Of course I didn't mind, knowing I could always use another friend. Mark would also be there, so I was sure there would be no problem. Anyway, Mark and I were having a very good day.

The party was successful, and everyone had a good time. However, there was one major problem. Mark had a friend named Bill that he'd known for years. He was a nice-enough guy, and he thought of him as a brother. He got real drunk this particular night. He and Roy were having a heated discussion out by the fire. Mark was standing nearby, just listening, not wanting to interfere. All of a sudden, all hell broke loose between Bill and Roy. Bill lunged toward Rod and punched him. I never saw Mark move so fast. He was immediately between them, pushing Bill backward and screaming, "Fuck you, man! That's my brother. You don't hit my brother, not ever. You motherfucker, you understand me!"

"Hey, man, I'm your brother too, man," Bill answered.

"No, you don't understand, fucker. That's my brother you hit. You get the fuck off my property. Now!" Mark ordered. He said it with such authority that Bill didn't hesitate in leaving immediately. They never saw each other again. Rod was okay. He wasn't the type to get in fistfights. He had to have been touched by Mark's loyalty and protective feelings for him. These brothers were very big on family loyalty. "You just don't fuck with my family," Mark had told me later.

The following day, in the late evening, Mark came over in a rage. Someone—I don't know who—had told him that our friend Jim had been trying to fix me up with his trucker friend, and supposedly, that was the only reason he'd come to the party. I couldn't believe my ears. Of course, he was really drunk by this time of night, and he was being totally irrational and illogical. He was going to go across the street and kill Jim for what he'd done, and no one was going to stop him. Poor Danny was in rage. He and Jim had become very close lately. He was Danny's good buddy. Jim was really good with all the young kids but had really latched on to Danny and Monty, Rory's little brother. They liked going four-wheeling together.

I couldn't understand Mark's behavior. He had hung around with me almost the whole evening the night before. When he wasn't right with me, he was keeping a watchful eye on me. He had to have known that nothing had been set up. What was happening to him? All this time that we had been split up, I never stopped telling him how much I loved and needed him. He knew me better than anyone. He knew I totally adored him. He was definitely losing it. The more he went on and on about how he was going to kill Jim for trying to set me up with someone, the more hysterical poor Danny got. Every time he would head for the door, he'd stop because of how upset Danny was. With me pleading over and over for him to calm down and come to his senses, before he did something that he'd be sorry for the rest of his life and Danny's hysterics, he finally came to his senses. He sat down with Danny, holding on to him real tight for a long time until he had calmed him down. Mark told him over and over, "Don't worry, Danny, I won't hurt your friend." Thank God. I'll never know what or who could have set him off like that, but I thanked God for a long time that we were able to bring him to his senses. The enormous compassion Mark showed Danny that night truly touched my heart, so as usual, I completely blanked out the damage he had done to my young son earlier. I seemed to only be concerned about myself.

Mark decided to stay all night. He knew he was pretty drunk and shouldn't drive. We had a good night, staying up for hours, just cuddling and talking about all the fun times we'd had and about what a special kind of love we had. He said over and over, "Why are we doing this to each other?" We talked about the dumbest things.

Like when it snowed, how we would make up two or three excuses a day why we needed to go to town for something. It was our explanation for getting to go fool around in the snow. We loved it when we'd get stuck. It was always such a challenge trying to figure out how to get out. It was fun just sliding the truck around in the snow. We laughed about the day he took me for a ride on his motorcycle in the snow. I was about three months pregnant, and dirt bikes had always scared me. I'd been dumped a few times while riding on the back with someone. He promised he wouldn't dump me. "Please, babe, come on. It'll be fun. I promise I'll go slow." Reluctantly I agreed, and as we took off, I urged him to go even slower than the crawling pace he was already going. Trying to oblige me, he went too slow, and over we went. We fell over sideways, in slow motion. I lay there laughing so hard, trying to yell at him at the same time and trying very hard not to pee my pants. It was funny. He was laughing so hard he couldn't get the bike off us. We ended up lying there for a minute, laughing until we cried. We must have been a sight. Needless to say, I never made him go that slowly again when he explained that it was our slow speed that caused us to fall.

We had so many fun memories like that. It was a good night, after all. It had been excellent therapy for us to stop and talk about all the special things in our life. About how close we were compared to other couples we knew, about how we were always best friends. That night, he held on to me all night, tighter than he ever had. It was like he never wanted to let me go. He'd come a long way for someone that didn't know what it was like to cuddle in bed with someone, someone that had never liked to be touched when he was sleeping. He'd become as cuddly as a teddy bear since he'd been with me.

Before he left for work the next morning, I reminded him about his appointment on Thursday for his brain scan. "You can't miss it, honey. It will take a long time for another appointment." He wouldn't forget. He said he probably wouldn't see me for a couple of days but that he'd call. Wednesday was the day we both went together to see Mary, our counselor. Mark never showed up. Mary explained to me that she knew he wasn't being honest with her about his feelings for me. She couldn't believe it when I'd tell her about all our good days and all the times he'd been requesting to come home. He'd been play-ing games with her, which was making it impossible for her to help. He would try to convince her that he wasn't drinking or smoking pot. I knew she could tell that he wasn't taking his medication. He'd found out that it just didn't mix well with the drinking.

When I got home, I tried to get a message to him to remind him that I'd be there early in the morning for his brain scan appoint-ment. I had no way of knowing if he'd gotten the message or not. The next morning, when I got to Moms and Pops's to pick him up, he was still sound asleep and almost impossible to wake up. "I need my coffee and doughnuts, babe," he insisted. "Someone always wakes me up with coffee and doughnuts." I'd heard about how Claudia had made this a habit, trying to get on his good side all the time. I went off to get him doughnuts and coffee, like a good little girl.

"We have to hurry, though, honey, or we'll be late for your appointment." When I got back and he had fallen asleep again, I was angry.

"I'm sorry, babe, but I'm still wasted."

It turned out that he and Pops had stayed up late smoking pot. They had gotten blitzed, he'd said. He really enjoyed having some special time with Pops. I know that was the truth, because I know how much Moms and Pops and their daughter, Gretchen, meant to him. By the time I got him awake enough and rational, it was defi-nitely too late to make our appointment. I was so upset with him. He'd waited so long for this test, hoping it would show a physical reason for his bursts of anger. I never thought there was anything wrong with him. He was too smart. In my opinion, he was grasp-ing for anything, and this was his last hope. I always thought that he knew for sure they wouldn't find anything, and that was why he didn't want to keep the appointment.

While I was still there, he'd convinced me to lie down and cud-dle with him for a little while. Then his buddy came over. He wasn't there for ten minutes, and I had to leave. I was sick to my stom-ach, watching Mark change from one person to the other almost the instant Fred walked in the door, and he knew I was mad when I left and very disgusted. We exchanged a few not-so-nice words as I left.

The next day was Friday, and Mark called in the afternoon. I reminded him that my brother Ronnie and his family and my dad and Virginia were coming over. It would be our last chance to be together for a while because Ronnie had to go back to Germany to finish his tour of duty. He'd only been home to attend Mom's funeral. Mark said not to worry; he'd be there. He loved my dad a lot and liked Ronnie also. He'd been very touched when Ronnie loaned us his guns. The guys were planning to go up in the hills to shoot, and I knew that Mark was looking forward to it. "Don't worry, babe, I'll make sure we have a good day. I won't embarrass you. You know how good I've been at that lately. See you tomorrow about ten. I love you." He hung up. Another Friday night without him, I thought to myself. For some reason, I felt especially lost and alone this night. I needed him very much. I read poetry and played my guitar out on the roof until I got too cold. I jotted down a special poem on paper and dated it, something I didn't usually do.

Lesson

One and one are two, of course,
But sometimes our steps would precisely match
And we knew that we two were one.
But now that you have gone away, I learned,
If you take one from two, there is nothing left.

This was exactly how I was feeling this night. I thought about what Mark had said during our phone call earlier. He said tomorrow was going to be a really special day. He promised. What did he mean? Were we both finally fed up enough with all the head games? Would it finally be the day that we decided to be together again? Was he finally through with his friend that had caused us so many problems? This was something that he knew I was insisting on. Time would tell. I fell asleep feeling very hopeful that everything was going to be better from tomorrow on.

The single most important healing force is hope.

My acrobatic circus dream,
To crash through the hoop of separation,
And land softly in your arms. My dream of Mark.

CHAPTER 12

IF ONLY

This Saturday in Oct was a very special day for my family. My dad was very surprised when I told him that Mark and I had been separated. "Don't worry, Dad, it's just temporary. We're real close to moving back in together, and he is seeing a counselor about his drinking, because he'd gotten a little violent lately." Dad was glad to hear that everything was going to be okay, and I had tried to make the situation sound not so serious. I knew that my dad loved Mark very much and was happy that I had him in my life.

The guys went shooting up in the hills right above us. They all had a good time. I was sad that I couldn't go, since it was such fun to do. I was eager to show off to my brother what a good shot I'd become. Mark bragged about me, his prize student, saying that I'd become a better shot than he was.

I couldn't shoot the twelve-gauge like he could, though. No matter how hard I tried, it would always hurt my shoulder. Mark never hurt his shoulder, because he almost always shot it off his hip. We'd joke about how cool he looked when he shot it that way. I couldn't believe how accurate he was. (This way of shooting would be an important fact later on.)

Danny and Monty, from across the street, went shooting also. Monty had a .22 rifle that kept misfiring while they were shooting. He said he'd been having trouble with it. When they got back, my brother cleaned it really well, saying that sometimes a dirty gun will misfire. It didn't help, so he came to the conclusion that the problem was with the firing pin. He said we probably needed a new one. It was no problem; they were cheap and easy to install for someone who knew guns. (This would be another important fact later on.)

Ronnie and his wife, Karen, had a new video camera. They had brought it with them last April when they'd come and left us the guns. We had a lot of fun "hamming" it up for the camera, especially Mark, as he played harmonica for Darla. She rocked her little head back and forth to her daddy's music.

It seemed he was never without a baby in his arms. At one point, for the camera, he gave Donny a beer to hold and a cigarette, thinking that it would be a cute picture. He did a Budweiser commercial from up on the deck, saying, "I still live in this damn barn, and I'm still with the old lady."

In the background, I was saying, "We all know he's a damn liar, 'cause he don't live here no more."

At one time, he was helping Richie work on the stereo in his truck. We gave all the kids rides on our horses, and there were a lot of fun family activities captured on film that day. I will treasure it always.

At the end of the day, Rory showed up. He drove his truck up the driveway very radically, as he usually did. It was where he parked it that caught my eye. He pulled it right up so it was parked nose to nose with Mark's truck. He had even bumped it a little when he stopped. Was this a warning of things to come? No, it couldn't be. Mark was embarrassed about all the jealousy he'd shown lately. When Rory got out of his truck, he called out, "Hi, Markie."

Mark answered, "We was gonna film you on your way in. You'll have to do it again." Dad and Virginia had already left, saying their goodbyes to everyone. It was late afternoon now, time for Ronnie and his family to leave also. They still had a long drive ahead of them to San Diego.

Before leaving, Ronnie took me to the back of his van to show me his guns. Mark was standing with me. Ronnie told us we were welcome to keep his guns for as long as we needed them. We told him how much we appreciated them and how many hours of fun they had provided us with. We promised we would continue taking excellent care of them. He showed me his .44 pistol, and I made a little joke about needing a bigger gun for protection. Did he want to trade me for the .22? I could tell he must have thought I was joking, since he never really answered me. I really hadn't been, though. I knew that I had mastered the .22, and I was ready for something bigger and more powerful. "Shooting a .44 makes you feel like Dirty Hairy," I joked. It was meant as a playful little hint that I wanted a bigger gun to use, but my brother did not take it seriously. (Another fact that would play into later: .22s are not very powerful.)

When Ronnie left, he took our dog, Maynard, with him. They had wanted a small dog for Margaret to play with, and we knew Maynard would be perfect. Now it was just Mark and me and our babies. We sat down on the love seat he'd made for us out of rock and watched our babies playing nearby, as our giant tree provided plenty of shade.

We talked about many important things on this special day. Mark talked about how badly he wanted us back together so Mason could come live with us again. He wanted to move back with us very badly, and Mason's mom had finally told him that he could. In September, when Mason had called, telling me he could come, I'd had to tell him that his dad and I were separated and that right now it would be impossible. He was sad.

Mark talked about how badly his trees needed trimming and said he'd be back the next week to trim them, if he wasn't living here already. Was that a hint? I wondered. He had worked so hard making everything green and beautiful. We had shade everywhere. He was so proud of all that he'd done to our place.

He reminded me of the seventeen sheets of plywood that he still had for fixing up the place. He'd do it alone, he said. He didn't need Fred to help. He was getting burned out on him anyway. He said, "Babe, we gotta get our shit together. This place is falling apart without me." I reminded him that we would see our counselor, Mary, next week. We would tell her now badly we wanted to move back in together and see what she thought about it.

"I want Mason back here with us, where he belongs," he said about the son he loved very much. "I want us all to be together again, babe." He smiled and gave me a sweet, tender kiss on the forehead. I loved this gentle, loving side of him when he made me feel like a queen.

"I know you do, honey," I answered sympathetically as I kissed my fingers and touched his lips with them. "Don't worry, we'll talk to Mary about all this next week."

He told me that being a bachelor wasn't all it was cracked up to be, that he wanted his family back. He said he wanted to get Danny and Mason some motorcycles, dirt bikes. He said that ATVs were much too dangerous; they were going to have to settle for dirt bikes. He was emphatic about it. There was no way those boys would ever get an ATV.

We walked around together for quite a while, watching our babies play while he watered the trees and bamboo. "You are such a good mom, babe. I love the way you take such good care of our babies," he said in his most mature, fatherly voice. "Bet you can't beat us guys, though," he said as he screeched off with Donny on his shoulders and Darla on mine. We raced a few times around our big tree, babies squealing and laughing, till I could go no more. The babies loved to do this, and of course, Darla and I always lost, but those babies had so much fun every time we had our little races.

Afterward, we'd crash out under our huge shade tree, exhausted. If it was a hot day, we'd always end up hosing each other down, laughing our butts off. Mark always hosed everyone down. When Lily used to come over from across the street, she always had to be on the alert. Lily was built very well for a girl of thirteen, and she was on her way to becoming a beautiful woman in a few years.

One day, Mark said to Danny and Monty, "Here comes Lily, you guys. When she gets close enough, hose her down good so you can see through her T-shirt." Shaking my head and smiling, I saw my young son look to me to see if I would say no, and when he saw the look on my face, he shrugged his shoulders. "Cool!" was all he said, heading for the hose. "You guys are silly" was all I could say, twirling my index finger next to my ear to make the crazy sign. Of course, they had obliged his wishes, thinking it was a great idea. Poor Lily, she was always very careful if any of them was holding the hose when she came over, but sooner or later, they would get her. She was always a good sport even though she would get a little embarrassed. She always knew that it was all in fun.

It was getting late, and it was time for Mark to leave. I felt a little sad, since we'd been having such a perfect time, and I wasn't ready for it to end. Why couldn't we always be like this? We always were before, for such long periods between our fights. "I don't think this separation has helped us at all. If anything, I think it has hurt us," I told him in a soft yet serious voice.

"Maybe not," he answered. "Maybe it'll make us try extra hard not to let it ever happen again. You know that old saying, 'You don't know what you've got till it's gone.'"

I knew what he was trying to say, but I wasn't sure I agreed that our separation had done anything except cause us problems. Today had been different. Today had been so special, and as he kissed and hugged the babies goodbye and me, we agreed to meet at Leroy's house in a couple of hours.

Richie and Dawn were staying tonight to play music with Jimmy and Rory. Mark had been practicing a lot on his harmonica, and he was very proud of himself. I'd heard him playing for Darla in his truck that afternoon, and my brother had it on video. She loved him to play for her. It was settled; he'd see the babies and me at Leroy's later on.

I hadn't told him about something that had been going on all day. My daughter Shelley had already called me three times from her apartment in Vegas. She desperately wanted me to come see her tonight. Her husband, Rudy, had gone hunting for the weekend, and she had found out that an old high school friend was going to be playing with his band in a club in Vegas. It was a kid that I was very fond of; he was a very talented musician. I had watched him start out at backyard parties when we had lived in Mira Loma. It was really exciting to know that he had progressed to Las Vegas.

"Please, Mom, please come," Shelley had pleaded with me in her earlier phone calls. "Get Rory to bring you. I know Rory will

bring you if you ask him. He'd have fun." I knew that she was probably right. There wasn't much that Rory wouldn't do for any of us,
especially if it was going to be fun. "Please, Mom, I'll never have this
chance again. Rudy's gone for the whole weekend." I didn't know
what to tell her. I'd kind of left her hanging all day about it. Ten
minutes after Mark had left, she called again. "Are we going to see
Jagger?" It was how we affectionately called him, referring to Mick
Jagger.

"Probably, honey. I'll get back to you as soon as I talk to Rory
and see if Gene and Linda will babysit."

She wanted me to come so badly, and I just couldn't turn her
down. We hated being so far apart, and we really missed each other.
We had been best friends for so long, and now we hardly ever got to
do anything together. I knew that it would be fun. I hoped that Mark
would understand.

I called Rory and got an okay from him. Gene and Linda were
a probability, and they'd let me know when I got to Leroy's. Because
Donny had a nasty cold, they were the only ones that I would have
left him with. Since I was going to Leroy's for the night anyway, I'd
be taking everything I needed for the babies and myself to spend the
night away from home. The decision was up in the air until I got to
Leroy's and heard from Gene and Linda, but how would I tell Mark?
He was really looking forward to being with us tonight, and I didn't
want to hurt him, since the day had been so perfect.

He hadn't been to a party at Leroy's with me since we had separated. When I'd been there on weekends, he'd been considered the
enemy because of the way he acted around me. Lately, he'd only
spent time at Leroy's during the week, when I wasn't there. Before
our separation, the five of us had been like best friends, Leroy, Rory,
Jimmy, Mark, and I.

Rory was the mechanic of the group. There wasn't much he
couldn't do with a car, and we all depended on him constantly. He
and Jimmy had been best friends for a long time. It was neat that
three of our very favorite people had finally ended up all living at the
same house, Leroy's. Jimmy was still working very hard during the

week as an electrician. He worked with all four of Mark's brothers, and we were all pretty close.

The drive to Leroy's seemed to take forever tonight. I was still very torn between going to Vegas and staying at Leroy's with Mark. Nothing was definite yet since I had only solved one out of three problems. The transportation wouldn't be a problem, because Rory and Shelley were pretty close, and he wouldn't miss a chance to see her. Gene and Linda would have an answer for by the time I got to Leroy's. They only lived a few miles from him. The biggest problem would be trying to figure out how to break the news of my new plans to Mark.

As soon as I got in the house, Leroy said, "Mark called a little while ago. He said to tell you he'd be here just as soon as he got cleaned up. He didn't want you to think he wasn't coming." That hurt, because now I really knew how much Mark was looking forward to tonight. What was I going to do? Then everything seemed to happen at once. Mark arrived, kissed the babies and me, and upon hearing the music from the boys, went into the bedroom with them to practice his harmonica.

"Will you be in soon? Babe?" he asked. "You've got to hear how good I am getting," he said, beaming proudly. Gosh, he was handsome, and I adored him.

"Yeah, honey, just as soon as I change the babies."

Not five minutes later, Gene and Linda got there and told me they could babysit. When Dawn heard that I was going to Shelley's, she asked if she could take Darla home with her and Richie. It would be fun for them, she insisted. I said okay, knowing that it would be a little easier on Gene and Linda, with Donny sick and all. Now was the hard part. How would I tell Mark? Rory was rushing around, getting ready and telling me to hurry.

"I've still got to tell Mark I'm going. I don't want to hurt his feelings, and you know how weird he's been about you lately. I hope he doesn't pull his jealous act again. I'm going to ask Leroy if he wants to go with us." Leroy said there was no way that he wanted to go, so there went that hope. Then I got a great idea. Why hadn't I thought of it before? I'd ask Mark to go with us. When I told Rory of my plan, I could tell he wasn't too excited about it. Mark had put him through hell lately with all his stupid accusations. Rory was flexible, though, and he went along with it for me.

I walked down to the end of the hall, to Jimmy's room, where they were playing. I was so proud listening to him play his harmonica. He was sitting on the end of Jimmy's bed. It was great to have him be a part of us again, like he always used to be. I stood there through quite a few songs, hardly believing my ears. He really was playing along with them, and he sounded good. His practice had definitely paid off.

When there was a pause in the music, I said, "Honey, you're getting so good I can't believe it. I'm so proud of you." His face showed so much pride, and he looked happier than I had seen him look in the last six weeks. He was finally happy and content, and I had no way of knowing how soon it all would change.

How was I going to tell him that I was going to Shelley's, and with Rory, of all people? I almost decided right then not to go. I'd give anything to be able to make that decision over. If only I hadn't gone. If only I'd been more worried about Mark than I'd been about disappointing Shelley. If only I'd followed my innermost feelings. If only this and if only that. It was the beginning of all the "if onlys" that would haunt me for the rest of my life.

Gene and Linda had walked up to me by this time. I knew that Mark was wondering what was going on, with all the whispering and puzzled looks. I managed to get his attention and waved him to come out and talk to me. I needed to talk to him alone, without the loud music overpowering us.

We were alone in the hallway, and the music paused briefly. "Honey, a good friend of ours is playing in a club in Las Vegas this weekend. Rudy's gone hunting with his dad, and Shelley wants me to come with her to go watch him play," I explained excitedly. "She wants to go so badly, but she says she won't go unless I come." The look on his face told me exactly what he was feeling, sad. He was very sad and disappointed.

"When are you leaving? How are you going to get there?" he asked.

"Rory said that he would take me. We're supposed to leave pretty soon. Why don't you come with us, honey? It'll be so much fun. I've got a little money to gamble with." There, I'd done it, and much to my surprise, he was handling it quite well. Even though he was sad, he was being very calm about it.

"I thought that tonight might be the night we'd get back together, babe. I wanted to go home with you and the babies really bad."

I had broken his heart—the look on his face told all. "We'll still get back together, honey, you know that," I said as I reached up and cupped his face in my hands, so I knew that I had his full attention as we looked into each other's eyes. "I'm only staying one night, and as soon as we watch him play tomorrow evening, we'll head for home. Come with us, please," I urged. "I already asked Leroy if he wanted to go, and he doesn't want to."

"Babe, there's no way I can go. I've got business to take care of tomorrow. I've gotta be here. There's a lot of money involved."

Knowing full well what kind of business he meant and that it involved his new buddy, Fred, I said, "Let him take care of it for you." I knew there was pot and meth involved.

He answered firmly, "I can't, babe. I can't trust him to do this for me. I have to take care of it myself." It had been one more time that he had inadvertently let me know he was definitely burned out on this guy and that he could not be trusted.

"Then it's okay with you if I go? You won't be mad? I don't want to hurt you, honey," I gently explained. "I want to make sure you understand. I don't want anything to ruin the special day we've had."

I was so relieved when he said it would be okay. "I'm not happy, but I understand. Like I said, I was hoping we'd get back together tonight, babe," he said as he lovingly stroked my hair. He knew how much I loved that. "That's why I've made plans to wrap up some business tomorrow. I've gotta be here to take care of it, so we can start off with no problems." Thank God he was okay. I could tell how disappointed he was, but I thought he'd be all right.

Even though Mark was acting okay, I was still a little worried about him. I had seen his happy face while playing music turn to a sad face the moment I told him of my plans. It was so different from the happy, peaceful look he'd had only moments before. A special look that I would never see again. I'll never forget how happy and content he'd looked that night. I know now that I made the wrong decision that night. Why had he seemed so strong to me when the fact was that he was already beginning to fall apart?

The babies were all taken care of, and Mark convinced me not to worry, that he was fine. He would stay for a while and play a little more music. It was time to say goodbye.

We stood at the beginning of Leroy's hallway, straight across from the front door. He kissed me and held me tight, as if he never wanted to let go. I was glad no one was around, so that we had this special moment alone. Rory was warming up his truck. We talked about how much we loved and needed each other and that we were glad we'd be together pretty soon for good. I said we'd be home late Sunday night and that I was leaving the car here if he needed it.

"Honey, if you get a chance, will you go by Gene and Linda's tomorrow and see your son? I know how happy it would make him, being sick and all. He loves his daddy so much."

"Of course, I will. You know that," Mark said. I gave him one more hug and kiss and told him not to forget how much I loved him.

"Thank you for understanding. It means a lot," I said as I turned to leave.

He pulled me back to him for one last hug. "I love you so much, babe." I'll never forget how tender he had been. As he held me tightly, I felt that familiar quiver of his, the same quiver that always made me sure of how very much he loved me.

I left that night feeling assured that all was well and things were only going to improve from that moment on. He had handled everything just fine, and I was a little upset with myself for the way I had overreacted, which had become one of my famous traits these past few years. All that worrying for nothing, I thought to myself, smiling and shaking my head. Or was it? If only I had known his true feelings, but I didn't.

The Clock of Life

The clock of life is wound but once, and no man has the power
To tell just when the hands will stop, at late or early hour.
Now is the only time you own, so live and toil at will.
Place no faith in your tomorrow, for the clock may then be still.

—Coby

No one ever knows when their time will be done.

CHAPTER 13

THE BEGINNING
OF THE END

B y the time Rory and I arrived at Shelley's, it was early Sunday morning. The drive had been fun. Since I'd never done much traveling, any type of a trip was exciting for me. Rory was very compromising on the music situation: I could only handle so much of the loud rock-and-roll; after a while, it made me a nervous wreck. I could listen to my kids play it for hours, but the radio was different. Maybe it was because when my kids played rock music, I was so proud of them and their talent that it didn't bother me.

Rory introduced me to a group called Styx. He couldn't believe that I had never heard of them before. I fell in love with their music that night, and I've loved them ever since.

I always enjoyed riding in Rory's truck. He had so many lights and gauges on his dash it seemed like you were in a jet plane. He was known to drive a little fast, but I always felt safe with him. Rory was smart; Mark and I had always thought so, and we were never too proud to ask him for help. Rory appreciated our asking and always wanted to help out. I was very sad about all the recent tension Mark had caused between them lately.

Our adrenaline was going strong by the time we had said our hellos at Shelley's, so naturally it was time to go gamble. I couldn't believe what happened at Circus Circus. There was a great big silver dollar machine that you could put in from one to five dollars. The more you put in, the more you'd win. Rory only put in one and told me to pull the giant handle. When I did, we couldn't believe our eyes. We won $200 on that one pull. We were set for the weekend. From that moment on, all I can remember about Rory is hearing him say over and over, "I love this town. I love this town." He was so funny. I'm pretty sure that this was his first time gambling. He wasn't even going to be twenty-one until the following July.

Needless to say, we had a really good time gambling with all the Circus Circus money and visiting with Shelley. The next day, we slept for a while, or at least rested a little. We had planned to see Jagger's last show that night. We had been in and out most of the evening. We'd come back to Shelley's apartment one last time, and the phone was ringing. It took a while for her to get the keys out and open the door, but when we finally got in, the phone call was for me. It was Linda.

"Linda, maybe you should leave to come home now. Donny's cough is really bad." I was surprised to hear her say that. I had always been secure in knowing that she could take care of my babies as well as I could, sick or not. I knew how much Donny loved her, and I knew that he would respond to her just as well as he would to me. Gene and Linda had a special, very loving relationship with our babies.

I was very puzzled by the call, as she had known I would be. I reminded her that she could do as much for him as I could. I explained that we were just getting ready to go see Jagger play and that we'd be home late tonight. She was at a loss for words, knowing all too well that I was right. As I hung up, I assured her that as soon as we watched him play for a while, we'd be leaving to come home. She had acted weird, I thought to myself.

About ten minutes later, the phone rang again. It was Linda. "Don't worry about Donny. He is fine," she informed me. She hadn't been able to talk before because Mark had been standing right beside her. He had just gone out to the garage with Gene, so she could talk now. I'll never forget the desperation in her voice when she spoke. "Linda, you'd better get home right away. Mark is acting crazy. He's been here most of the day, drinking and pacing the floor. He told me to call you and get you to come home right now, no matter what it took. He's the one that said to say Donny was really sick, not me." That, at least, had explained that mystery.

"Don't worry about Donny, he's okay," she assured me once more. She went on to say how worried she and Gene were about Mark. He was really acting weird and had been drinking all day. They thought I should get home as soon as possible.

I definitely didn't like the sound of her voice. I could tell she was really worried. She and Gene had never been one to make a bigger deal of something than was necessary. She said again, "He told me to say anything I had to say, but to get you home now."

What was wrong with him? He'd been fine when I'd left. He said he'd be fine, not to worry. I was so disappointed that I had to leave without seeing Jagger, but I had no choice. By now I was very worried about Mark. How could he let himself fall apart like this?

I told Shelley and Rory how sorry I was but that I thought it best that we leave right away. Something was really wrong. I'm not sure they understood, but they went along with it for my sake. We were all disappointed. I was still apologizing to Shelley as I hugged her goodbye. "Don't worry about it, Mom. It's okay, really." My ever-dependable daughter hardly ever let me down. We had a very special relationship, thank God.

As we drove off, I was trying to convince myself that he'd be okay. Once I got home to him, he would calm down right away. Feeling a little cheated, we decided to stop at Cactus Kate's on the state line. It turned out to be our big chance to lose about half of what we had left of our Circus Circus money. It probably caused about an hour's delay. The way Rory drove, though, we probably weren't that much later than most people would have been if they hadn't stopped. I knew Rory wasn't all that thrilled about leaving early, but there was nothing I could do. Being the easygoing guy that he was, he handled the little inconvenience caused once again by Mark just fine.

Rory had bailed me out of problems with Mark quite a few times. He had put up with all the stupid jealousy lately and had spent hours listening to me talk about all the bullshit that was going on since we'd been apart. He was just plain old fed up where Mark was concerned, and I really couldn't blame him.

The long ride home gave me lots of time to think. I knew how easily and quickly Mark could lose control and how sorry he always was later. We knew the type of violence Mark was capable of, and it always made Rory as mad as it made me scared. I wondered what could have set him off. He'd been fine when I'd left. I'd been looking forward so much to going home and being with him. Why this? He's crazy and someday he is going to kill someone.

A million things went through my mind during the long drive home. I developed a nasty headache in no time. All the excitement and hope I'd had only hours earlier about my life with Mark had suddenly vanished with one phone call. The hope and excitement had turned into a worrisome, unsuspecting mess. Why me? What was happening to my life?

Rory was silent most of the way home. I knew him really well. Rory was always in total control of himself. Usually, when he was quiet, it was because he was upset. That was how he controlled it. He had learned a long time ago not to bother putting in his opinions about Mark and me. We always ended up back together, so it was best not to get involved. He hated it when I would involve him. Sometimes I needed his help. What could I do? His irritation was totally understandable, and I really appreciated the silence at this time.

When we got off the freeway, I realized just how upset with Mark Rory really was. Something happened that really shocked me. We saw, together, right in front of us, the longest, brightest falling star I had ever seen. It seemed to last forever. "Wow," we both said.

"Did you see that?" Rory asked.

"Yes, make a wish."

"That Mark dies," Rory said very harshly.

"Rory! How could you?" I said in shock.

"Mark dies," he said again very angrily. Assuming he was kidding, I kind of shrugged it off, saying he shouldn't joke like that.

"You never want to wish someone dead," I said.

Did Rory have some kind of special power? Was his wish an omen of things to come?

We were almost home. I was going to pick up my car and go straight to Gene and Linda's. I knew Mark would be okay as soon as I got there. He was probably asleep by now. Linda had said that he was real drunk, so I was really hoping he was asleep by now. I would lie down with him and cuddle him the rest of the night. It would be hard to sleep. Rory and I were wide-awake from the drive.

I was worried and Rory was pissed as we turned the corner by Leroy's house. We were surprised to see Mark's truck parked out on the street. He must have come over to wait for me. We turned into the driveway. My car was still there, and Rory pulled in just to the right of it. Then, all hell broke loose. I couldn't believe it.

The minute Rory opened the door of the truck to get out, the passenger door of my car opened. Mark jumped out like a raving maniac. He had a gun, a pistol. "I'm gonna kill you, motherfucker," he was saying over and over as they wrestled for the gun. I ran to Leroy's front door, hysterical. It was locked. I banged on the door with my fist as hard as I could, screaming for Leroy as loud as I had ever screamed before.

"Leroy, help! Help me, please. Let me in. Mark is trying to kill Rory! He's got a gun." It was no use. Still, I kept screaming and banging on the door. The dogs were going crazy inside. Why wasn't Leroy waking up? My god, what was I going to do? I'd never been so scared in all my life. Two men that I loved so much were trying to kill each other. This was real. This time there was a gun. Why was this happening?

I had to get in the house somehow and get some help. They were still fighting and screaming at each other. I prayed with all my heart that I wouldn't hear a gunshot. There was one more chance, Jimmy's room. I could see that his light was on as I ran to his bedroom window, and I could see him sleeping on his bed.

I banged and banged as hard as I could through the bars on his window. All the while, I was screaming at the top of my lungs, "Help me! Jimmy, wake up! Help me, please. I can't get in. They're going to kill each other. Please, somebody help me!" He didn't move. He couldn't even hear me. He was sound asleep. By now the fight had been going for a long time. How long could they keep this up?

Everything happened at once. Rory had the gun in his hand now, pointing it at Mark. "Back off now, you motherfucker," he ordered. Thank God Mark had responded. Just then, Leroy opened the front door and started screaming at us all.

"Get out of here right now, all of you. I'm sick and tired of having to deal with all this craziness. Just get out of here, now!" Poor Leroy, he had no idea what was going on. He thought it had been just another crazy fight as he slammed the door and went back to bed. He felt bad later when he found out what had happened.

With Mark still screaming at Rory that he was going to kill him, me crying hysterically, and Rory still keeping him at a distance with the gun, Rory somehow managed to throw me his keys from the truck. "Unlock the door, quick!" he yelled to me.

After I got the door unlocked, Rory joined me just inside. By now Mark had moved in a little closer and was standing by my car. He had a jack handle in his hand, waving it and screaming like a madman, all the while ordering Rory to give him back his gun.

"Give me my motherfucking gun, you motherfucker. Now!"

"No fucking way, you asshole! No fucking way." Rory answered through the slightly opened door. Rory didn't want Mark to see what he was doing. He'd immediately taken the bullets out but was not satisfied with that, assuming Mark probably had more.

We heard the sound of glass breaking. Mark broke a window in my car with his crowbar. "Give me back my gun now, you asshole, or I'll break every window in the car."

"The cops," I said, "I've got to call the cops."

"No," Rory said. "Wait." What was he doing? He was trying to do something to the gun.

"Rory, what are you doing? You've got the bullets. He can't hurt us now. If you give it back to him, maybe he'll leave now that we're inside."

"Give me a minute. I'm trying to mess up the firing pin so it won't go off. He's probably got more bullets." We heard more glass breaking.

"My god, Rory, what are we going to do? He's gone crazy. He's going to destroy my whole car. He wants to kill you. God, what are we going to do? Somebody please help us. Mark, please stop this. Think of your babies!" I screamed.

Rory was still fidgeting with the gun. His hands were shaking. I'd never seen Rory scared before. What was happening to us? It was like a nightmare, but it wasn't. It was real. We couldn't just wake up and have it over with. Not this time.

"One more chance, motherfucker. Give me the gun, now! When I'm done with this one, I'll start on your truck!" Mark screamed. He only gave Rory a few seconds to respond before we heard the third window break. From where we were, we couldn't tell which ones he was breaking. At that time, it didn't matter anyway.

"Rory, please give him his gun. I know he'll leave. If it were your truck he was destroying, you'd give it to him," I pleaded.

"Just one more minute. I've almost got it."

Crash. A fourth window smashed.

"You've had enough warnings, you motherfucker. Where are the cops? They should be here by now. I know you called the cops, bitch." It almost seemed like he really hoped we'd called the cops. Maybe he wanted to be stopped. Maybe he was hoping he'd get arrested. If only I had called the cops.

Rory was finally satisfied with whatever he did to the gun. He started walking toward Mark. He was standing between my car and Rory's truck. Both doors were still wide-open. "Throw the crowbar across the yard, motherfucker, and I'll give you your fucking gun. It doesn't work anymore. Then you get the fuck out of here and don't ever come back," Rory said with much authority. There was no question that he meant it.

Mark threw the crowbar, and Rory tossed him the pistol. "Please, Mark, just go. Please go before it gets worse," I begged, tears streaming down my face.

Hearing my voice must have set him off again. When it seemed like he had turned to leave, still between the vehicles, he lunged toward the open door of my car. Reaching right behind the passenger's seat, he grabbed another long bar. Rory though it was a shotgun when Mark turned around with it. It happened so fast.

Mark pushed him backward and held the bar across him. Rory went backward inside his truck, on his back across, the seat. He looked up behind his seat and saw the barrel of his shotgun sticking out. He pushed Mark back with his feet, and that gave him the time he needed. He grabbed his gun and cocked it defiantly, "Get the fuck out of here, now, motherfucker, and be thankful I didn't kill you!"

Mark looked like a fool. He was trying to stand up and back up all at the same time. He kept falling and stumbling since he was very drunk. I don't know how he managed to put up as good a fight as he did, being so drunk. He was in a rage. People who are in a rage can usually find more strength than those who aren't. Thank God Rory was so strong.

He had definitely gotten Mark's attention when he cocked that shotgun, and he was finally leaving, but not without a few final words. "I'm gonna kill you, Rory, you motherfucker. You won this time, but I'll get you."

Once again, I pleaded, "Mark, please don't do this." I was still crying hysterically.

"Shut up, you fucking bitch! You're nothing but a fucking slut."

I couldn't believe he was saying that. What had happened to my Mark? What happened to set this off? He'd been fine. How did he allow himself to lose control like this? Why did he do this? By now we would have been together in each other's arms. Instead, I was more scared than I had ever been in my life, wondering what else could possibly happen.

We stood outside until he drove away. Somehow, Rory managed to get me in the door. I was so shocked, and I felt like I was going to throw up. My heart was beating so fast that I thought I was going to have a heart attack. I couldn't calm down. Poor Rory was trying so hard to calm me.

"It's all right now, he's gone. I won't let him hurt any of us. Just calm down," he said, trying to give me a comforting hug. Nothing seemed to work. His hug made me realize just how scared he had been, as I could feel his whole body shaking. We could hardly believe what we had just gone through. This sort of thing only happened in movies, we said later.

Now, what should we do? And where was Mark going? Would he come back, maybe with another gun? Would he park somewhere and watch us? He had done that before. Would he go to Gene and Linda's and try to take Donny?

We knew that in his frame of mind, he would be capable of almost anything, because he was totally out of control and Rory had made him look like a fool. We knew this fact would bother him more than anything. Nobody made Mark look like a fool and got away with it, especially in front of me.

When he sobered up, he'd know he had messed up big-time. This was serious. How would he ever get out of this one? You can't just say sorry when you've tried to kill someone. No, sorry wouldn't help this time. It wasn't me he had threatened, it was Rory, and Rory was unbelievably mad.

During their struggle with the gun, there had been a very loud, definite click. Mark had actually pulled the trigger when the gun was buried in Rory's stomach and had really tried to kill him; there was no doubt about it. Thank God there was something wrong with the gun, or Rory would be dead because of me. Mark tried to kill Rory because he'd done me a favor, and now Rory wanted him dead. "Don't call the cops," he insisted. "I'll take care of this myself." How would this end?

Please, God, let it all stop, I prayed.

Jimmy, where was Jimmy? I needed him badly. Feeling sick to my stomach, I started to walk down the hall toward his bedroom when I realized I was going to throw up. I just made it to the toilet, but it wouldn't have mattered if I hadn't, since all I had was dry heaves, just like I had in the shower after Mom had died. It was so weird.

Feeling better after I finally stopped vomiting, I continued my journey to Jimmy's room, wondering if he could have slept through the whole thing. The answer was no. He was awake when I opened the door. "Boonie"—it was his affectionate nickname—"do you know what just happened?" I sat on the bed beside my son, feeling physically and emotionally exhausted. "I banged on your window so loud, honey, we couldn't get in. Mark has gone crazy. He pulled a gun on Rory and broke all the windows in my car." I began to sob. Trying to comfort me, he reached for my hand. "Boonie, I was so scared!" I continued on, voice quivering and pulse racing. "I screamed and screamed for you. Didn't you hear me? Leroy's so mad. He just came out and screamed at us and went back to bed." I went on and on. "He doesn't even know what happened. I can't believe Mark did this, honey!" I was shaking my head in disbelief. "Why didn't you come out?"

"Why can't you believe he did this?" he said in a stern but loving voice. "This is Mark, remember? He goes crazy sometimes, and I am not stupid. He scares me real bad when he acts like this, and I'm not ashamed to admit it." He stood up angrily and walked toward the window to close his drape. "I heard what was going on, and I was scared. I wasn't going out there. He's crazy." I knew he was right. Mark had gone crazy. I didn't blame Jimmy at all. My Boonie had always been the most easygoing kid I had. He hated problems. He hated people who couldn't control their tempers. He had seen enough of that from his dad when he was young. He hated violence. Violence frightened him badly, just as it should. People get hurt from violence—sometimes they even die. He just wasn't a fighter like Richie. Richie would never back down from a fight. My two eldest sons had always been very different in that way. I admired Jimmy for it. He never had a problem with admitting that violence really scared him. Sometimes being scared could be the smartest thing of all. Thank God he hadn't been involved this time.

We had to decide what to do next. I finally calmed down, although my whole body was still shaking. We needed to get out of here. We didn't want to upset Leroy any more or involve Jimmy in any way. He worked with all of Mark's brothers every day. He didn't need any problems concerning Mark. We called Gene and Linda and told them what happened. They had feared something like this, the way Mark had been acting. When he left their house earlier, they had hoped he was going home to bed. He'd been very drunk. "Had he been there in the past half hour?" I asked. "Could he have driven by and not stopped?" No, he hadn't been by, and they didn't think he had driven by either. They probably would have heard his truck. "I need to get my baby. I'm afraid he's watching for us to leave. He knows I'll be going to get Donny. What should we do?" Gene had a good idea.

By now, it was at least two in the morning. There was hardly anyone out on the road at this time. "Meet us in fifteen minutes in the field behind the market. We should be able to tell if either one of us is being followed. There's no way he could follow us this time of night without our knowing it." It seemed like a good idea. No one else had a better suggestion. It was now or never. For the second time that night, I was scared to death. We had to get out of Leroy's house and get my babies. I needed them so badly. When I got in Rory's truck, he was loading his shotgun.

Not even thinking about what he was doing, I said, "Thank God for that shotgun. Who knows what could have happened if it hadn't been behind the seat." For the first time since all this had started, Rory cracked a smile. "Why are you smiling? You scared him to death the way you cocked that gun. You could tell that there was no question in his mind as to whether or not you'd pull the trigger if he hadn't left."

He smiled again. "Thank God I didn't have to pull the trigger. The minute I cocked it, with all that authority, I realized it wasn't loaded. It's amazing the kind of power you can have with an unloaded gun. It's all in your attitude, I guess."

Even I had to smile. "You might say that this was our lucky day, huh?"

"Yep, we sure were lucky, more than once."

Gene's plan went very well. We met them in the field, got Donny, and said our thank-yous and goodbyes. Now what? I'd told Gene and Linda that I hoped Mark didn't come over, causing them problems, pumping them for information. I was so scared someone was going to get hurt. I wished they hadn't been involved.

Holding on to my precious baby boy felt so good, but I knew I would not be happy until I was holding his sister also. "Mommy loves you so much," I repeated a few times as I gave him big hugs and kisses.

"Don't worry about us. I'm not. I can handle Mark if I have to," Gene assured me as we drove off. "He's not going to hurt us."

Gene's attitude made me feel a little more relaxed. I was glad that he didn't seem scared, since all this was because of me. I wished I could be more like him. I knew I was scared to death, no question about it.

As we headed down Main Street, I assumed we were going to Dawn and Richie's to get Darla. Without warning, Rory pulled into the shop where he worked, Tires West. His boss, Dave, was really nice. Rory was a very trusted employee at that time, so naturally, he had his own set of keys to the shop. Still puzzled as he pulled in, I was wondering why he had stopped.

He jumped out of the truck and unlocked one of the big steel garage doors. He got back in, drove inside, hopped out, and closed the door behind us.

"We'll be safe here," he assured me. "No one can get through those doors."

During the five-minute drive since we'd picked up Donny, Rory had noticed a few questionable headlights behind us. He explained that he was just being cautious. "Don't worry, there's a phone here in the office." I was glad to have this chance to relax a little.

"Rory, I don't believe that this is happening to us. I feel like I'm in a scary movie and we're the main characters." My voice was strained, and I was so tired. "I'm so scared. Isn't it all just like a movie, what's happening?"

"Yep," he said as he nodded in agreement.

"I don't want to be in this movie, and I just want it all to stop," I continued on. "I don't even watch these kind of movies, because I can't stand all the tension, they scare me to death." I just kept wondering how it was all going to end. "Rory, I don't want to be scared anymore. I can't believe how scared I am." He was trying so hard to ease my mind, and I knew that he hated having to deal with me when I was like this, always because of Mark.

"Don't worry, I'm not going to let anything happen to you or me. I don't want anyone to get hurt."

"Not even Mark?" I questioned him immediately.

He didn't care much for that statement after what he'd just been through. "Mark's going to die, if I have anything to say about it. I'm sorry, that's just the way it is," he said very matter-of-factly and with no hesitation. It was very painful having to hear Rory say that, knowing all too well that he meant every word of it.

Even I couldn't make an excuse for Mark this time. I knew that what he'd done this time was very bad. It was so bad that he had pulled a gun on Rory. I hated to have to admit that I understood why Rory felt the way he did. Mark had done the unthinkable thing, and it was unforgivable, as far as Rory was concerned. I didn't blame him at all for having this attitude. I had just gone through the whole thing with him. Rory just doesn't get upset about anything very often, and there was no doubt that he was very upset and really pissed him off.

Before we left the tire shop, we tried calling down to Dawn and Richie's so we could tell them we were coming to get Darla and let them know what was going on. They didn't answer. A few minutes later, we tried again. Still no answer. We came to the very logical conclusion that they must be sound asleep and couldn't hear the phone. Oh, well, we headed that way and would try again when we got closer to their house.

It was about a forty-five-minute drive to their place. When we were about thirty minutes away, we changed our plans. Having lost all track of the time and wondering if we'd be able to wake up Richie and Dawn when we got there, we decided we'd just get a room for the rest of the night. We were both exhausted, and it had been a very long time since I had slept.

Since we still had some of our Vegas winnings, the money was no problem. We decided it would be nice to be able to lie down and relax; morning would be here soon enough. Much to our surprise, we quickly learned just how soon that would be. You should have seen our faces when we got settled in our room and found out what time it was. It was almost five o'clock in the morning! We had a good laugh about what a stupid waste of money it was. "Oh well, it wasn't our money anyway," I told Rory.

"Yeah, but it would have been if we hadn't just spent it." We both laughed.

By now, I had stretched out with Donny on one of the two beds. I was beginning to realize that it had been a good idea. It felt great to lay down with my baby boy cuddled in my arms. He was very fussy but finally went to sleep for a little while. As it turned out, it was well worth spending the Vegas money, after all.

All of a sudden, Rory was waking me up. "No, not yet," I said. "Have a little compassion," I whined. He didn't listen. It was time to go. He was missing work because of all this, he reminded me. By the time we got to Dawn and Richie's, it was around nine o'clock.

I'll always have this picture stuck in my mind of what I saw when we opened the front door that morning. It was one of those pictures that you keep on file in your mind forever so you can refer back to it anytime you want.

Darla was sitting in her little car seat. She was right in front of Richie, on the coffee table. She was in the best mood, smiling and laughing at his funny faces and funny noises. In one of his hands was a simple bowl of cereal, in his other hand a spoon. A very simple picture, I know, and yet it will always remain one of my very favorites. To see my eldest child, now a man, sitting there with one of my priceless twins, projecting so much love toward her, had definitely filled my heart with pride that day. Even with all that I was going through, I was still able to stop and think about how truly lucky I was. I loved my kids so much, and I knew how lucky I was to have them.

Before we left, I decided to try calling home. Danny and Becky were staying across the street at Jim and Iona's, so I tried their house first. I got Danny on the phone, and I was trying to fill him in on what was happening. I didn't want them going to the barn for any reason until I got there. I was afraid that Mark might go there. Before I could finish, Danny interrupted me. "Mom, he's there now. I just talked to him. He called over here, wondering if we knew where you were." Mark was at the barn. I couldn't believe it.

"How was he acting?" I asked. "What kind of attitude did he have?"

"I didn't notice anything. He was real nice. He said that he needed to talk to you. He was just trying to find you. He was being the nice Mark," my young son said in a very strong voice. "He was real nice to me."

Wow, I was shocked. I was assuming, because of what Danny said, that Mark had come home to apologize, once again, with his heart in his hand. Didn't he know how serious this was? Did he really think it would be that easy this time? Didn't he realize what he had done? This was no game. He pulled a gun on Rory, our good friend Rory. He'd even pulled the trigger. Rory could easily be dead. Didn't he realize that Rory wanted him dead? This was unbelievable.

I could tell from what Danny said that his mood was the one he was always in when he was sorry. It was his "I know I really fucked up this time" mood. I'd seen it so many times. The saddest part about it was that I knew for sure how really sincere this mood was. It was no bullshit. It wouldn't be so easy this time, though. His last stunt had involved much more than me. His last stunt had affected lots more than just me.

I immediately hung up the phone with Danny and called the barn. This would be interesting. What could he possibly have to say? It was ringing, but no one answered. Just when I was about to hang up, he answered. "Hello." My voice was very firm and direct.

"What are you doing there? I can't believe that you have the nerve to show up over there after what you did last night."

"I just needed to talk to you. I've been looking all over for you, babe," he said in a sad, weakened voice.

"Did it ever enter your mind that maybe I was hiding from you because you scared me to death last night? You were crazy! You pulled a gun on Rory for no reason, and you tried to kill him!" I scolded him relentlessly. "I can't believe you did that. All the times you've preached to us about respecting guns. What bullshit it was all this time." By now, I had really made him mad. It always did whenever I pointed out things that he did that he was ashamed of. He was actually mad at himself, not me.

"It's obvious that I made a big mistake coming here," he said, "thinking we could talk." His voice was becoming very angry.

"You ruined everything last night. What you did was real bad. We would've been together today. I can't believe you did that. You convince Rory that you're sorry. If you can manage to do that, then come see me."

"Fuck you, bitch! I'll take care of both of you. It won't be pretty either." He hung up on me. He was back in his badass attitude again. What did I do? I was just too mad to give him a chance to explain. I couldn't help it. Didn't he realize what he had put us through last night?

I felt bad, realizing the way I immediately attacked him, not even giving him a chance to talk. There was nothing I could do about it, though. I was really upset this time. This was much too serious, and even though I still loved him, and knowing how sorry he was, I wasn't sure that I would ever be able to forgive him this time.

Within minutes, Richie's phone rang. It was Mark, for me. "Hey, bitch. Say goodbye to the chain saw and your brother's shotgun. They're both mine now. You'll pay for this." He slammed the phone down. Was this ever going to stop? How much more could I take? I didn't ever want to be afraid again.

What had happened to the man that I loved so much? The man that had always made me feel like a queen? The man that I knew loved me with all his heart? How did he let himself become so weak? Why couldn't he learn to control himself so that he wouldn't do things he would always be sorry for later? I had so many unanswered questions running through my mind that I wondered if it was finally really over between us.

With all that was happening, Richie decided he should come home with me. He didn't want me to be so afraid, and he knew Dawn would understand. It would just be for the night, until Mark had calmed down.

My eldest son was really worried about me. Rory thought it sounded like a good idea, and I agreed. I was afraid of what Mark might do, and now things had worsened since he had taken the shotgun. It seemed that our movie wasn't over yet. I hated scary movies. I hated movies with sad endings, and I hated movies that ended tragically. I didn't want anything more to do with this, and it didn't seem possible that it could have a happy ending.

A few hours after we returned to the barn, the inevitable happened. Mark called again. He thought I'd bring Richie back with me, and it had made him even madder since I had someone to protect me. He knew that this was not the day we would talk, and the threats began.

"Hey, bitch! Do you have your little army there to protect you? They can't stop me. I'll get you all," he said as he slammed down the phone. A few hours later, he made one more call, saying pretty much the same thing.

He'd scared us badly enough that we stayed up all night with our guns loaded, wondering if he would really go through with it. We weren't taking any chances. Too much had happened, and by now, Mark was a desperate man who was slowly losing control once again. He proved that when he stole my brother's shotgun.

In less than twenty-four hours, he had become totally unpredictable. He was up against a wall, and nothing he tried was working this time. He was so angry with himself that he lost all his self-respect. He turned his anger toward us as he became a tough guy again, the one he hated so much. He'd always learned so much from his mistakes in the past; that was why it was always so easy to forgive him. His apologies were always sincere, and he was easy to forgive.

I knew him so well since we had always talked deeply about our feelings. We had spent hours and hours discussing how he felt during our fights and after our fights. He learned early that he could tell me anything he was ever thinking. It was very important to him to know that he cold tell me anything he was feeling. Many times he had admitted to me what an ass he had been at times. He never hesitated admitting that he'd been wrong about something.

For a long time, he had worried about his brothers seeing too much of the new him. The tender, caring, gentle, loving side that I loved so much. He was so proud when he could finally say that he didn't care if they made fun of him any more. That had been a big step for him.

Little things like finally being able to tell his mom "I love you" meant so much to him. I'll never forget that day, seeing how proud of himself he was, having him tell me that I'd taught him the real meaning of love. It was because of me, he'd said, that he was able to tell his mom "I love you" so easily.

On this Monday afternoon, I was remembering a lot. I knew how easily he could carry something too far. So far that he didn't know how to stop it. He didn't know how to get out of it. Nothing he tried was working, but he wouldn't give up. There was still tomorrow. There was too much at stake to just give up. Everything he had ever wanted was at stake. He could learn an important lesson from all this craziness. Just two days earlier at the barn, he had said that very same thing to me. "Maybe our separation has helped us," he'd said. "Maybe it would make us appreciate our special love a little more. Drinking along with pot and meth could change him in an instant. How did I ever let all of this happen?"

There had to be a way out of this. There had to be a way to stop all this craziness. Maybe tomorrow he'd find the answer. There's always hope. How many times had I told him, "Any problem can be solved if you want to solve it bad enough"? It was true. It had been true for me my whole life.

I wonder if this is how he felt. It is a good saying.

The journey of life
Takes us through many times of happiness and sadness.
We remember the happy times
As the most loved and enriching experiences of all.
Although the sad times
Do not outwardly appear to benefit us,
They are, in reality,
What builds character and strength in all of us.

—Scott Palmer

CHAPTER 14

TERROR

It was morning, and my whole body was numb from the cold, and I realized I'd been sitting on the metal roof above my stalls for quite a long time. Richie and Rory had been outside most of the night with loaded guns.

Before I came outside, Danny and I had been lying on my bed, talking and watching, remembering and watching. We wondered how this could have happened, if Mark would really be coming as he'd said he would. "Someone's gonna die." Those were the exact words he'd used.

This time was so different from any other time before. Something had been added to his violent outbursts; he was playing with guns now. Wasn't he the one that had always told us that you just don't play with guns, not ever? That guns can kill?

The night had seemed so long, and now the darkness that I feared all throughout the night had finally, slowly disappeared. The sun was about to peak over the mountain. I knew its secret—Mark had told me all about it when we had first met, and I had teased him when I heard him telling his babies the same story not too long ago, knowing that they could not understand yet.

"You see, every morning before the sun rises, it always takes a little peak first. That way, it can decide whether or not it wants to come out. If it's going to be a gloomy, rainy, cloudy, yucky day, it just doesn't come out. But if the day is going to be pretty, clear, and warm, it'll be happy and keep coming up higher and higher and shine bright for us the whole day." This was the Mark that I loved so very much.

I smiled a little when I saw that the sun had decided to come out today, even though my eyes were filled with tears by now. I thought about how many times Mark and I had watched it together. Morning was always his favorite time of day. I wondered if we'd ever share this special time again, and it was hard to believe what he had done, but I knew that it was true.

I was so angry with him, but at the same time, I had this terrible pain and sadness in my heart. I loved him so much. How do you just forget a million happy times? I knew that the bad was very bad, but the good was so, so good. The good had been so special and perfect, and it seemed like we had always been together. He was my man, my lover, the best daddy ever, and my very best friend. He was my life. Was it all gone forever?

Richie came up the stairs, rifle in hand. What a terrible sight to ever have to see, my eldest child carrying a loaded gun. We had feared for our lives all night, and the man I loved had fallen apart on me, practically right before by eyes. Still, I was trying to be optimistic. All my life, I had been an optimist. Why was I having so much trouble today?

I prayed that today would be a good day. The sun was shining bright and pretty. Maybe today would be the day that all this craziness would finally end.

It was Tuesday, a beautiful fall day. If only I'd known what the day had in store for us. If only I'd known what would happen that night and how badly our hearts and minds would be scarred forever. As I sat there this Tuesday morning, wondering what the new day had in store for me, I still had plenty of hope left in my heart. No one had been hurt yet. For that I was very glad.

As I glanced around our two and one-half acres, there were happy memories of Mark everywhere I looked. We had managed to fill two years and three months together with more happy memories than most people have in such a short time. We were just beginning; there were still lots of happy memories to make. The best part of all was still ahead, raising our priceless babies together. I wasn't ready to stop making memories. Not yet.

All of a sudden, the beautiful, peaceful silence was broken. A baby was crying. It was Darla, of course, always the early riser, like her daddy. The moment I picked her up, she wrapped her tiny little arms around my neck and squeezed her tightest squeeze. I really needed that. We peeked at Donny, still sound asleep. "Ssh, ssh," she said, putting her little finger to her lips, smiling her beautiful, sweet smile, her big eyes as large as saucers.

They were fifteen months old, and they did the cutest things. We spent hours just watching them. They were starting to say so many words now, and we knew that they were very smart. They had been saying Da-Da for a while already. It was a word that was going to break my heart a million times for a long time to come.

While I was feeding Darla her breakfast, Rory said he was going to work, since everything seemed okay. Besides, Richie was here with me, and Rory knew that I wasn't as scared when it was light outside. The poor guy was totally exhausted; he'd hardly slept at all for days, thanks to Mark.

I told him how sorry I was to be such a problem and thanked him for everything. "It's not your fault. You don't have anything to be sorry for except that you met Mark! That's all you should be sorry about." It was an attitude that would never change, and I understood why.

"I don't blame you for the way you feel, Rory. I was there, remember? It would be so easy if I didn't love him so much." My eyes were filling with tears. "It would be so easy to just walk away from it all," I continued on. "We all can't be as strong as you all the time, always totally in control."

Rory's expression was one of total disgust. "It's a weakness that he hates himself for. He needs serious help, and he knows it. He should never drink again."

Trying to change the mood, I gave him a hug goodbye, and I said, "Maybe we'll all be able to get some sleep tonight. Maybe it will all stop today."

"Don't count on that," Rory said. "Hey, Rich, you want to go hunting with me tonight? Mark-hunting?"

He looked up. "Sure, I do," answered Richie with a smile of vengeance on his face as Rory left.

I was totally exhausted, both mentally and physically. I was sure glad that I didn't have to go to work like Rory did. I could have never done it. Becky was up by now, and poor Danny had fallen asleep on my bed with Monty's .22 rifle still next to him. He'd stayed up most of the night too, helping us watch. Richie said he felt fine because he'd gotten plenty of sleep the night before. "Go lie down for a while, Mom. You look terrible," my protective son urged.

"Thanks, honey." I smiled, knowing that he was right. I felt like a zombie. Why not look like one too? I was surprised that I couldn't sleep. My stomach was still in knots from worrying. I had this gut feeling that something really bad was about to happen. My optimistic attitude wasn't working very well.

I couldn't stop thinking about what Rory said as he was leaving. Would he really kill Mark? I wondered just how far he would really go. I certainly didn't want him dead, even though I understood Rory's feelings. Was Mark worth going to jail for? I knew that I had to try to convince Rory not to go through with this. Do I have the right to ask that of him? I wondered. I just didn't want anyone to get hurt, and I was very frightened.

Soon after I lay down, the phone rang. Please, God, don't let it be Mark. I knew it was real early for the phone to be ringing. No one ever called this early. I was so happy that it was my sister-in law. We had talked for a while when someone beeped in on the line, and this time, it was him. Saying I had to go, she understood, and I clicked back to Mark nervously.

He sounded very depressed. Yesterday's calls from him flashed through my mind. I would be very careful not to set him off this time. I would let him talk, but I was nervous and hoping so much that he would be decent to me. "Hello," I said very calmly.

"Hello, babe. I just called to tell you not to worry. You know I could never hurt you or the kids. You don't need any protection from me. I know how you are, and I didn't want you to be afraid of me."

Still being extra calm, I said, "Don't you realize that I'm only afraid of you because of the things you've said and done? Why would you ever want to hurt Rory? Rory has been our good friend for a long time. He hasn't done anything except help me out since you've been gone."

I was scolding him as tenderly as possible. "I'm lucky that he's helped so much. You should be glad too. Why did you try to kill him? What has he ever done to you? I don't understand, honey." I spoke very softly and gently. My last sentence drew a very dirty look from Richie.

"I can't believe you're being nice to him. Just hang up," Richie said. He was very upset with me.

"I don't have anything against Rory, you know that," Mark said. "I don't know what happened to me. I don't know why I did that." He continued to explain, staying calm and soft-spoken. I was glad for that.

"Babe, I just started going crazy thinking about you being in Vegas, the place where we'd had so much fun together. I'm just a stupid fuckup, and I know that I don't deserve someone like you." He went on and on. "I know it's probably too late, and I know you're tired of hearing it, but for what it's worth, I'm really sorry."

I was stunned, and I could not believe what he was saying. "I'll tell Rory I am sorry, and believe me, it'll never happen again, babe. I just didn't want you to be afraid of me anymore."

He still had more to say.

"I'm not going to steal your brother's gun, so don't worry about it, and the chain saw is safe. It's over at Fred's house. I'll bring it back as soon as I can." This call lasted about forty-five minutes.

During our entire conversation, Richie sat ten feet away, never missing a word I said and giving me one dirty look after another. I knew that he was upset that I was being nice to Mark, and I could not blame him for his feelings.

After a while, the conversation turned to our relationship. His earlier strength was fading, and I could tell he was falling apart, as his voice would quiver and sound very strained. At one point, I could tell that he was crying, and I knew his words were coming from his heart. He'd asked me if there was still any chance at all for us, any little hope to cling to.

"I'm falling apart, babe. I can't imagine life without you and the babies, and I don't want to lose you. I'm nothing without you. Nothing means anything to me without you and the babies. I'm lost, and I don't know what to do. I just want to hold you. I know if I could hold you, I'd be okay."

My god, he was breaking my heart. He was falling apart, and he was begging me to please help him. I was helpless, and I knew it was out of my hands this time. There was so much more involved. I couldn't just forgive him and tell him to come home this time. I had to think of Rory and all that Mark had put us through. I couldn't just listen to my heart this time like I always had before. This time was very different.

"Honey, you know how much I love you. That kind of love just doesn't go away overnight, but you did something really bad the other night. You jumped Rory with a gun. What if you'd killed him? What if he was dead now? Could sorry bring him back? If that gun hadn't been broken, he'd be dead. You pulled that trigger—"

He interrupted me immediately.

"What?" His voice was surprised and shocked.

"You pulled the trigger when the gun was against Rory's stomach." I repeated very matter-of-factly in a stern voice.

"Babe, I didn't. I swear to you I didn't. If I had, the gun would have gone off. Think about it. Please believe me. I know I've done some terrible things, but you know I wouldn't lie about something like this. Please?" he begged.

I didn't know what to say. Rory had been sure. He had no doubt that Mark had pulled the trigger, and yet I would have sworn on our babies' lives that he was telling me the truth. He'd never lied to me about his actions in our fights before. He'd always been big enough to admit how wrong he was, sometimes feeling ashamed for days and days.

The only thing I could figure out that would explain it was that he'd been so drunk and so out of control he'd had no idea that he'd done it. That was still no excuse. He shouldn't ever allow himself to get in that condition if he couldn't control himself, and I couldn't make excuses for him.

"Babe, please. I just need to come see you for a little while. I know if I can just hold you, I'll be okay." He repeated it again. "Tell Richie he can leave. I'd never hurt you. You don't need him to protect you. Please? I'll never ask anything of you again."

I was very confused, and my heart wanted to tell him yes so badly, but I knew that everyone would hate me if I did. They always said that he did the things he did because he knew that I'd always forgive him. Richie was still sitting in the chair, glaring at me, listening to every word I said. I had to be stern.

"I'm sorry, honey. You can't come over right now. This is a big thing that happened. Rory is so mad. Rory wants to kill you for what you did. You have to try to talk to him. You convince Rory that you're sorry, then you can come see me." His whole mood changed immediately.

"Fuck you, then, bitch. You'll be sorry!" His mood had changed instantly. "You give your priceless Rory a message for me. Tell him he's a fucking liar and killing me won't be so easy. He'll wish he'd called the cops the other night when I'm through. A lot of people will." Before I could say a word, he slammed down the phone.

Almost instantly, the phone rang again. I was so relieved it wasn't Mark. It was for one of the kids. I was a nervous wreck, and I was shaking all over. I was angry with Richie, and I knew I had no right to be, so I couldn't let him know how I was feeling.

About half an hour passed when the phone rang again. When I answered it, Richie could tell who it was. He was still sitting in the same chair, never taking his eyes off me. His look told me exactly what he was thinking. "Don't you dare weaken. Don't you dare be so stupid. Don't be so nice to him. You're an idiot if you let him come over!" His message was loud and clear. Wasn't that exactly what he said to me after the first call?

"Babe, I'm sorry. I don't know what's wrong with me. Please let me come home. I can't live another day without you. I won't live another day without you."

"Honey, I can't stand to hurt you. I hate hurting you. It's just not up to me this time. Rory could have died for no reason. You know that Rory hasn't done anything wrong. He could be dead just because he's my friend. This is so serious." Once again, Mark denied pulling that trigger, begging me to believe him. "I don't think you're lying. I think you just don't remember, because you had gone crazy. You can't let yourself get like that. You have to stop drinking."

"I will, I promise," he said. "I'll do anything you want. Please just let me come home. I need to hold you. I'll be okay if I can just hold you."

"I can't, honey, I just can't. Please try to understand. Look how fast you got violent with me a little while ago. I'm afraid of you. For the first time since we've been together, I'm really afraid of you. I have been since the other night."

He wasn't giving up. His voice was so desperate. "Please, babe. I need you. Please?"

"I'm sorry, honey. You have to clear this up with Rory first."

"You bitch! I'll clear this up with Rory, all right. I'm gonna hurt you more than you could ever imagine. How would you like it if your Rory and your Richie were both dead? Would you hurt then? You bitch! If I can't have you, I'll make sure no one can have you. And your priceless son Jimmy won't have a job anymore either. All I've gotta do is say the word, and my brother will fire him. Say goodbye to your son's job. You're gonna pay for this, bitch. Just watch. You're gonna hurt more than you ever hurt before," he threatened before hanging up on me.

"Wow, I don't believe this. He's crazy. He's really crazy," I whispered sadly as I hung up the phone.

"Yep" was all Richie said, grinning from ear to ear.

My car. I had to figure out how to get my car from Leroy's. The windows had to be fixed. What a mess it must be, I thought. I hadn't even had a chance to look at it the night it all happened. Rory said that Mark hadn't broken the windshield or back window. He'd only broken the four on the sides. Only! I thought to myself. What a neat guy. I figured that I could drive it home okay as long as I didn't have the babies inside. Rory said there was shattered glass everywhere.

Leroy must be upset that it was still in his driveway. I hadn't talked to him since that night. I was angry with him for the way he'd screamed at me and slammed the door. I just wanted to get it out of there. Richie said that he'd take me over there and put the babies in his truck on the way home. No, the babies could stay here with Danny. We'd leave at about one o'clock, I told my son. It was already around eleven.

Before we left, Mark called one more time. This call started out exactly the same. He apologized and begged me to let him come home. He used the same phrases every time he called. "Babe, I can't live without you. I won't live without you." It was back and forth with love and threats. "If I can't have you, I'm gonna make sure no one ever has you."

Usually, he started out with, "I just want to hold you, babe. I know I'll be okay if I just could hold you. I'm lost without you. Nothing seems important without you." Another one he used over and over was, "I won't live another day without you." Why was I letting Richie's attitude influence me? Why wasn't I following my heart? If I followed my heart, I'd only have myself to blame if things went wrong. If I took Richie's advice and things went wrong, would I blame him? Richie had a perfect right to feel the way he did.

During this call, Mark said something that really worried me. He said that it wouldn't be a good idea to start up my car. We wondered if he'd done anything to it. I didn't think he'd take a chance of hurting his babies, but then again, I never thought that he could do what he was doing either. He definitely scared me, which was exactly what he'd wanted to do.

Richie was very brave. He started it up for me as I stood back— way back, in fact. Aside from all the glass inside, it was fine. As we pulled out of Leroy's, I yelled to him that I had to stop up at the corner for gas. He followed me in and parked in front of the store while I went to the pumps.

I couldn't believe our timing. I heard someone screaming from across the pumps and looked up to see that it was Mark. He was screaming at me. "You fucking bitch, you're gonna pay for this! You're gonna be sorry, you slut!" There was that word again. I couldn't believe it.

I replied with such quickness that it amazed me. "I thought you were with the slut!" I screamed back. He was with Claudia in her little pickup truck. For the first time in my life, I had been able to come back with the perfect comment. I was a little embarrassed about the scene we made, but I was still proud of myself. Then Mark noticed Richie parked in front.

"You got your gun, motherfucker?" Richie obliged him by lifting his rifle high enough so he could see, and Mark nodded. "Good, 'cause I've got mine too." With that, he jumped in the passenger side of Claudia's truck and whizzed by me. I managed to get in one more vicious little comment as she drove past.

"You said you couldn't stand that slut, honey," I said proudly. I'm sure that he was able to convince her that I had lied, even though I hadn't.

When we got back home, I felt much safer. I'd been afraid that Mark was going to show up. Where was he going in Claudia's truck? If he was coming out here, I'd soon know it. The way our barn was situated, it was impossible for anyone to sneak up in the daytime.

We felt very secure this afternoon. Mark knew we'd be watching for him, so he wasn't stupid enough to try to sneak up on us in the daylight.

He called two more times after we got home. The conversations were almost exactly like the three earlier calls, only much scarier. After he changed into this mean guy when I once again told him no, his threats were only of death. This scared me badly.

We decided to call the cops and ask them what we should do. It had definitely been the right decision. They told us they would send someone out immediately to take a full report.

The officer they sent was very nice. His name was Joe Morgan. He urged us to leave. "You're too far out for us to get here fast enough if he does come," he said. I tried to explain to him that I knew Mark would never really shoot me. I was more afraid that he might do something like burn the barn down if I wasn't here. I thought it was important to put all the threats that he was making on record.

Officer Morgan agreed that it was a smart thing to do, but in his opinion, it was even smarter to go somewhere for the night. Knowing that Mark had the shotgun and I only had my .22, he warned me, "If he breaks the door down and has the shotgun raised to shoot, don't let him shoot first. You'll know he means business once he breaks down the door."

Again, I assured him that I knew he would never shoot me. "He loves me too much. He's just upset because I won't let him come home. He'd never shoot me, I know."

Officer Morgan's comment about the shotgun being raised to shoot would unfortunately stick in my mind.

Between late afternoon, when Officer Morgan left, and seven o'clock, there were three more calls. The mean side of him was meaner with every call, and I could tell he was getting very drunk. My rejection, no matter how gentle I would be, would set him off instantly, and by this time, all his threats were of death. It was scary, but I still was convinced that he would never hurt the kids and me.

I wasn't leaving my home. I wasn't going to let him scare me like this. I talked to Gene and Linda that evening, and they said Mark had been there earlier. Linda had been short and to the point with him. He had asked if he could talk to Gene. "No," she told him. "Gene's in bed. His back's bothering him a lot. He doesn't want to be bothered."

Mark hadn't given up easily. He said he really needed to talk to them, that it was very important. "No, I'm sorry, Mark, another time." Her orders had come from Gene himself. He hadn't wanted to deal with him today. Like the rest of us, they were very upset with him because of his recent behavior, since they were completely aware of everything that was going on. This was one more rejection for Mark to handle.

That same afternoon, Mark had also gone to see Leroy. He respected him and knew he could talk with him. When he'd gotten there, he sat up at the bar with his back to the front door. Other people were there also, and soon Rory came home. When he saw Mark at the bar, not wanting to cause a problem in Leroy's house, he went straight to his room.

Mark desperately needed someone to talk to, but instead of help, he received another rejection. Leroy told him that it would be best if he left. Mark didn't want any trouble. He knew that Leroy was just as upset with him as the rest of us were. He quietly walked out the door. During the day, we all had rejected him. What would he do now? Had he lost everyone that he loved?

It was starting to get dark at the barn. Danny and Becky were scared. They wanted to leave like the cop said we should. I didn't want them to be afraid like this. I called Jim and Iona. They knew what was going on. It would be fine with them if Danny and Becky spent the night. I would send them over after we ate. We were cooking dinner, fish sticks. The kids loved them. The kids relaxed a little, knowing they were going to Jim and Iona's.

Earlier that afternoon, I had called Rory to see if he was coming back tonight. He'd said no, that he had to get some sleep. He was exhausted. "Don't worry, you'll be okay. Richie's there with you." What could I say? Rory felt pretty sure that there wouldn't be any problem with Mark, but by this time, Mark had gotten the word that Rory wanted to kill him. Mark's anger was aimed more toward him than me, he'd said. I hoped he was right.

Later, I tried Jimmy. "Please come stay here with me tonight. I'll feel a lot better."

"Mom, you know how I hate this. Please don't ask me. Mark scares me so much when he's acting like this."

"Please, Boonie," I begged, "just tonight. I promise I won't ask you again. Rory's too tired. He hasn't slept in days. Please, please?" What could he say? I was begging.

"Okay. I'll be there in a little while," he promised.

I felt better. It was eight o'clock, and Mark had called eight times today. The violent threats had gotten vicious, all pertaining to death. My whole family was going to die. He was going to hurt me more than I could ever imagine. He wouldn't live one more day without me. Could I stop him if I just let him come home? Were people going to die because of me? This was serious.

I called Roy and Nicki to see if they'd seen him. Roy told me he had talked to Mark a little while ago and he was acting crazy. "When

I talked to him earlier, he was acting crazy. He's not himself, and if I were you, I'd get out of there." His brother's voice was stern, and I knew that he was serious. I immediately changed my plans.

No problem, I thought to myself. I was getting out of here, no hesitation now. Roy's comment was all I'd needed to hear. Mark had crossed over the edge, and I knew we weren't dealing with the real Mark anymore.

The kids and Richie were very relieved that I had finally decided to leave for the night. Richie called Dawn and told her he'd be home tonight after all. He was leaving soon. He had to get gas in town before nine o'clock, or he wouldn't make it home.

Just to be safe, I decided to pack a few things that were very special to me, things that couldn't be replaced. Mark had threatened more than once during the day to burn the barn down.

I called Leroy to tell him the latest news, that I was going to leave.

"Tell Jimmy he can pick me up now." He'd already left. "Good. When he gets here, he can just take me and the babies back to your house." That was okay with Leroy.

I tried to gather my most special things. I put everything in a small box I'd set on the couch, right by the front door. The kids were done eating and wanted to leave now. "No, wait until Jimmy gets here. He should be here any time now, and we'll drop you off on our way out." They didn't care much for that idea.

At eight thirty, Mark called one more time. "I'm only gonna ask you one more time, babe. Are you going to let me come home or not? All I want to do is hold you," he said in a beaten-down tone. I could tell he was sad and that he was also very drunk as he slurred his words.

"Mark, why are you doing this, honey? Why are you scaring us so bad?"

"Shall I come home now, or is someone going to die?"

"Honey, please don't talk like this. You know we love each other more than anything in the whole world. We'll be together soon. We'll talk to Mary."

"I'm coming to get you now, bitch." He hung up the phone. Was it just another threatening call? This was number nine. This last call didn't really scare me any more than the previous eight had, but just as a precaution, I did what the officer had told me to do if Mark called and said he was on his way.

I called 911 and told them about the phone call. I knew that they would not be able to respond on a phone call only and that Mark had to be on the property before they considered it a threat. Well, at least they had been alerted.

By now I was anxious to get out of there, just in case he'd finally been serious. Where was my Boonie? Shouldn't he be here by now? I was still gathering things to take. I was so thankful that the babies were asleep.

There was one on each couch. I would let them sleep until Boonie got here. At around eight forty-five, Richie couldn't wait any longer or the gas station would be closed. It was just a small town market with gas pumps. Mark's Mom was the night manager there at the time. When Richie hugged me goodbye, I started to fall apart a little. "I feel like I'm being deserted," I told him.

"Don't worry, Mom. You'll be all right. Boonie will be here soon. Mark won't do anything. He's not that stupid."

"Not in his right mind, anyway," I added. "It's when he's not that I worry." He knew exactly what I was trying to say. "Thanks, honey. You be careful. I love you so much."

"I love you too," he said. As he started to open the door, he saw Monty's .22 rifle sitting there. He picked it up and leaned it against the stove. "Danny, this gun can't help you if you're unable to get to it if you need it. Keep it back here with you, just in case." Richie was smart. We never would have thought of that.

"Tell Dawn I love her," I said as he left. I hope he makes it to town in time to get gas, I thought to myself.

CHAPTER 15

MY WORSE NIGHT EVER

For the first time since Mark's death threats began, Danny, Becky, the babies, and I were all alone. The nervous churning in my stomach would not go away. I was very tense on the inside as well as the outside, and I worried that my behavior would frighten the kids. I called Leroy again.

"Leroy, Boonie's not here yet, and Richie just left," I said in a serious, concerned voice. "He had to get gas by nine before the store closed, or he would not make it home tonight. I'm so scared, and we are all alone," I said softly, with my back turned to the kids, hoping they could not hear the obvious fear in my quivering voice, not wanting to worry them.

Remembering my earlier call when I told Leroy that Mark had just called saying he was coming to get me now, he feared that I was going to break down as he sensed the urgency in my shaky voice, realizing how frightened I really was.

I thought back to the earlier call when I had heard him telling Rory that Richie had left and that Boonie hadn't arrived yet and that we were all alone for the first time.

"Rory's coming, don't worry. He's already gone out the door," Leroy said as he kept me on the phone, trying desperately to calm me down. He thought I was going to have a nervous breakdown, knowing me as well as he does. "Just stay calm. Rory's on his way.

Boonie will probably be there any minute. Everything will be okay. Just stay calm."

"Leroy, I'm so scared. What if he comes right now? We're all alone."

He just kept talking to me, trying to think of anything that would make me feel better. "He's been calling all day. He hasn't done anything yet, has he? He won't come. Don't worry, you'll be okay. Boonie and Rory are both coming." It was just a few minutes until nine o'clock now. Leroy was still talking. He never let me know how scared he really was for us. He stayed very calm and optimistic the entire time. He didn't want us to feel so alone, and as long as we were talking on the phone, I didn't. "Don't worry. You know you worry way too much," he said.

Danny and Becky were glued to the window. I don't know why, since it was so dark out they couldn't see a thing. There was only one lamp lit, and it was on the bar, directly across from the front door, about ten feet away.

My box was packed; it was on the couch right by the door, and it was too full to close. On the very top was my crucifix, which had hung in my living room for the last twenty years, wherever I'd lived. I knew that God was always protecting us, always watching over us. Mark knew how much my crucifix meant to me. I told the kids to get away from the window a couple of times, but they weren't listening to me.

All I could think of as I was trying to talk to Leroy was, "Please, somebody hurry. I didn't want to be so scared anymore. I couldn't stand seeing my kids afraid like this." It was amazing the way Leroy was able to think of one thing after another to say, trying to act so nonchalant about everything. If I hadn't had him to talk to, I know I would have fallen apart.

"I'm okay, don't worry," I'd say one minute. The next minute, I'd say, "Leroy, I'm so scared. I can't believe I'm so scared." What were the kids looking at? "You kids get away from that window now!" I said sternly. "I'm not going to tell you again." They finally listened to me, thank God. I didn't want to tell them that I was afraid Mark could be watching; they were scared enough already.

If only I had some way of knowing what was about to happen. I had no idea of how lost and alone and rejected Mark felt and that he was falling apart. It wasn't a game this time, and it wasn't a bluff. It was real. Now it was a few minutes past nine, and I was still talking to Leroy. We were still all alone, and he was trying to calm my fears. For the past two days, we'd had constant protection, and I was not being very brave, being by myself with my kids.

Now that we were alone, I wasn't doing very well, and we were all very nervous, a fact that we could not hide from each other, no matter how hard we tried. I was trying so hard to be strong for them on the outside. On the inside, I was panicky.

"Linda, you've got to calm down. You're not helping the kids any. If they know how scared you are, it's only going to make things worse." I'd never been able to hide my true feelings from my kids before. Why did I think that I could do it now? They knew me too well. They could always tell instantly if something was wrong with me.

"I know, Leroy, I'm trying so hard. There's no one here to be strong for me." "I just know something bad's going to happen. I can feel it." I took a deep breath, trying to relax. I let it out real slow. It always helped me during childbirth, but it wasn't working now. Leroy never failed me. He never gave up on me. Somehow, he managed to keep me from falling apart. He kept me on the phone, and I listened to his words of comfort.

If only Mark hadn't scared us so badly. I couldn't believe this was happening, and I didn't want anyone to get hurt. I just wanted it all to stop. As I listened to Leroy, I glanced over at the bar and saw my gun next to the lamp. I knew it was loaded. There were six bullets next to it. I started to pick it up and changed my mind. I know I won't need it, I thought to myself. Mark would never hurt us. He would never shoot me, never. Still, I picked it up and tucked it in the front of my jeans. I put the six extra bullets in my back pocket. No one should ever have to do that, not ever. What have I done to his mind? I told him how much I loved him. If only he had listened.

"Mom, it's Mark. We heard Mark's truck," Danny said, his voice quivering.

"No, honey, don't worry. It can't be him."

"No, Mom, it was," Becky added. "We know what his truck sounds like. We know it's Mark. He turned the corner and stopped."

"She's right, Mom. I know it's him." They were so afraid, and I couldn't believe the fear in their eyes. Leroy was right. My actions were affecting my kids, and I hated Mark for scaring us all like this.

"Kids, please. You're breaking my heart. I can't stand to see you so scared. It couldn't have been Mark. He's hiding his truck. He thinks the cops are looking for him. That's why he was with Claudia in her truck today, so please don't be afraid," I urged. "Boonie or Rory will be here soon. Please, kids, this is breaking my heart to see you like this."

Leroy heard the whole thing. I was still doing my best, trying to stay calm. I couldn't stand seeing my kids like this. How much more could they take? How much more could I take? "You're doing fine," Leroy said.

"I tucked my gun in my pants, Leroy." All of a sudden, we both heard a click on the phone. "Leroy, are you still there?"

"I'm still here. What was that?"

"I don't know. I thought you hung up on me." I was so glad he was still there. I realized how much talking to him was helping me. We continued. "Anyway, I've got my gun now. I tucked it in my pants. I know I won't need it. I just feel better. God, I wish Rory would get here. The kids are so scared. They just want to get out of here."

Click. This one was louder, much more distinct. We both heard it clearly.

"Mom, there's a little truck out front. It's going real slow. It started to turn in, but it had passed the first driveway." Danny had returned to the window, thank God.

"Leroy, it's Mark. I know it's Mark. It looks like Claudia's truck. It's passing the second driveway, and now it stopped. God, it's backing up now. It's pulling in. It's him. He's here. I know that's Mark." I continued on as my entire body quivered in fear. "He's coming in the driveway. He's coming real slow." The kids were terrified. "I don't know what to do, Leroy. I have my gun."

"Calm down. It might not be him." The truck had stopped.

"It stopped right below us, Leroy. Oh god. It is Mark. I heard his voice. He's yelling."

"You motherfucker! Get the fuck outta here!" Mark yelled as he slammed the door with much force.

"He must have gotten out, and the truck's driving away." I heard his powerful steps coming up the stairs two or three at a time. "Leroy, he's coming up the stairs fast, real fast." My voice was quivering as I bravely fought back tears.

"Don't worry! Be strong," Leroy said in a comforting voice. "I'm calling 911 right now." We both hung up.

The barn door was locked, the bolt slid across. Would he knock? If he did, should I open it? I didn't have to make that decision. Instantly, he started pulling on the door. Back and forth, back and forth.

"You kids get in the back. Right now!" I screamed. They each grabbed a sleeping baby off a couch. They'd be safer back there. Back and forth, back and forth. He wouldn't stop. He wasn't trying to talk. He just kept pulling and pushing on the door, trying to get it open.

My .22 pistol was still tucked in the front of my jeans. I took it out, but my hands were shaking so much that I could hardly hold it. I backed up a little, and I felt the bar against my back. The lit kerosene lamp was directly behind me, and it was the only light in the front area of the barn.

Back and forth, pulling and pushing. He wouldn't stop. "Mark, what are you doing? What are you doing? There's no one here. There's no one here. It's just us. What are you doing?" There was no answer. He didn't make a sound. He just kept pulling and pushing on the door.

I knew he must be crazy. I aimed my gun at the door, watching it as it moved back and forth. It was opening more and more each time. I held my gun with both hands, arms fully extended, with my eyes focused on the middle of the door.

I knew it was about to open. The back-and-forth banging became louder and faster. "Mark, please. What are you doing? There's no one here. There's no one here!" I pleaded over and over. The door opened, and he had his gun. God, why did he have it? It was okay, though, the gun was down low, off his hip.

Never taking my eyes off it, I watched it, just watched it. He hadn't raised it to shoot, and I was remembering Officer Morgan's earlier warning. "If he raises it to shoot, shoot him first. He will kill you with that shotgun," he had urged. He kept it low, and he didn't speak, and it happened so fast. I didn't think he'd shoot me. I didn't want him to shoot me. The gun was still low.

Boom! I heard the deafening noise and saw the bright-red flame all at once. There was something wrong with my arm. It was hot, very hot. I knew he'd hit me, and I fired my gun as fast as my index finger would move, my arms still fully extended.

He'd shot me. Oh my god, please, I didn't want him to shoot me, I thought to myself as I pulled the trigger as fast as my finger would move. Click click click came the cap gun sound of my .22 pistol. Boom! I saw one more flame. Thank God he had missed me. I heard the wooden walls shatter to the left just behind me.

Seven times I fired. Die! You shot me, die! I thought intensely. Click click click. The horrifying sound of our gunfight continued. "You might kill the babies. Die, you might kill us all!" I pulled the trigger the seventh time, and I knew there were no more bullets. I couldn't believe that he'd shot me.

Where was he? He was gone. My gun didn't work anymore, so I threw it down, never thinking of the extra bullets I'd put in my back pocket. I couldn't see him anywhere; he had disappeared from my view. He'd never stepped inside the barn. My kids were screaming, and the babies were crying. "Are you all right, Mom? Are you all right?" they cried. I knew that I was in shock. Everything seemed to be moving in slow motion.

"I'm okay. I'm all right." Trying to calm my hysterical kids down, knowing all along that I was not all right. "I had to have hit him. I couldn't have missed. He shot me! I can't believe he shot me." I started to cry. Stay calm, I thought to myself. Don't upset them any more.

"Where is he, Mom?" my young son pleaded. Becky was shaking and crying and trying to comfort the babies all at the same time, something a nine-year-old should never have to experience. They were terrified.

"I don't know where he is. He just disappeared. He's just gone." I was holding my arm together; I couldn't let them see it. I could feel the bone, and I didn't think it was all there anymore. I tried to hold it close, so the blood would stop coming out so fast. It wasn't working, and I knew I wasn't really okay.

I knew my whole torso was full of bullets. My chest and stomach were as hot as my arm, and by now, the whole front of me was covered with blood. "Mommy, you are bleeding so bad," my daughter cried, seeing the enormous amount of blood through the dim light of the oil lamp.

"I'll be okay, honey. It's not very bad, baby," I said as I tried to take a deep breath and couldn't. "I'll be okay," I lied, knowing that I was going to die soon. I could barely breathe, and I knew that my lungs were not working right.

I walked slowly back to my bed and sat down on the corner of it. I couldn't let go of my arm. I could feel the blood rushing through my fingers, and it was very warm. I remember rocking back and forth, slowly, very slowly, something I'd always done to comfort myself. I couldn't stop rocking.

Everything was moving in slow motion, and I knew that it was just a matter of time before I died. There was so much blood, and I was very dizzy, growing weaker by the moment.

Danny was standing right next to me with his gun. Where was Becky? I didn't know where Becky was. The babies—where were the babies? I didn't know where my babies were. I didn't know where Mark was, and I didn't even know if I'd hit him. It was so dark.

My body had been in front of the light. The night was black, and the figure of the man that I had loved so much had been no more than a dark silhouette as he stood at the open door. I had never seen his face as I had watched his gun so intently.

"Danny, he shot me, honey! I can't believe he really shot me," I cried. "He loves me. I didn't think he'd shoot me." I couldn't say that again; it would make me cry too hard. I had to be calm. I was afraid I was going to bleed to death as the weakness began to overpower me.

"Just shoot him, Danny. If you see him, just shoot him. Find him and shoot him. He might kill his babies. He might kill you. He might kill us all. Just shoot him over and over, Danny," I pleaded over and over. Where was he? I didn't know where he was. I didn't know if I'd hit him or not.

Please, God. Don't let my kids see me die, I prayed. Don't let my kids die. Don't let my babies die. Please, God. I'd never prayed so hard before. For about five minutes, we didn't know where Mark was. We were terrified, and the horror was unexplainable.

I knew I was dying. I was helpless. How could I save my kids now? During the five minutes since the shooting, I was either telling Danny to shoot Mark, find him and shoot him until he's dead, or else, praying to God with all my heart that he wouldn't let my kids see me die.

I heard my babies crying on and off again. I still didn't know where they were. I wasn't coherent enough to realize they were in the bathroom, right next to me, with their big sister. She was trying so hard to protect them as she stayed as calm as she possibly could, knowing that their care was entirely up to her at this moment. She loves them so much, and she was just a baby herself, but she was doing an amazing job protecting them both, not thinking of herself and how scared she was.

Where were my babies? Where was my Becky? I asked myself over and over. Where was Mark? We were so scared. Danny was shaking, and I could hardly understand his quivering voice. I knew he was terrified. Still, he never left my side, and I knew that he would do everything he could to save us all.

He was ready to protect me with his life, and all that he had was his friend Monty's rifle, the one that kept misfiring. Would Danny ever be the same? I wondered. Would any of us? Please, God, let this end, I prayed. Why was this happening?

"Where is he, Danny? Find him. Find him and shoot him. Shoot him over and over. Where is he? He's not on the roof, is he? He's not coming back here on the roof? Find him, Danny. You have to find him, honey." My voice was becoming weaker as I spoke. "He shot me! He might kill us all." I struggled to get my words out loud enough for him to understand me.

Be calm, be calm, I reminded myself. I didn't want to die. I couldn't die. Please, God! Help us, I prayed with all my heart. Somebody, please help us. Everything was moving in slow motion as it became slower by the moment. My head felt like it was going to rise off my shoulders, and I felt like I was going to pass out.

I heard the sound of glass breaking as Danny broke out my bedroom window with something. He poked his head out, trying to see where Mark was.

"Mom, he's coming back in now. He's coming up the stairs, Mom. I see him. He's coming in." For so long, we hadn't known where he was; now we did, and we had no idea what he was about to do.

"Shoot him, Danny! Just shoot him if he comes back here. As soon as you see him, shoot him. He shot me, he might kill us all," I repeated slowly and firmly. I could hardly hold my eyes open, and I felt like I was going to fall over. I couldn't. Not now. It would scare my son, and he would feel alone.

I still didn't know where my Becky and my babies were. They had briefly stopped crying, and now the deafening silence seemed as terrifying as the screams had earlier. We could hear Mark's struggling, slow-moving footsteps coming closer and closer. We had no idea that I had wounded him in his thigh and abdomen just moments earlier as I returned fire, and we were terrified.

Once he'd shot me, I knew he was capable of anything. What was he going to do? Suddenly, I heard his voice. It was the voice of a desperate, confused man, not a crazy man.

"Linda, why did you shoot me? Why did you shoot me?" He just stood there near the bedroom area, behind one of the baby cribs. Danny could only see half of Mark, the only light coming from the oil lamp on the bar.

My god, why is he asking why I shot him? I wondered. Doesn't he know that he had shot me? Danny took careful aim, raising his rifle, his body trembling as he never lost his courage. Just then, Becky peeked out of the bathroom door and heard Mark's plea as he saw the boy that he loved ready to shoot him.

"No, no! Please don't shoot," he begged. It was too late.

Bang click…bang click click…bang click click click. Armed with his misfiring rifle, my brave young son was chasing him out of our barn as his rifle misfired often.

"I hate you, I hate you! You shot my mom! Die! Die! I hate you, you shot my mom!" I heard him repeat over and over. Danny stopped by the bar to grab more bullets. Mark also made a stop near the front door and picked up my crucifix as Danny followed him out the door and continued to shoot and yell at him in a courageous, controlling voice.

My son was in total control of this situation, and he had managed to protect us all as he somehow managed to put his own fears aside. The relief I was feeling was impossible to explain, and I was so very proud of my young son.

My Becky had done her job perfectly, as she had protected the babies, and I knew that they were all okay in the back of the barn. She had been amazing. Thank you, God, for helping her and for saving all my kids, I prayed with the little strength I had left.

Would this pride I feel for my kids be one of my last thoughts before I died? I wondered sadly. Please, God, could I stay alive for just a little while so that they don't have to see their mom die?

*****

The door to the ambulance is opening now, and I know that we must be at the hospital. Reality is setting in, and it is overpowering the happy memories I have of my life with Mark. My closed eyes fill with tears as I silently pray to God to let me live. I have no idea what happened to Mark, and I am sure that it is just a matter of time before I die.

CHAPTER 16

THE END

They are wheeling me into the emergency room. I am irritated because someone keeps asking me what my name is, and I am unable to answer. Don't you realize that I am too weak to speak? I think to myself, feeling confused, as I wave my hand away from my body, trying to make them understand.

I wonder, in my dazed state of mind, why they don't go ask my family all these questions. I know that they are all out there and that they are all worried about me, and I don't understand why they don't even know my name.

"Have you been at this hospital before?" someone says in a soft, gentle voice. I move my head a little, up and down, very slowly. "Did you have a baby here?" I can plainly hear as a strange voice pleads, sounding much more intent than the last. Raising my right hand slightly, slowly, with every ounce of energy that my badly damaged body has, I am able to put up two fingers. "Two babies?" I nod. "You had twins? How long ago? One year ago?" she asks when I lift one finger.

"Yes," I whisper softly with great relief.

"Wait a minute," I hear her tell someone. "I'll be right back!"

A short while later, I hear the same voice. "Are you Linda Anne?"

"Yes." I nod as I am able to open my eyes halfway for the first time in a long while. There is also a policeman standing next to me, asking the nurse questions and writing his report among the scurrying of many people all around me.

"On this day, at approximately 2217 hours, I was dispatched to the Hospital Emergency Room in regards to an attempted homicide victim allegedly shot in her left chest area and having the possibility of becoming a fatality. I was assigned to obtain a dying declaration from this victim in the emergency room," he wrote.

I hear him discussing the incident with a nurse, and I get his attention as I slowly begin to speak. "Mark said, 'You shot me,' but he shot me first," I say slowly in a low murmur, carefully choosing my words, tears threatening. My subconscious mind is working as I wonder why Mark had asked that puzzling question after he'd been the one who shot first, and his words have already begun to haunt me.

I tell the officer exactly what happened, a little at a time, with spontaneous statements, as my breathing becomes a little easier. "Linda! Linda, wake up, please," I hear over and over, realizing that I am having trouble staying awake. I see the bright flash of a camera and wonder why they are taking pictures of me, and I can't believe that this is happening to me. Soon I am back in an ambulance. "Where are you taking me?" I ask weakly.

"You're being transported to the trauma ward at San Bernardino County Hospital," the attendant replies.

"Please, I need something for the pain," I beg. It has been about four hours since the shooting, and for the first time, I am starting to hurt badly.

"Don't worry, as soon as we arrive, they'll be giving you something. You'll be going right into surgery." His words would give me a little more strength.

"Thank God," I whisper, feeling I could make it a little longer.

I feel the motion of the ambulance come to an abrupt stop, and quickly the cool air of the night is upon me as the door opens. Feeling the gurney hit the ground, I wonder how much longer I can be strong, since my pain is practically unbearable.

"Please help me. I hurt so bad. I can't stand it anymore, please," I beg as they wheel me inside. No one is answering my desperate pleas.

There are people walking all around me, touching me as they work on me, but no one seems to hear me.

"Somebody, help me!" I scream as loud as my weakened body will allow. I wonder if this is really happening, since everyone is ignoring me. What's wrong? I wonder.

"Somebody help me! My god, I hurt so bad. This is a hospital, and you are supposed to help me!" I say through tear-filled eyes. "Please, I beg you, please!" It's no use, because no one is listening.

"I hate you. You're horrible people! How can you be so mean to me?" I screech as loud as I can with the little strength that I have. My pain is totally out of control, and my tantrums are only making it worse as my pulse races inside my shattered body.

"Let me die, just let me die, please! I can't stand this pain! God, please let me die," I beg over and over, tears streaming down my face. The hours have worn me down, and my pain is excruciating. I can't believe that I'm still alive after experiencing so much pain.

"I hate you, God. Please let me die," I plead, trying to take a deep breath. "I don't want to live anymore. This hurts too bad!" I glare intently at the nurse by my side.

"It'll all be over soon, sweetie. Just hang on," she says in a low, soothing voice as she holds my hand.

Thank God, someone seems to care, I think to myself, feeling the comfort of another human being for the first time.

"Linda, we need you to sign this paper before you go to surgery," a new voice requests as a clipboard is held in front of me. "Your bowel is damaged, and there is a possibility that we may have to rest it for a while and put a colostomy bag after the damage is repaired."

My eyes open wide in disbelief. "Oh my god, I don't want that, please!"

She continues on in a soft, soothing, and reassuring voice, "It may not be necessary, but we need you to sign just in case, honey. Just put an x, and I will witness that you signed," she urges. I hold the pen that has been placed in my hand, reaching toward the clipboard, making a mark.

In a matter of seconds, I am on my way down the long corridor, heading for surgery, ceiling lights whizzing by, frightened and feeling very alone as I pray that this unbearable pain will soon be gone.

I am in a room now, and the pain becomes even more intense as I am moved to another gurney. I see the faces of numerous people above me, and my tear-filled eyes are blurred. "Soon it will be better, I promise you." It is the reassuring voice of a man this time. There is a mask on my face, and for a brief second, I feel a little high.

It is the next afternoon, and my surgery is over. I am awake for the first time since the early morning hours, when my surgery had begun. Trying to focus my eyes, I see images of people all around my bed in the shape of a horseshoe.

Blinking away the fuzziness as my vision begins to clear, I can see my kids and Leroy and Rory. With brilliant smiles and a look of relief in their beautiful faces, their voices pierce my ears like a knife as they seem to be talking all at one time. I am not trying to speak as I feel the effects of the pain medication that flows into my veins.

"We love you. You're going to be fine, Mom," one of them says.

"I'm glad you're okay" comes from the other side of my bed. All of a sudden, I remember what had happened.

"Mom, you're out of surgery. It's Wednesday afternoon."

I give them a weak smile as my eyes fill with tears, happy to see them for the first time since they had taken me away, thanking God silently that they are all okay.

Mark, what happened to Mark? I wonder. I know that I could probably speak if I wanted, but I am not ready to ask. I don't want to know, not right now, because I'm afraid of the answer, assuming the worst. I cannot handle any more right now, and I know that it would not be good to ask.

I feel terrible. The pain is intense, and all I want is to fall back asleep. I don't want to hurt them, but I don't want to talk right now. I mouth the words I love you, and they are able to read my lips as I wave my hand toward the door, knowing they will understand.

"I love you, Mom. We'll be back tomorrow," each one tells me as they give me a careful hug.

"Take care, see you later," Rory and Leroy say, and they are gone.

I am still awake and all alone for the first time since all this has begun as I try to put the past few days out of my mind.

Tears streaming lightly down my cheeks, pooling in my ears, as I lie flat on my back, pondering the many unanswered questions that are racing through my mind. Over and over, I see the bright orange flame and hear the loud bang of Mark's shotgun as he broke the door down and shot me without a word.

Now I focus on Mark's words as he reentered the barn and came into the bedroom. "Linda, why did you shoot me? Why did you shoot me?" I hear his voice over and over as if he were standing right next to me. Why did he say that? He shot me! I didn't think he'd shoot me. Why did he ask me that?

I search my mind for answers as I begin to cry out loud. As I become hysterical, sobbing uncontrollably, I notice a nurse at my side. She's doing something to me. What is she—

I fall asleep.

The next thing I know, it is morning. Thursday morning, the nurse tells me.

I realize where I am, and once again, I remember what happened. I start to cry and drift off to sleep as I exhaust myself once again.

The next time I wake up, I see three different IV pumps to the right of me, and I remember the paper I had signed for the colostomy bag. I thank God when I hear the nurse tell me that there is only one bag hanging next to me, containing my urine. The doctors had been able to repair my bowel, avoiding the colostomy bag that I had feared earlier.

The nurse has a very nice smile, and her voice is very quiet and comforting, and I remember seeing her several times this morning.

"Hello," I murmur softly, voice cracking, somehow finding a smile for her. "Am I okay? Did my surgery go well?"

With raised eyebrows, I anxiously wait for her reply. She smiles back, and her expression tells me what her words would verify.

"The damage wasn't quite as bad as they first thought. Your bowels have been repaired enough to use. How do you feel?" she asks, rubbing my arm softly. "You're a lucky lady, you know, lucky to be alive." She is very nice, and I know that she means well, but I can't stop thinking about how unlucky I'm feeling. I know she is right about one thing—most people die when they get shot with a twelve-gauge shotgun from ten feet away.

Every time I wake up, I gather a few more thoughts as I try to piece everything that happened together. My left arm is heavily bandaged and propped in place and in a slightly raised position. I can see that there is also a large dressing all across the front of me beneath my hospital gown.

Soon the pain and confusion, along with the shock of it all, overpower me, and I drift back to sleep for a while. I still have no idea what happened to Mark, and I am not sure if I want to know just yet. Soon the pain and confusion overpower me, and I drift back to sleep. The entire day would be spent this way, being awake for only short periods of time.

It is late afternoon on Thursday, and this time, I am awake when my family and friends arrive. I was half hoping that no one would come see me today. The possibility that Mark might be dead hasn't left my mind since he had disappeared Tuesday night, and I'm afraid of the answers to all my questions.

Once again, everyone is here, and they are so thankful that I'm alive and happy, that there is nothing to be afraid of anymore. Their mom is alive and okay, and they know that I will remain that way.

They all seem to be experiencing total relief. Everything is okay in their eyes, and they are very happy and in high spirits.

"Hello," I utter with a slight smile. "I love you guys!" are the first words to come from my quivering lips. For a while, they all wonder if I would ever talk again.

"You must keep this door open at all times," a nurse says gruffly as she opens the door.

"We can't. We want to talk to our mom, and that reporter won't go away from the door," my daughter Shelley replies in a very stern but sweet voice.

"I'm sorry, hospital rules. This is the trauma ward. It must stay open."

"It's okay," Richie says. "I'll go out and talk to him a little."

Everyone is happy and excited. There is a lot of chatter going on.

Then it happens. They are talking about the shooting with great relief in their voices. Someone says his name, and I know the time has finally come. The question has to be asked. I can't put it off any longer; my voice is strained, and I am very afraid of what the answer might be.

"Where's Mark? What happened to Mark?" There is no pause, and I know the answer to the question I have been afraid to ask immediately.

"He's dead. Danny killed him," Jimmy says with a smile.

It has happened. My world is shattered, and I don't even realize it yet. The shock I feel is overpowering. "He's dead?" I ask, hoping I had heard my young son wrong.

"Yep, he's dead. We don't have to worry about Mark ever again." As the main details flood my mind, I realize what a hero my eleven-year-old son is as my eyes turn to his.

I remember the horror that we somehow managed to survive a few nights before and the unbelievable courage he had shown as he stood next to my blood-soaked body, clinging to his rifle, taking care of us all. He was my strength and my protector. I would never ever forget how brave Danny was on that tragic Tuesday night.

"Honey, I don't want you to ever feel guilty, not ever! Do you understand?" I plead with my son. "Mark didn't give us any choice. He shot me." Danny knows that my words are sincere, even though he is a little confused by them, knowing the truth already.

"Don't worry. I won't, Mom," he answers. "I'm going out with Richie for a minute, okay?" My young son asks gently as he hugs me carefully, seeming a little confused.

The kids are giving me more details of the shooting, but I am wearing down, and soon everyone decides to leave so I can rest.

"Mom, there's something else you'll want to know," Shelley says.

"What, honey?"

"We found your crucifix by a bush, right near where Mark died."

I can't believe it. "Are you sure?" I'd put it in the box I was packing to take with us that night, and there was no question it was mine.

"Yes, I'm sure. He must have taken it with him and dropped it right before he fell." She is right. I definitely want to know that since it tells me that he has prayed before he died, telling God how sorry he was and asking for forgiveness.

By now, I'm having trouble staying awake, so after more hugs and "I love yous," they leave me alone once again, for my own good. I need to rest and get strong again. This time, it isn't for my own good, though. Being left alone right now is the worst thing that can happen to me.

Mark's dead, he's really dead. I can't believe it! My mind would not stop repeating it. This is not a bad dream or a movie. This is very real, and I cannot escape the shocking reality any longer. He's dead. He's gone forever, and he'll never be back. I will never see him again. His babies will never see him again. They don't have a daddy anymore. He loved them so much and wanted so badly to see them grow up.

My mind is racing as the tears begin to well up in my eyes. Now I'm screaming. "I hate you, God! Why did all of this have to happen?" I sobbed hysterically. "Why couldn't you help him learn to control himself, God?" I pleaded.

My whole body is quivering as I totally lose control. Shock and sadness will not help me this time. Reality is pushing it aside. I am sedated, but I continue to cry uncontrollably.

"Just a little more, to help you sleep," the nurse says. "You can't get up, Linda, you have to be still." Soon, there are two of them holding me down, and I have no strength to fight. I don't know why I'm trying to get up. I don't have any idea what I am trying to do.

As they hold me gently, trying to keep me still, I am mentally and physically exhausted. My voice becomes weak and faint as everything begins to blur from the strong medication.

Having the answer to the question that has haunted me for the past two days, I finally know the ending to this horrible, sad, and very scary movie. Oh god, what have I done? I prayed. What have I done to my precious kids? How many lives have I destroyed? Oh god, this is all my fault! As I fight to stay awake, I lose the battle as my eyes close lightly on my glistening cheeks. I won't wake up for a long time.

FINAL THOUGHTS

I have struggled for a very long time about how I wanted to end my story—my final thoughts, so to speak. So much has happened to my kids and me in all of these years that I could probably write a whole other book. I know that it is finally the right time to finish my longtime effort, so I am.

I wanted to make sure that telling my story would be okay with my kids. It allows you all into the worst time of our lives, a horrible, tragic, and very personal time. A time that many would be embarrassed of, but my kids have all assured me that they want it finished.

There were two reasons that I needed to write these words down. The first thought was that I wanted his babies to know the real story, the complete truth. I know that there was so much bad, but I wanted them to always know the good side of their daddy as well. There was so much good; if there hadn't been, I would not have loved him so much. That's why my story is as sad as it is terrifying and as inexcusable as it is tragic.

The second reason came years later, when I began to think more clearly and more logically as time slowly began to heal. I thought about the millions of abused women out there that were going through what I had been through, and my need to reach them became overwhelming.

That was how I became involved in Advocates to End Domestic Violence in Carson City, Nevada. Twice a year, during their training sessions for volunteers, I would tell my story to the trainees. For a few years, I would take the phone calls of the shaken and sometimes-terrified, abused women that would call in the middle of the night, desperately pleading for help and for safety for their children and themselves.

It was my one small chance to reach as many women as possible in hopes that my story may save one family from going through what I had put my own children through.

It makes me very happy to know that there is so much help for abused women today, with shelters for safety, support groups, programs to allow them to make it on their own and take care of their precious children at the same time. Because of the advocates, many laws have been changed in favor of women, and they will continue their efforts as long as it may take in order to protect our women even more.

The most important thing these women learn is that they do not deserve to be abused and that this kind of a relationship is a bad relationship, one that needs to end immediately. They learn to hold their heads up high and proudly, and they know that none of this is their fault, something that I struggled with for many years, blaming myself. They regain their self-esteem and independence and realize that life without him is so much better for herself and her children.

Of course, there is lots of help for the men, but that is entirely up to them. It is totally out of your control. Your job is the beginning of a long, hard journey to fix yourself and to once again feel good about who you are and all that you do. The men that really and truly want to learn to control their anger must work harder than in their entire life, with the effort never ending.

I often wonder, if my story had happened today, if it would have ended differently. Maybe he would have been one of the 4 percent that could learn to control his anger, and maybe he would have been here to love and to guide and be a good example to the babies that he adored. The honest answer is, probably not, for I know how badly he wanted to change but, no matter how hard he tried, he could not.

Through all the past years of learning and trying to forgive myself, there is one thing that I heard along the way that I will always know is the absolute truth, and I want to share it with you, if you have ever been in an abusive relationship. The first time he hits you, it is his fault. The second time he hits you, it is your fault.

It is up to us as moms to do all we can to protect our children, to not let it happen that second time. Be responsible, be smart, and above all, be afraid. It is a very bad story, a bad kind of love, and I could have stopped it all from progressing into such a tragedy.

I needed my story to emphasize the entire truth, the happy, the sad, the good, the bad, the love, and above all, the intense fear. If I hadn't, you would not be able to relate. I wanted you to see yourselves in my story and to know how horrifying and tragic an abusive relationship can be.

There are many reasons we stay. For me, it was love and knowing how badly he himself wanted to change and to learn to control his anger. I know now that he loved me more than anyone else ever has—there was never a doubt because of the way he could make me feel. None of that should have mattered, and to let it matter was very selfish of me. The bad was enough to erase all the good. I know that now.

As far as advice goes, who am I to give advice? you are probably thinking. The past years have taught me so much about the damage I caused my children. I never realized the ugly guilt I caused them, always begging them to forgive Mark, reminding them, "You want your mom to be happy, don't you?" Of course they did, always pretending to forgive him.

As far as ruining my kids, I am sure that I have not done that. I am so very proud of each and every one of them. Along with being successful in life, I know that they have all the qualities that matter most to a mom. They are kind, caring, loving, compassionate, sensitive individuals who know how to love in a very special way. They know the importance of being able to forgive and to put the past in the past, to look at the positive side, and to always try to have a more-than-half-full glass.

Everyone has failures in their lives and lots of wrong choices, but if we learn from our mistakes, it is all for a reason. My mom taught me that, and I have tried to teach that to my own kids, and I am so proud when they thank me for the way that they are. The best part is seeing them passing it on to my precious grandchildren.

The hardest part of all this for me is the fact that Donny and Darla have never had their daddy, because, of course, I always imagine that he would have learned to control his anger and that it would have been a wonderful life for them. Deep inside, I know the truth, though; he tried so hard without success.

I feel his presence so strongly when I am doing things that concern the kids that he adored. He was always with me at his son's sporting events, bursting with pride as he watched Donny with his above-average, exceptional athletic ability. When he acts like a clown, I know it comes from his dad. He can be so funny, just like Mark. Just like his dad, his outgoing personality, never ceases to amaze me. I have no doubt that either one, could sell an Eskimo ice.

He loves to watch his daughter and the beautiful, special gift that she has with babies and small children, seeing what an amazing mom she is and how very much they adore her. She whistles at babies, just like he always did, and that is something that she never knew about. I know it makes him smile every time.

It works both ways, though, and I can't forget the chills that run through my body when one of them loses their temper and I see that part of their dad in them. It scares me so badly and can bring back so many bad memories, memories that I try hard to keep in the past.

I am better now, and I truly like the person that I have become. I am proud of me, and I am so thankful to be alive. I try to live my life as if every day could be my last. I want people to know that I care about them, never holding back a compliment, praise, or encouragement. I have even been called a suck-up at times and am proud to say that I have learned not to let it upset me as it once did, knowing it's sincere and that it all comes straight from a kind, loving heart, the same heart that my mom had passed down to me.

I know how sorry Mark was for all his bad choices, because of the way he carried my crucifix. I am sure he was praying, asking God to forgive him with his last breath as he fell to his death. That only adds to the sadness of it all. Why couldn't he have just changed? I will always wonder.

Six months after he died, I am convinced that he came to me in the night, at the barn that he loved so much. I had gone to bed early and suddenly awoke. I went into the living room and picked up my tablet of continuous notes that I had been writing ever since he had died. I did not want to forget anything, so I would be able to share my life with their father with my babies, the good and the bad. Not wanting to forget any details of our life together.

I wrote nonstop by kerosene lamp before returning to bed. In the morning, I glanced at what I had written, and to my amazement, I knew that it was a letter from Mark. There was no doubt in my mind that every single word had come from him. I knew that this letter told me exactly how he felt. I put it into a song and titled it "Letter from an Angel," changing only a few words for rhyme's sake. It still gives me great comfort to play his song on my guitar and sing the words he has blessed me with that night.

Is it real or not? I guess I will never really know. But one thing I am sure of is that he will always be in my heart. I will always have my "if only" and my "what ifs." I will always have my sadness, and I will always feel an unimaginable, deep loss.

But the most important thing I need for you to know is this: It took years and years for me to forgive myself for the irresponsibility I showed to my children for my own selfish reasons. It took years for me to see things clearly, the way that I should have always seen them. My choice to stay with him was a bad choice, and I know now that no matter how strong this love was, it was not a good love.

I will never forget the horror of it all, those last few days. I know it will never go away, I can still remember every single terrifying detail as if it had happened yesterday. Most of all, I will never forget the unimaginable, unbelievable fear that my children and I experienced that final night.

Why wasn't I more afraid? The red flags were everywhere. Why was I so irresponsible to my kids, the most important thing in the world to me? I know things would be different, if only I had another chance.

If you are reading this story and you live with abuse in your life, you are very lucky. You still have that chance. I always said that if my story could save one woman and one child from going through what we went through, then writing it down and working on it for all these years would have been well worth my time.

Do you have red flags, and are you afraid? Don't make the same mistakes I made. Become the mom that I failed to be. Think of your priceless children. Get the help that is there for you. All you need to do is reach out.

The most important thing I can say to you is, be afraid!

I hope my story scares you one quarter as much as it scared all of us. If it does, you will make the necessary changes. Remember the most important fact: I never thought he'd shoot me!

Letter from an Angel

I'd come to you, you know that I would.
If I could only find a way.
You know exactly how I feel,
But there's some things that I still want to say.

I can't believe that I lost my way that night,
And that I lost your special touch.
Remember all the times I said it scared me, babe,
Because I loved you way too much.

(Chorus)

Finally got this letter to you,
Wished it didn't hurt so bad,
For you to finally know the truth.
I loved you more than life itself,
I knew I couldn't last another day,
But I wish I didn't have to go away,
I had to send this letter with an angel.

Remember me with laughter now,
You know your tears are so hard for me to bear.
Always share your thoughts with me,
And know that I'm with you everywhere.

And when you see the things that I've done for you,
Please try not to let it hurt you quite so bad.
Remember that I love you just the same from here,
And I'm always gonna be their dad.

ABOUT THE AUTHOR

L inda Rhoutsong was blessed to be able to spend most of her early years, being a stay at home wife and mother. In 1992 she moved to Catalina Island, where she and her young twins lived with a wonderful Pastor and his wife, Enrique and Santa at the Catalina Bible Church. With their help, and by the Grace of God, she got her first job, at the small Island hospital, there she became a C.N.A. (certified nursing assistant) and later moved to Carson City Nevada. Where she was a pediatric C.N.A, eventually becoming an OB. Technician, assisting in deliveries and C-sections. It was at this time that she became certified with Advocates to end Domestic Violence. She spent many nights, taking calls from abused women who needed emergency help and shelter for themselves and their children. It was during this time that she realized just how important her story could be to abused women everywhere. After 10 years she moved back to her beloved Island, and lived on her sailboat, for a few years, until finally moving into a small apartment. She became a C.N.A/ Activities Director to the full time, hospital residents.

Now residing in Arizona, recently retired, she enjoys traveling, (visiting her kids and many grandchildren), and boating and camping on the Colorado river, that she loves so much. She has finally found peace in her life! She still works hard every day, to forgive herself for the lifelong damage she has done to her friends, both families, (that will never be the same) and most importantly, her precious children. With her deep faith in God, she will always be grateful, for the love he has blessed her with, thanking him every day that her precious children have forgiven her. She knows sadly, that the unimaginable terror she caused, will remain with them forever. If sharing her story can help to save one woman or one child, from this type of horror, it will all have a purpose.

CPSIA information can be obtained
at www.ICGtesting.com
Printed in the USA
LVHW090948240919
632099LV00001B/4/P